Science Fiction Films
of The 20th Century
1950 - 1954

Theresa M. Moore

◇ANTELLUS®
www.antellus.com

SCIENCE FICTION FILMS OF THE 20th CENTURY
1950 - 1954

Published by **Antellus**, Los Angeles, California USA
Catalog no. 019C1 - ISBN 978-1-938752-98-8

Other nonfiction books by Theresa M. Moore:
- A BOOK OF FIVE RINGS: A Practical Guide To Strategy by Miyamoto Musashi
- Feast Or Famine: Blogs And Essays About Writing, Publishing, And Other Things
- The Most Important Science Fiction Films of The 20th Century: Vols. 1 to 3
- Principles of Publishing In The Digital Age: 4th Edition
- Science Fiction Films of The 20th Century: The Early Years
- Science Fiction Films of The 20th Century: The 1940s
- Science Fiction Films of The 20th Century: 1955-1959

TABLE OF CONTENTS

Preface

This is the third volume of a series of books covering the whole panoply of science fiction films of the 20th century. It is a collection of essays about films which were popular in culture and the genre of science fiction. Each essay includes a complete plot synopsis, additional analyses and notes, anecdotal information and data about each production. Each film has been selected for addition to this volume based on the my experience as a fan of science fiction and a film critic. Some of the films listed may seem like cheaply made popcorn thrillers but when seen for their themes and impact they were actually quite educational. I want to include only those films which fit the criteria: they must be mostly science fiction and include technology, social themes as they relate to science, and also real science. So you will excuse me if I publish brief notes about some of the films which were on the list but which actually fall under romance or other themes, only for their inclusion of robotics and other scientific methods which skim the genre. Some of the films have already been included in the previous trilogy, *The Most Important Science Fiction Films of The 20th Century*, with additional notes which have been picked up post publication. I hope to present a complete chronology where possible. -- **Theresa M. Moore**

Introduction

Before we begin I must post a brief note about serials and their importance to science fiction: each involves a cowboy, g-man or a hired agent and his assistant or sidekick, who work with scientists who have invented and developed various weapons powered by a radioactive substance (mostly radium), robots, and special detectors; even a time machine.

There are always gangsters and their minions, bent on stealing the devices or intimidating the scientist(s) into cooperating with their plans to enrich themselves; and/or or aliens bent on destroying or taking over the Earth. In one, the villain is entirely insane, yet he manages to command a whole squad of gangsters.

There is at least one fist fight, gun shootout, and car chase per chapter, as well as a cliff hanger ending which resolves differently in the next chapter and is something of a cheat to lure the audience back to the theater.

The budgets for these serials being extremely small, the entire lab usually occupies one room and is full of scientific clutter. The robots are badly put together, and a couple of them have really ugly face plates which do not correspond to their body types. They must be remote controlled, which means that they do not function well as super soldiers.

Chemicals are stored in jars on an open table or a shelf in the cubbard, and the fist fights erupt in the middle of everything. There are no security guards, and the facilities are placed in deserted warehouses or cabins in the woods; sometimes caves in the remotest boulder-strewn areas. A great many of them were shot in the hills above Chatsworth, California. There is little to explain how the scientists get their electricity, or why they are hiding out there apart from a need for security.

The costumes are extremely primitive, too, ranging from plain suits and hats to recycled costumes from previous serials, t-shirts and capes. The devices themselves are somewhat primitive, too. The lone exception is the door to the teleporter in "Brick Bradford", which sparkles with glitter and crystals. Otherwise, everything else looks plain as mud.

1

There is also one and only one female hero in each serial. Apparently, this feature was to appease the female audience. She would be a reporter, someone's daughter, a fiancee' or a sister. Toward the end of the 1940s, the heroine began to be regarded as a partner to the hero, but always ended up being menaced or kidnapped by the bad guys. She was always a bit smarter than the hero, yet she always held last place in the pecking order.

If one were to reprint the serials in continuous form they would make for some epic adventures, but I have fallen asleep while reviewing these things and I have to warn you that you would need a score card to keep up. The serials were produced from about 1936 to 1953, when television finally killed them off. After all, why pay the theater to get a weekly chapter when one can get them for free through the screen at home? I suspect that people were also tired of the cheating cliffhangers.

In any case, these serials were cumbersome and not really worth viewing in their entirety, though out of a sense of duty to accuracy I stuck to each one to the end. A story should have a beginning, a middle, and an end. The long protracted fist and gun fights, as well as the cliffhangers, detracted from their value as entertainment.

The 1950s soon broke out of the pattern provided by the preceding films and serials of the 1940s. Many of these films began to take on a distinctly anti-communist strain as the cold war broke out. And yet, somehow that too was left behind and more and experimental films were created devoid of propaganda.

The 1950s were also the most prolific and creative decade of the 20th century, exploring space, utopia, dystopias and post apocalypse scenarios. Some films were utterly brilliant despite their poor budgets. Others broke the mold with experimental sights and sounds. And some became iconic classics which can never be remade. As there were so many films produced in the 1950s, I broke the volume up into two pieces. This is the first book of this period. The second is also available.

Read on and prepare to be gobsmacked.

DESTINATION MOON (1950)

Directed by Irving Pichel
Produced by George Pal
Screenplay by James O'Hanlon, Robert A. Heinlein, and Rip Van
Ronkel; based on "Rocketship Galileo" by Robert A. Heinlein
Music by Leith Stevens
Cinematography by Lionel Lindon
Studio: George Pal Productions
Distributed by Eagle-Lion Classics Inc.; release date: June 27, 1950
(New York); running time 91 minutes

Cast:

John Archer as Jim Barnes
Warner Anderson as Dr. Charles Cargraves
Tom Powers as General Thayer
Dick Wesson as Joe Sweeney
Erin O'Brien-Moore as Emily Cargraves
Franklyn Farnum as Factory Worker (uncredited)
Everett Glass as Mr. La Porte (uncredited)
Knox Manning as Knox Manning (uncredited)

Plot: The story is about a successful first flight to the moon, made by four adventurous men who travel in a spacecraft (designed by Willy Ley) built by a private company. In a presentation to various industrial investors, the men show them a cartoon featuring Woody Woodpecker (produced by Walter Lanz) explaining the principles of space flight as was understood at the time. At the end, most of the investors are convinced that it would be good in practical terms to put their money behind the project, chiefly because they cannot stand the idea that a foreign power could conceivably beat them to the Moon and control the spacelanes.

Cargraves's company builds the rocket in only a few months, on a schedule to land the ship on the Moon when it is at the closest perigee. Then, the 4 man team learn of a court order to stop the launch and decide to take off early before the government officials can stop their departure. Due to public opinion, which is fearful of the possible consequences of any such effort, there are supposed issues with the idea of a nuclear powered rocket taking off, the potential for a nuclear

3

accident in the air, and also the response by other governments. (The problem with a rocket's spaceworthiness was made real by the tragic explosion of Shuttle *Challenger* in 1986 after almost 2 decades of successful shuttle and rocket launches.)

The astronauts are 3 highly educated men: retired Army general Thayer (Tom Powers); a famous scientist named Dr. Charles Cargraves (Warner Anderson); a technical executive, Jim Barnes (John Archer). The fourth is a man named "Joe Sweeney of Brooklyn, New York, USA" (played by by comedian Dick Wesson), who will operate the communications equipment.

Sweeney is a wise-cracking, cowardly "everyman" who does not believe the space ship will ever fly but needs the job for the money after his pal, an electrical engineer, becomes ill and cannot do it himself. He is comedy relief for the entire story. Sweeny's character also provides a foil for the other three men's more serious interactions, but later becomes a hero as well.

On the way to the moon, a problem develops which requires that crew members must go outside of the ship in space suits and make repairs, the first instance of an EVA space walk ever filmed. One of the team members accidentally loses his grip and drifts off into space, but is rescued by another crew member who uses an oxygen tank to propel himself toward him. The rescue scene is all done dramatically and believably, and this is true of additional dramatic moments in the movie. The astronauts are faced with all the same problems the Apollo crews experienced during the 1960s and 70s, and treat them with the same deliberate caution. The only difference is they are having to learn in situ instead of weeks of simulation beforehand.

After a narow miss with an asteroid, the space ship lands on the moon safely, and the commander claims the moon for the USA on behalf of all mankind, in a statement quite similar to the declaration the first NASA Apollo astronauts made famous in July of 1969, when astronaut Neil Armstrong declared, "that's one small step for a man; one giant leap for mankind."

But after making a cursory exploration of the Moon's surface, they discover a rich deposit of uranium ore. There is discussion of this find as justification for their trip. Sweeney is skeptical that their flight can be repeated. But Cargraves is certain that this opens the way for other expeditions to the Moon in the future.

When the explorers return to the space ship, they discover that they expended too much fuel already to make a safe return trip to Earth, and it is now too heavily loaded for a safe departure. They will need to unload large quantities of equipment and supplies to lighten the ship and make departure possible. (I wonder if the tons of moon rocks the Apollo astronauts gathered would have had to be left behind. That would have been a terrible turn of events!) After contacting the Earth by radio, they are told by calculation how much weight they must get rid of. They pitch out unnecessary items including used oxygen tanks and other large and unidentified metal objects; but after removing everything they can think of, an extra 110 pounds still remain to be shed!

Each traveler separately volunteers to remain behind, but Joe Sweeney actually suits up and leaves the ship while the other men are arguing. This is a moral dilemma they had not anticipated. When they find out what he has done they call him to return to the ship. Sweeney says he is redundant, that he will stay behind so his remaining three comrades can leave safely. There is to be no debate about it. The other three men declare that he is just as valuable as they are, refuse to launch without him and begin to look for alternatives.

Finally, Cargraves says "to hell with this," and decides to ditch the radio equipment, which weighs about that much; and there is no point in sending transmissions anyway. He tears the thing out of the wall, then declares that one of the suits, which weighs about 80 pounds, should suffice to make up the difference. Sweeney reluctantly climbs back aboard and is relieved to find that his personal sacrifice is not needed. Together, the astronauts rig the suit to be dragged out the airlock by the remaining oxygen tank. When the airlock is closed, the ship takes off.

The ship returns to the Earth with all four travellers, now good friends, safely aboard. The final end credit appears over the ship as it returns. (A somewhat inadequate close to what has been a great adventure so far. I would have loved to see the landing.) The credit reads "This is THE END... Of The Beginning."

Analysis and Additional Notes: *Destination Moon* was the first major science fiction film produced in the United States which deals realistically with the prospect of space travel. Science fiction writer

Robert A. Heinlein contributed significantly to the script and served as a technical advisor. Heinlein also published a novella, *Destination Moon*, based on the screenplay after the film's premiere.

The film advances the premise that private industry will finance and manufacture the first spacecraft to reach the Moon, given the Soviet threat at the time, and that the U.S. government will bring itself to buy or lease the technology. Visionary industrialists are shown cooperating to support the venture; to presage a great era of innovation and industrial progress in which they can exploit the Moon's resources to raise mankind's prosperity to new heights.

We now see that we are fulfilling this premonitory vision as the U.S. space program has been forced to rely on private enterprise in order to advance its goals in the 21st century; while visionaries like Sir Richard Branson, Paul Allen, and Elon Musk are working frantically to innovate new ways to get off the planet. That such projects will serve to enrich them even more is secondary.

The film was promoted through an unprecedented onslaught of publicity in the print media. 7 years before Sputnik, and 19 years before the actual moon landing, the film clearly spells out a rationale for the space race: unnamed enemies (clearly understood at the time to be the Soviet Union) are sabotaging the American space program, and unless the U.S. beats them to the Moon they will establish forward bases with which to conquer the world.

I am sure that President Eisenhower had this film clearly in mind when he wanted to create a space program in order to beat the Soviets into space. It took a few years to find men with "the right stuff" to take on the task, but he succeeded. (The book *The Right Stuff* by Tom Wolffe is a recommended historical read. The film will be reviewed later in another book.) It was not until President John F. Kennedy made his inaugural speech in 1960 that the effort redoubled with a vengeance. The U.S. would make its mark on history by landing men on the moon, never mind the Soviet threat; and clearly succeeded in July of 1969.

For its daring and exciting plotline, and good acting, I give this film 3 stars out of 4. IMdb give it 6.4 out of 10, while Rotten Tomatoes gives it 60% fresh, with an audience of 47%.

Production: *Destination Moon* includes an animated segment of Woody Woodpecker illustrating the basics of space flight. The segment serves to educate not only certain characters in the story but the audience as well. As a narrative device, this technique has been employed in subsequent films of that decade. Walt Disney employed Donald Duck in a similar capacity for other science fiction films.

The film shows the rocket being constructed in the desert, and the Lockheed aircraft plant in Southern California is shown with workers examining a model of the nuclear spacecraft, called a Constellation Class rocket. Additional sequences show several Lockheed rockets being assembled. The fictional rocket uses thermonuclear propulsion, a method that has never been employed in actual rocket launches to date. (The idea of a class of ship was repeated later in *Star Trek*. The Enterprise is a *Constitution Class* starship; carried over from Navy parlance since the starships are clearly treated as space submarines in the show.)

The sets and costumes were used and reused in later films, and even appear in the second episode of *The Time Tunnel*.

Both *Destination Moon* and a competing film called *Rocketship X-M* contain a polemical element, but with almost diametrically opposed messages: where *Rocketship X-M* (1950) contained a seriously intended antinuclear message, *Destination Moon* promoted a nuclear powered spacecraft. Once on the moon, the crew find evidence that the moon is a rich source of uranium, one of the main components of nuclear power. The idea is that resources are limited and that any subsequent missions would involve recovering more.

In Heinlein's novel *Rocketship Galileo*, the astronauts are high school boys led by an older scientist, and the enemies are the Nazis rather than the Soviets. In the film the sabotage is only vaguely hinted at. The concept of a space race is introduced; the voyage is a massive industrial rather than scientific undertaking, and the plot revolves around the practical dangers of the voyage. A common element in both stories is that the rocket takes off in defiance of a court order. *Destination Moon* is in fact more similar to Heinlein's novella *The Man Who Sold the Moon*, which according to its copyright date was written in 1949, although it was not published until 1951, the year after *Destination Moon* premiered.

Destination Moon's matte paintings, used for the departure of the space ship from Earth, its approach to the Moon, the spaceship's landing on its surface, and the panoramic lunar landscape, are by noted astronomical artist Chesley Bonestell. He was intrumental in promoting space for NASA and other aeronautic companies by creating realistic landscapes and space paintings evoking a desire to explore space.

Director: Irving Pichel was selected to direct the film, his 30th since 1932. Pichel began his Hollywood career as an actor during the 1920s and early 1930s, in such films as *Dracula's Daughter* and *The Story of Temple Drake*. Pichel had been blacklisted after he was subpoenaed by the House Unamerican Activities Committee in 1947, despite having never been called to testify before the committee. He would go on to direct five more films after *Destination Moon* before his death in 1954.

Woody Woodpecker: Cartoon character Woody Woodpecker's creator Walter Lantz and producer George Pal had been close friends ever since Pal left Europe and arrived in Hollywood. As a result, out of friendship and good luck, Pal always tried to include Woody in all his film productions. (On the commentary track of the Special Collector's DVD Edition of George Pal's science fiction film *War of The Worlds* [1953], actors Ann Robinson and Gene Barry point out that Woody can be seen in a tree top, center screen, near the beginning of the film.) George Pal incorporated Woody into *Destination Moon* as a vital part of its unfolding storyline.

In a cartoon shown within the film, Woody (voiced by Grace Stafford) explains the scientific principles behind space travel and then a trip to the Moon. This engaging cartoon is shown to a gathering of U.S. industrialists, who it is hoped will patriotically finance such a daring venture before an (unnamed) non-western power can do so successfully. The Woody cartoon actually serves the purpose of explaining, in layman's terms, to the average 1950 moviegoing audience, the practical details of a manned space expedition to the Moon and how it might be accomplished.

Soundtrack: The soundtrack music, written by composer Leith Stevens, is noteworthy for its atmospheric themes and musical motifs, all of which add subtle but important detail and emotion to the various dramatic moments in the film. According to George Pal biographer Gail Morgan Hickman, "Stevens consulted with numerous scientists, including Wernher von Braun, to get an idea of what space was like in order to create it musically." The Stevens *Destination Moon* film score had its first U.S. release in 1950 on a 10 inch 33 rpm Monaural LP by

Columbia Records. I owned this LP in its 20th reissue until vinyl went out of popularity for a time.

Release: Despite its half-a-million dollar budget and a large national print media and radio publicity campaign preceding its delayed release, *Destination Moon* ultimately became the "second" space adventure film of the post-World War II era. Piggybacking on the growing publicity and expectation surrounding the Pal film, Lippert Pictures' small budget ($94,000) and quickly shot (18 days) *Rocketship X-M*, about the first spaceship to land on distant Mars, opened in movie theaters 25 days before the Pal feature.

Critical reaction: Bosley Crowther in his review of *Destination Moon* for The New York Times, opined, "... we've got to say this for Mr. Pal and his film: they make a lunar expedition a most intriguing and picturesque event. Even the solemn preparations for this unique exploratory trip, though the lesser phase of the adventure, are profoundly impressive to observe".

In a later appraisal in a <u>Time Out</u> (UK) review, editor John Pym saw *Destination Moon* as having both good and bad aspects", ... characteristically thin on plot and characterization, high on patriotism, and impressive in its colour photography and special effects; a true precursor to Star Wars."

Author and film critic Leonard Maltin awarded the film two and a half out of four stars, calling it "modestly mounted but still effective", Maltin also praised Bonestell's lunar paintings as being visually striking.

In his autobiography, Isaac Asimov called it "the first intelligent science-fiction movie made."

Awards and honors: Destination Moon won the Academy Award for Visual Effects in the name of the effects director, Lee Zavitz. The film was also nominated for the Academy Award for Best Art Direction, by Ernst Fegté and George Sawley.

At the 1st Berlin International Film Festival it won the Bronze Berlin Bear Award, for "Thrillers and Adventure Films."

Retro Hugo Awards: A special 1951 Hugo Award for Best Dramatic Presentation was retroactively awarded to Destination Moon by the 59th World Science Fiction Convention (2001) exactly 50 years later for being one of the science fiction films eligible in calendar year 1950. 50 years, 75 years, or 100 years govern the time periods

9

when a Retro Hugo can be awarded by a Worldcon for the years prior to 1953, when the Hugos were established and first awarded.

Adaptations: Episode 12 of the *Dimension X* radio series was called *Destination Moon* and was based on Heinlein's final draft of the film's shooting script. During its broadcast on June 24, 1950, the program was interrupted by a news bulletin announcing that North Korea had declared war on South Korea, marking the beginning of the Korean War.

Robert A. Heinlein published an adaptation in the September 1950 issue of <u>Short Stories</u> magazine.

A highly condensed version of the Dimension X *Destination Moon* radio play was adapted by Charles Palmer and was released by Capitol Records for children, who had become familiar with their recordings through a "Bozo the Clown approved" record series. The series featured 7 inch, 78rpm recordings and full color booklets which children could follow as they listened to the stories. The *Destination Moon* record was narrated by Tom Reddy, and Billy May composed the incidental and background music. The record's storyline took considerable liberties with the film's plot and characters, although the general shape of the film story remained.

In 1950, Fawcett Publications released a 10¢ *Destination Moon* film tie-in comic book. DC Comics also published a comic book preview on the Pal film. It was the cover feature of DC's brand new science fiction anthology comic book <u>Strange Adventures</u> #1 (September 1950).

The same year, <u>Tintin Magazine</u> released a serialization from *The Adventures of Tintin* stories titled *Destination Moon* by the Belgian cartoonist Herge'. It ran from March 30, 1950 to September 7, 1950.

FLYING DISC MAN FROM MARS (1950)

A serial of 12 chapters
Directed by Fred C. Brannon
Produced by Franklin Adreon
Written by Ronald Davidson
Music by Stanley Wilson
Cinematography by Walter Strenge
Distributed by Republic Pictures; release date: October 25, 1950
Running time: 12 chapters / 167 minutes
Budget: $152,640 (negative cost: $157,439)

Cast:
Walter Reed as Kent Fowler, pilot
Lois Collier as Helen Hall
Gregory Gaye as Mota, martian invader
James Craven as Dr Bryant, scientist and Nazi supporter
Harry Lauter as Drake, one of Mota's henchmen
Richard Irving as Ryan, one of Mota's henchmen
Sandy Sanders as Steve, Kent's sidekick
Michael Carr as Trent, discship pilot and henchman
Stunts:
Dale Van Sickel Kent Fowler/Watchman (doubling for Walter Reed)
David Sharpe as Henchman Ryan/Technician (doubling for Richard Irving)
Tom Steele as Henchman Drake/Trent/Taylor (doubling for Harry Lauter and Michael Carr)
Carey Loftin as Truck Loader Thug

Plot: Martian invader Mota (Gregory Gaye), comes to conquer the Earth since Mars is worried about its use of new atomic technologies. They consider that it would be much safer, and beneficial for both Earth and Mars, if the Martians were in charge. Having his flying disc shot down by an experimental ray gun from Earth, Mota blackmails an American scientist and former Nazi, Dr. Bryant (James Craven), into assisting him, and hires some criminals to be his henchmen and do the rougher chores.

Kent Fowler (Walter Reed), the private pilot who shot down Mota's flying disc with Dr. Bryant's ray gun, gets caught up in these events while in charge of security for various atomic industrial sites.

Mota appears to be one step ahead of him when he must contend with the henchmen. Fist fights, gunfights, and car chases abound. With the help of his girlfriend Helen Hall (Lois Collier), he manages to foil Mota's plans.

Mota has been keeping his flying disc in the sinkwell of a volcano and flies sorties from there. Kent sets a trap, but Mota manages to kidnap Helen and takes her to his hideout in order to force Kent to give him the plans to the ray gun and other weapons in development. Kent traces him down to the volcano and frees Helen, but in the fight Kent accidentally kicks a bomb into the lavabed.

The volcano reacts to the explosion with explosions of its own. In the chaos Kent and Helen get into the disc and take off, while Mota and his henchmen are killed in the eruption. The eruption damages the disc as it takes off. Kent and Helen are forced to parachute out to save themselves. The disc is destroyed forever.

Later, Kent announces to Helen and a friend that he is going to train for the Air Force as a fighter pilot. END

Analysis and additional notes: This one was a tedious stinker. For one thing, one man alone cannot hope to save the day against what is supposed to be an overwhelming force. He would require the backing of the Army or Air Force with considerable firepower to defeat an enemy like Mars. For another, the ray gun may have been nifty, and the disc "invincible", but the disc could hardly hold 3 men at a time. In fact, the interior of the disc was bigger on the inside than it was on the outside. And I don't see how Mars would send one of theirs alone and without any help, when it would require at least 3 Martians to do the job. Not to mention that, owing to the lighter gravity on Mars, Mota could not have done a 6th of his tasks. Pffft.

In fact, I did not see the whole thing, but watched the first and the last chapter to get the lay of the land. After recording at least two fist fights, and a huge gunfight in the end chapter (with revolvers that held more than 8 bullets at a time, by my estimation), the capper was the eruption of a volcano which destroys everything. That is called a cheat. The resolution should have involved turning Mota and Bryant over to the government. Instead, science is forced to go back to the drawing board.

For its plodding and fight-ridden plot, I give this film 1.5 stars out of 4. IMdb gives it 5.8 out of 10, and Rotten Tomatoes gives it no rating at all.

Chapter titles: Menace from Mars - The Volcano's Secret - Death Rides The Stratosphere - Execution by Fire - The Living Projectile - Perilous Mission - Descending Doom - Suicidal Sacrifice - The Funeral Pyre - Weapons of Hate (recap chapter) - Disaster on the Highway - Volcanic Vengeance

Production: *Flying Disc Man From Mars* was budgeted at $152,640, although the final negative cost was $157,439. It was the most expensive Republic serial made in 1950. It was filmed between August 21 and September 12, 1950 under several working titles: *Atom Man From Mars, Disc Man From Mars, Disc Men of The Skies, Flying Planet Men,* and *Jet Man From Mars.* The serial's production number was 1709.

This was a sequel to Republic's earlier serial *The Purple Monster Strikes.* The villain Mota reuses the Purple Monster costume from that serial.

Special effects: The flying disc aircraft from Republic's *King of The Mounties* was reused for this serial (note that the Japanese rising sun logo is still visible). In some shots the flying wing footage was from Republic's *Spy Smasher* serial, where the tail fin is missing.

Stock footage from several earlier Republic serials was reused to pad out *Disc Man* in order to lower its production costs. This includes the rocket crash from *The Purple Monster Strikes*, a car chase from *Secret Service In Darkest Africa*, and various scenes from *G-Men vs. The Black Dragon*.

All special effects in this serial were produced by the Lydecker brothers, the inhouse duo who designed most of Republic's special effects.

Release: *Theatrical: Flying Disc Man From Mars*'s official release date is October 25, 1950, though this is actually the date the 6th chapter was made available to film exchanges. A 75 minute feature film version, created by editing the serial footage together, was released on March 28, 1958 under the new title *Missile Monsters*. It was one of 14 feature films Republic made from their serials.

THE FLYING SAUCER (1950)

Produced and directed by Mikel Conrad
Written by Howard Irving Young and Mikel Conrad
Music by Darrell Calker
Cinematography by Phillip Tannura
Edited by Robert Crandall
Production company: Colonial Productions, Inc.
Distributed by Film Classics Inc.; Release date Jan 5, 1950;
Runtime: 120 minutes
On Disc/Streaming: May 8, 2001; Running time: 75 minutes
Studio: Film Classics

Cast:
Mikel Conrad as Mike Trent
Pat Garrison as Vee Langley
Hantz von Teuffen as Hans
Roy Engel as Dr. Lawton
Lester Sharpe as Col. Marikoff
Denver Pyle as Turner, a spy
Earl Lyon as Alex, a spy
Frank Darrien as Matt Mitchell
Russell Hicks as Intelligence Chief Hank Thorn
Virginia Hewitt as Nanette, bar girl
Gary Owens as Bartender

Plot: American Intelligence officials learn that Soviet spies have begun exploring a remote region of the Alaskan Territory in search of answers to the worldwide reports of "flying saucers".

A wealthy American playboy, Mike Trent (Mikel Conrad), who was raised in that remote region, is recruited by intelligence officer Hank Thorn (Russell Hicks) to assist a Secret Service agent in exploring that area to discover what the Soviets may have found. At first Mike is highly resistant to the idea. He wants to continue partying at his own pace. After a night of "fun", he finds himself hijacked and taken to an isolated island in the Aleutians with a woman who is there to "take care of him". Her cover is that she a nurse and that Trent is a reclusive patient who had suffered a nervous breakdown and has come to take in the air.

To his pleasant surprise, Mike discovers the agent in charge of him is an attractive woman named Vee Langley (Pat Garrison). After some adjustments to his situation, they slowly become attracted to each other, with the proviso that it's the job which is important. At Mike's family's wilderness lodge, they are met by a caretaker with a foreign accent named Hans (Hantz von Teuffen), who is new to the job.

Meanwhile, a group of Soviet agents have followed Trent and party, and are planning to steal the flying saucer to reverse engineer it for their leaders. They make plans and make plans, but never seem to succeed. Hans sneaks away to make reports to them.

Mike is very skeptical of the flying saucer reports until he spots one flying over the mountains near the lodge. Assorted complications ensue until Mike and Vee finally discover that Hans is one of the Soviet agents who is trying to acquire the flying saucer.

But, it turns out that the saucer is an invention of American scientist named Dr. Laughton (Roy Engel). His assistant Turner (Denver Pyle), is a communist sympathizer and has other ideas. He tries to make a deal to sell the saucer to the Soviets for 1 million dollars. Laughton keeps the saucer in a basement hangar underneath his mansion. There are issues with its engineering, and all the bugs have not been ironed out yet.

Mike starts suffering from cabin fever and makes a trip to Juneau to see old friends, which has been ill advised. He meets up with Matt Mitchell (Frank Darrien), and when Vee tracks Mike down he is in the company of a bar girl named Nanette (Virginia Hewitt). Matt gets mixed up with the Soviet agents who are trying to obtain control of the saucer. When he tries to strike a bargain with ring leader Colonel Marikoff (Lester Sharpe) at his headquarters, Matt is knocked unconscious. When the agents leave to do errands, Matt comes to and manages to escape.

Matt seeks out Mike, but they are attacked by the agents, who kill Matt. Before he dies, however, Matt reveals the location of the saucer: Twin Lakes.

Mike rents an aircraft and flies to where the saucer is hidden in an isolated cabin. The wunderkindt is not as big or as formidable as he thought. After flying back to his lodge, Mike tries to find Vee, who has tried to spirit Lawton away. The trio are captured by the turncoat Taylor and a group of Soviet agents. The Soviets lead their prisoners through a secret tunnel hidden under the glacier, but an avalanche begins which wipes the spies out.

Mike, Vee, and Lawton escape the tunnel just in time to see Turner flying off in the saucer. It suddenly explodes in midair, due to a time bomb that Lawton had planted on board for such an eventuality.

Their mission now accomplished, Mike and Vee embrace and kiss. END

Analysis and additional notes: After watching this film I was seriously on the fence whether it is science fiction or simply industrial espionage with a political tie-in. For one thing we don't see the actual flying saucer until halfway through the film. For another, there was too much time spent traveling back and forth from one place to another. In fact it looked to me like a travelogue with scientific underpinnings. The Soviet spies were totally ineffectual, even though their plans appeared sound. The problem was with execution.

As for Mike Trent, he is unable to take the situation seriously. He does not realize the true danger he is in, until Matt dies. He does not want to be there. He thinks that someone else can do the job better, but he is in a position to make something of his life for his country. So, as a reluctant hero he fits the bill to a T.

On the whole it was a long, plodding, unsatisfying film. So I give it 1.5 stars out of 4. IMdb gives it 3.8 out of 10 (ouch), and Rotten Tomatoes gives it a 0 (ouch, ouch).

Production: Principal photography for *The Flying Saucer* took place from late September to early October of 1949 at Hal Roach Studios. Additional B-roll photography was shot in Alaska on location where, according to a September 21, 1949 article in the <u>Los Angeles Examiner</u>, Mikel Conrad claimed to have obtained footage of actual flying saucers while shooting *Arctic Manhunt* in Alaska in the winter of 1947. This is open to wide speculation, but there were many rumors that the Soviets had developed flying saucers in order to attack the United States, but none of them panned out. To date, the US has never been attacked by a flying saucer or saucers, Martians, or anything else of that ilk.

The opening prologue appears before the onscreen credits and states: "We gratefully acknowledge the cooperation of those in authority who made the release of the 'Flying Saucer' film possible at this time." The message obliquely alluded to some authorized government films of flying saucers. None of that footage was actually included in *The Flying Saucer*.

Reception: The Flying Saucer did not rise above its B film origins. Its low budget production doomed it to the bottom end of theater playbills and drive-ins.

<u>New York Times</u> film critic Bosley Crowther observed: "A film called 'The Flying Saucer' flew into the Rialto yesterday and, except for some nice Alaskan scenery, it can go right on flying, for all we care. In fact, it is such a clumsy item that we doubt if it will go very far, and we hesitate, out of mercy, to fire even a critical shot at it". For fear of destroying its balsa wood construction, no doubt.

Copyright: Striking while the iron was hot, actor/producer Mikel Conrad registered the title *The Flying Saucer* for copyright not long after UFOs were allegedly spotted in Washington State. Filmed on location in Alaska, *Flying Saucer* stars Conrad (who also co-wrote the script) as a reluctant secret agent dispatched by the government to find out whether or not the UFO reports constitute a threat against American defenses.

All rights to *The Flying Saucer* have been owned worldwide and in perpetuity since 1977 by Wade Williams. Copyright was renewed on November 29, 1977 (R 677308), Library of Congress Copyright Office.

THE INVISIBLE MONSTER (1950) A serial of 12 chapters

Directed by Fred C. Brannon
Written by Ronald Davidson
Produced by Franklin Adreon associate producer
Music by Stanley Wilson
Cinematography by Ellis W. Carter
Film Editing by Cliff Bell and Sam Starr
Art Direction by Fred A. Ritter
Set Decoration by John McCarthy Jr. and James Redd
Makeup Department: Bob Mark
Hairstyles by Peggy Gray (uncredited)
Production Management: Roy Wade and Lewis T. Rosso (uncredited)
Sound Department: Earl Crain Sr.
Special Effects by Howard and Theodore Lydecker
Camera and Electrical Department: Bud Thackery (uncredited)

Costume and Wardrobe Department: Adele Palmer (uncredited)
Music Department; Stock Music: (uncredited composers) Robert
Armbruster, R. Dale Butts, Joseph Dubin, Mort Glickman, Jerry
Roberts, Walter Scharf, Nathan Scott, Roy Webb
Dog trainer: Earl Johnson (uncredited)
Production company: Republic Studios; release date: May 10, 1950;
streaming: Nov 21, 1991; **runtime:** 167 minutes
Budget: $152,115 (estimated).

Cast:

Richard Webb as Lane Carson
Aline Towne as Carol Richards
Lane Bradford as Burton
Stanley Price as The Phantom Ruler
John Crawford as Harris
George Meeker as Harry Long
Keith Richards as Doctor [Ch.12]
Dale Van Sickel as Otto Wagner / Frank Martin [Chs. 1, 10]
Tom Steele as Bill 'Mack' Haines [Chs. 5,10]
Marshall Reed as MacDuff - Roadblock Cop [Chs.1, 7-9]
Forrest Burns as Joe - Watchman [Ch.5]
Ed Parker as Stoner - Barn Henchman[Ch.9]
Frank O'Connor as Hogan [Ch.5]
Chas Regan as Art
Charles Sullivan as Grogarty - Squad Car Cop [Chs.7-8]
Howard Mitchell as 2nd Garage Watchman [Ch.7]
Bud Wolfe as Harding - Henchman [Ch.8]
Rest of cast listed alphabetically (uncredited):
Douglas Evans as James Hunter [Chs. 1, 3, 7, 12]
Harold Goodwin as Kirk - Body-Shop Henchman [Ch.11]
Roy Gordon as Mr. Moore [Chs.8-9]
John Hamilton as Henry Miller [Chs. 1, 8, 12]
Edward Keane as Warren Madison
Bert LeBaron as Crooked Watchman [Ch.2
Carey Loftin as Dirk - Dynamite Thug [Ch.6]
George Magrill as Sam - Thug-Truck Driver [Chs.4-5]
Tom Monroe as Gates - Cop in Cave [Ch.7]

David Sharpe as 3rd Garage Watchman [Chs. 3-4] / 2nd Armored Car
Guard [Ch. 11]
Mark Strong as Bank Watchman [Ch.1]
Duke Taylor as Second Roadblock Cop [Ch.1]
Guy Teague as Al - Decoy & Dump-Truck Thug [Chs. 5, 7]
Ken Terrell as Kern - Henchman [Chs. 8-9]
George Volk as Second Armored Car Guard [Ch.11]
Stunts (uncredited): Bert LeBaron, Carey Loftin, George Magrill,
Eddie Parker, David Sharpe, Tom Steele (doubled for Richard Webb),
Duke Taylor, Guy Teague, Ken Terrell, Dale Van Sickel (doubled for
George Meeker and Roy Gordon), and Bud Wolfe

Plot: An evil villain called The Phantom Ruler (Stanley Price) plots to
take over the world using an army of invisible soldiers. He has
developed an invisibility serum to make this possible. Using four
illegal European aliens as his minions, The Phantom Ruler goes on an
unchecked crime spree to finance his project. Insurance company
investigator Lane Carson (Richard Webb) is assigned to determine the
identity of The Phantom Ruler and to put the cuffs on him once and
for all. Both Carson and his assistant Carol Richards (Aline Towne) are
subjected to any number of life threatening perils before justice is
meted out in the final chapter. END

Analysis and additional notes: As usual so far, this serial is less about
the chemistry and more about the fist fights and gunfights, chewing
up scenery and in other ways proving to be basically a waste of time.
After watching several serial adventures of this ilk I felt it was time to
just list them and their chapter titles and put them to bed, because so
far the most complete part of *The Phantom Ruler* is the credits.

I will not even rate this one. IMdb gives it 3.8 out of 10, while
Rotten Tomatoes gives it nothing.

Production: beyond the cast and crew, the notes are pretty sparse
to nonexistent. For a serial dubbed "the best Republic serial ever"
there does not appear to be any real fan following, enough to show
any actual notes which I could list here.

ROCKETSHIP X-M (1950)

Produced and directed by Kurt Neumann
Executive producer: Robert L. Lippert
Screenplay by Orville H. Hampton, Kurt Neumann, and Dalton Trumbo
Music by Ferde Grofé
Cinematography by Karl Struss
Edited by Harry Gerstad
Production company: Lippert Pictures
Distributed by Lippert Pictures; release date: May 26, 1950
Running time: 78 minutes; budget $94,000

Cast:

Lloyd Bridges as Col. Floyd Graham (Pilot)
Osa Massen as Dr. Lisa Van Horn (Ph.D. in Chemistry)
John Emery as Dr. Karl Eckstrom (Physicist and RX-M designer)
Noah Beery, Jr. as Maj. William Corrigan (Flight engineer)
Hugh O'Brian as Harry Chamberlain (Astronomer and navigator)
Morris Ankrum as Dr. Ralph Fleming (Project Director)

Plot: Four men and a woman blast into outer space from the White Sands Proving Ground aboard the RX-M (Rocketship Expedition-Moon) on humanity's first expedition to the Moon. Halfway there, after jettisoning a runaway first stage and avoiding a meteoroid storm, their engines suddenly quit. Recalculating fuel ratios and swapping fuel tank positions fixes the problem temporarily. After the engines finally fire, RX-M rapidly careens out of control on a rapid heading beyond the Moon. Lower oxygen pressure also causes the crew to slowly pass out.

They gradually revive much later and discover that they have traveled some 50,000,000 miles and are now on a direct heading toward Mars. Quick calculations reveal that RX-M is only 50,000 miles away from Mars. Dr. Karl Eckstrom (John Emery) is forced to "pause and observe respectfully while something infinitely greater assumes control".

RX-M passes through the Martian atmosphere and lands safely. The next morning the scientists, clad in aviation oxygen masks due to the low pressure, begin exploring the desolate surface.

They come across physical evidence of an advanced Martian civilization which is now dead. They find a partially buried, stylized, Art Deco or Tiki culture metal face sculpture and, in the distance, ruins like Moderne architecture. Their Geiger counter registers dangerous radiation levels, keeping them well away from exploring further in that direction. Based on the levels detected, there was once an atomic war on Mars sometime in the distant past.

The scientists find a cave refuge from which to reconnoiter further. Then, they notice the primitive descendants of that civilization emerging from behind boulders and creeping toward them. They are skinny, wasted, clad in rags, all burned or maimed by the radiation.

Dr. Eckstrom mutters, "from Atomic Age to Stone Age".

Soon after leaving the cave, two of the explorers encounter a dark-haired woman who has lost her footing and rolled down a hill toward them. She is blind, with thick, milky cataracts on both eyes. She screams upon hearing their voices through their oxygen masks.

The ragtag tribesmen attack, throwing large rocks and stone axes. Armed with only a revolver and a bolt action rifle, the explorers defend themselves, purposely missing the primitives, but they appear to be determined to kill the newcomers. Dr. Eckstrom is killed by a stone axe; navigator Chamberlain (Hugh O'Brian) is badly injured by a large thrown rock. The survivors finally make their way back to the RX-M as fast as they can and take off just in time.

As the RX-M nears Earth, the scientists calculate that they have no fuel for a landing. Col. Graham (Lloyd Bridges) contacts their base and reports their dire status to Dr. Fleming (Morris Ankrum), who listens intently and wordlessly over headphones.

Col. Graham's report is not heard on screen, but Fleming's subtle reactions tells of the crew's odyssey, their discovery of a once advanced civilization destroyed long ago by atomic war, and of the crew fatalities at the hands of Martian descendants who have reverted to barbarism.

Col. Graham and Dr. Van Horn (Osa Massen) embrace as the RX-M begins its uncontrolled descent, consoling one another in the moments left to them. Through a porthole, they bravely watch their rapid descent into the wilds of Nova Scotia.

The press is later informed by a shaken Dr. Fleming that the entire crew had perished. When they ask if the mission was a failure, he confidently responds with conviction that all theories about manned spaceflight and exploration have now been proven. He continues, underscoring the point that a dire warning has been received that could very well mean the salvation of humanity: "a new spaceship, the RX-M-2, begins construction tomorrow."

The pioneering exploration continues. END

Analysis and additional notes: This film was about as gripping in scope as *Destination Moon,* only it goes quite a bit farther than that film. We are shown a possible destiny if we ever to engage in nuclear war. We are shown the consequences in stark terms through the behavior of the tribe on Mars.

These are the doomed survivors of nuclear war, who do not have anything left to claim but their lives. They resent anyone intruding on their desperation, they little understand what the scientists mean to them. Anyone who is different from them becomes the enemy, to be destroyed however they can manage it. And also the scientists mean food. Who knows how many of the survivors of this ancient war had fed on each other in order to stay alive? But it appears hopeless. Soon they would be dead, and there would be nothing left.

At the same time, there appears to be no heroic return to Earth for the scientists aboard Rocketship X-M. They all die tragically, after losing two of their own on Mars. There is to be no ticket tape parade, no celebrations of their accidental success. They were headed to the Moon, and instead ended up on Mars. They were not prepared for the shock of reaching farther than they intended, and their ship was dysfunctional at best. They had two choices: die on Mars, or die on Earth. They chose Earth.

For this panorama of science fiction warning, I give it 3 stars out of 4. IMdb gives it 4.9 out of 10, possibly for its negative plot, and Rotten Tomatoes gives it no rating, yet.

Production: Because production issues had delayed the release of George Pal's high profile *Destination Moon, Rocketship X-M* was quickly shot in just 18 days. It was then rushed into movie theaters 25 days before the Pal film, while taking full advantage of *Destination Moon's* national publicity. Talk about a space race!

Given the film's minimal special effects budget and limited shooting days, the surface of Mars was much easier to simulate using remote Southern California locations than creating the airless and cratered surface of the Moon. The location where the crew exits the spacecraft and begins to explore is Zabriski Point in Death Valley National Park. The film's original 1950 theatrical release prints had all Mars scenes tinted a pinkish-red color.

The RX-M's design was taken from rocket illustrations that appeared in an article in the January 17, 1949 issue of Life magazine. The interior structure of the spaceship's larger second stage is shown as having a long ladder that the crew must climb; it runs "up" through the RX-M's fuel compartment, which has on all sides a series of narrow fuel tanks filled with various propulsion chemicals. By selecting and mixing them together in various proportions, different levels of thrust are attainable from the RX-M's engines. The crew ladder ends at a round pressure hatch in the middle of a floor bulkhead that leads to the crew's upper living and control compartments.

Instruments and technical equipment were supplied by Allied Aircraft Company of North Hollywood.

Historical and factual accuracy: The five Mars explorers wear U.S. military surplus clothing, including overalls and aviator's leather jackets. It has been noted in other film reviews that the explorers are wearing gas masks, but gas masks would include goggles to protect the eyes. Due to the thin Martian atmosphere, the explorers are actually wearing military "Oxygen Breathing Apparatuses" (OBA) like those used by military firefighters.

Various scientific curiosities and errors are seen during the film:

1) With less than 15 minutes to go until launch, the RX-M's crew are still in the midst of a leisurely press conference being held at a base building. There is no preparation procedure.

2) From its launch pad, the RX-M blasts straight up, and once it leaves the Earth's atmosphere, the ship makes a hard 90° turn to place the RX-M into Earth orbit. Its speed at an altitude of 360 miles is stated to be 3,400 mph (1.5 km/s); in fact at that height orbital velocity is 18,783 mph (8.397 km/s) [though escape velocity is approximately correctly stated to be 25,000 mph (11 km/s)]. In order to achieve the right orbital velocity the ship would have to execute a slow series of spirals once it entered the ionosphere.

3) Simultaneously with that 90° turn, the crew cabin rotates within the RX-M's hull around its lateral axis, so the ship's cabin deck is

always facing "down", orienting the audience. Though objects are purposely shown to float free to demonstrate a lack of gravity, none of the five crew members float, apparently unaffected by weightlessness. So the simulation of gravity is contradictory.

4) The RX-M's jettisoned first stage, with its engine still firing, and a later meteoroid storm (inaccurately referred to in dialogue as meteorites) both make audible roaring sounds in the soundless vacuum of space that can also be heard inside the crew compartment. The clusters of those fast moving meteoroids appear identical in shape and detail. Actually, the same prop meteoroids were shot from different angles and positions, then optically printed in tandem, at different sizes, on the film's master negative.

5) A point is made in dialogue that the RX-M is carrying more than "double" the amount of rocket fuel and oxygen needed to make a successful round trip and landing on the Moon. While impractical for various reasons, this detail becomes a convenient, then a necessary plot device in making the later Mars story line more plausible. Actually, the fuel consumption of the RX-M was negligable given that statement. In order to reach Mars, the fuel would have been consumed halfway there. So they would have continued to drift along carried by inertia until they crash landed on Mars.

Several scenes in *Rocketship X-M* involving the interaction between the RX-M's sole female crew member, scientist Dr. Lisa Van Horn, her male crew, the launch site staff, and the press corps provide cultural insights into early 1950s sexist attitudes toward women.

One notable scene involves Van Horn and expedition leader (and fellow scientist) Dr. Karl Eckstrom rushing to recalculate fuel mixtures after their initial propulsion problems. When they each come up with different figures, expedition leader Eckstrom insists they must proceed using his numbers. Van Horn objects to this arbitrary decision, but submits, and Eckstrom forgives her for "momentarily being a woman." Subsequent events prove Eckstrom's arbitrary decision to be wrong, placing them all in jeopardy.

Lippert's feature was the first film drama to explore the dangers of nuclear warfare and atomic radiation through the lens of science fiction. These became recurrent themes in many 1950s science fiction films that followed.

Dalton Trumbo, blacklisted during the McCarthy era, wrote the film's Red Planet sequence, adding the horror of an atomic war having occurred on Mars. His name does not appear in the film credits.

New footage added: A lack of both time and budget forced RX-M's producers to omit special effects scenes and substitute stock footage of V-2 rocket launches in flight to complete some sequences that otherwise would have been made using the Rocketship X-M special effects miniature. The V-2 inserts created very noticeable continuity issues and no doubt made the audience laugh. I know that I did. The V-2 footage was abandoned in favor of more modern designs after this film was made.

In the 1970s, the rights to *Rocketship X-M* were acquired by Kansas City film exhibitor, movie theater owner, and later video distributor Wade Williams, who set about reshooting some of the special effects scenes in order to improve the film's overall continuity. The VHS tape, LaserDisc and DVD releases incorporate this footage.

The new footage was produced for Wade Williams Productions by Bob Burns III, his wife Kathy, former Disney designer/artist Tom Scherman, Academy Award winner Dennis Muren, Emmy Award nominee Michael Minor, and Academy Award winner Robert Skotak.

Costumes were remade that closely replicated those worn by the film's astronauts; and a new, screen accurate Rocketship X-M effects miniature was built.

The new replacement shots consist of the RX-M flying through space, landing tail first on the Red Planet, a different shot of the crew heading away from the RX-M to explore the stark Martian surface, the surviving explorers quickly returning to their nearby spaceship, and the RX-M later blasting off from Mars into space. These six replacement shots were filmed near Los Angeles in color, then converted to black and white and retinted where necessary to match the original film footage.

Unlike the DVD release, the laser disc of *Rocketship X-M* contains extra bonus material documenting the making of the film and the creation of this new footage. The film's production and the making of these new scenes were also presented in feature articles in both <u>Starlog</u> magazine and later expanded in the first issue (1979) of <u>Starlog</u>'s spin-off magazine <u>CineMagic</u>.

Prints of the original theatrical release version of *Rocketship X-M* are still stored in Williams's Kansas City film vaults. They have not been converted to a home video format.

Rocketship X-M is not in the public domain. A copyright renewal for the film was registered under Certificate #R678491 from the Copyright Office of Library of Congress.

Image's 50th Anniversary DVD release (2000), under license from Williams, is oddly missing two of his refilmed Mars scenes: Lippert's original matte painting scene, which has tiny figures leaving an obviously painted RX-M, is retained instead of the Williams' replacement scene that has the 5 explorers heading away from a convincing RX-M effects miniature standing on a barren Martian plain. A new bridging scene, set at the end of the Mars sequence, shows the surviving explorers returning in a rush to the RX-M, and is also missing from Image's DVD.

Awards: Retro Hugo Award: Rocketship X-M was nominated in 2001 for the 1951 Retro Hugo Award For Best Dramatic Presentation, being one of the science fiction films eligible during calendar year 1950, exactly 50 years after the film's first release. 50 years, 75 years, or 100 years prior is the eligibility requirement governing the awarding of Retro Hugos.

Mystery Science Theater 3000: The film was featured in the 2nd season premiere episode of the cult film lampooning television series *Mystery Science Theater 3000. Rocketship X-M* stands as an important episode in that show's history, showcasing iconic set redesigns as well as the introduction of Kevin Murphy and Frank Conniff to their long-running performance roles as "Tom Servo" and "TV's Frank", respectively.

ABBOTT AND COSTELLO MEET THE INVISIBLE MAN

(1951)

Directed by Charles Lamont

Produced by Howard Christie

Screenplay by Robert Lees, Frederic I. Rinaldo, and John Grant

Story by Hugh Wedlock Jr. and Howard Snyder; based on The Invisible Man by H. G. Wells

Music by Erich Zeisl

Cinematography by George Robinson

Edited by Virgil Vogel

Production company: Universal-International

Distributed by Universal Pictures; release date: March 19, 1951

Running time: 82 minutes; budget: $627,000, box office $1,550,000

Cast:

Bud Abbott as Bud Alexander

Lou Costello as Lou Francis

Arthur Franz as Tommy Nelson/The Invisible Man

Nancy Guild as Helen Gray

Adele Jergens as Boots Marsden

Sheldon Leonard as Morgan

William Frawley as Detective Roberts

Gavin Muir as Dr. Philip Gray

Sam Balter as Radio announcer

John Daheim as Rocky Hanlon

Paul Maxey as Dr. James C. Turner

James Best as Tommy Nelson (Franz's stand-in)

Claude Rains appears in a photograph as Jack Griffin (now called John), the original invisible man from the 1933 film.

Plot: Lou Francis (Lou Costello) and Bud Alexander (Bud Abbott) have just graduated from a private detective school and are eager to use their newfound skills. Tommy Nelson (Arthur Franz), a middleweight boxer, comes to them with their first case.

Tommy had recently escaped from jail after being accused of murdering his manager, and asks the pair to accompany him on a visit to his fiancée, Helen Gray (Nancy Guild). He wants her uncle, Dr. Philip Gray (Gavin Muir), to inject him with a special serum he has developed which will render Tommy invisible, and hopes to use the invisibility to investigate his manager's murder and also prove his innocence.

Dr. Gray adamantly refuses, arguing that the serum is still unstable, recalling that the formula's discoverer, John Griffin, was driven insane by the formula and did not become visible again until after he was killed. However, as the police arrive to nab Tommy, Tommy injects himself with it and becomes invisible. He manages to escape the house and hides.

Detective Roberts (William Frawley) questions Dr. Gray and Helen while Bud and Lou search for Tommy.

Helen and Tommy convince Bud and Lou to help them seek the real killer, after Tommy explains that the motive for the murder occurred after he refused to "throw" a fight, knocking his opponent, Rocky Hanlon (John Day), out cold. Morgan (Sheldon Leonard), the promoter who had fixed the fight, ordered Tommy's manager beaten to death while framing Tommy for the crime.

In order to investigate undercover, Lou poses as a boxer, with Bud as his manager. They go to Stillwell's gym, where Lou gets in the ring with Rocky. Still invisible, Tommy gets into the ring with them and again knocks out Hanlon, making it look like Lou did it, and an official match is arranged.

Morgan urges Lou to throw the fight, but when the match occurs, poor Hanlon is knocked out yet again by Lou, with the aid of an invisible Tommy. Morgan plans Bud's murder and is thwarted by Tommy, who is wounded in the battle and begins to bleed badly. After revealing Morgan to Detective Roberts, the police are satisfied that they have their man, while Tommy, Bud and Lou manage to slip out.

The protagonists rush to the hospital, where a blood transfusion is arranged between Lou and Tommy. During the transfusion, Tommy becomes visible again. But some of Tommy's blood has apparently entered Lou's system, and he briefly turns invisible, only to reappear with his legs on backwards. Tommy and Helen bond again, while Lou and Bud are left to figure out how to get Lou's body straightened out. END

Analysis and additional notes: This film was dubbed a "comedy detective adventure", not science fiction. I think the injection of an invisible man into the mix was a sort of cheat to make the plot more exciting. Otherwise, it would have been a regular boxing show with some murder mixed in. It was not really funny. For me, Bud Abbott and Lou Costello were never really funny to begin with. Their movies involved hikinks of a sort that would not be seen as funny today, but more like tacit vandalism and disastrous blunders.

Nevertheless, the producers tried to use the invisibility gimmick to advance the plot, and Arthur Franz was credible as Tommy Nelson, a new Invisible Man. It's the serum, not the man, which figures in the plot. It is at least faithful to the original, which is why I have chosen to include it on the list.

For its fast pacing and plausible scripting, I give this film 2 stars out of 4. IMdb gives it 7 out of 10, and Rotten Tomatoes give it a rating of 80% fresh, while 65% of their audience liked it.

Production: *Abbott and Costello Meet The Invisible Man* was filmed between October 3 and November 6, 1950. The character names of "Bud Alexander" and "Lou Francis" are Abbott and Costello's real first and middle names.

The special effects, which depicted invisibility and other optical illusions, were created by Stanley Horsley, son of cinema pioneer David Horsley. He also did the special effects for *The Invisible Man Returns*, *The Invisible Woman* and *Invisible Agent*.

As a reference to the first *Invisible Man*, a photo of the serum's inventor, Dr. John Griffin (Claude Rains) who played the role in Universal's first *Invisible Man* (1933), was displayed on the wall in Dr. Gray's laboratory.

When asked by a reporter whom he has fought in the past, Lou answers, "Chuck Lamont, Bud Grant." The film's director and screenwriter, respectively, are Charles Lamont and John Grant.

Home media: This film has been released several times on DVD. First on The Best of Abbott and Costello Volume Three, on August 3, 2004, and again on October 28, 2008 as part of Abbott and Costello: The Complete Universal Pictures Collection. Later, the film was included in the 3 disc The Invisible Man: The Complete Legacy Collection and the 21-disc Universal Classic Monsters: Complete 30-Film Collection both released on September 2, 2014. It was released on Blu-ray on August 28, 2018.

CAPTAIN VIDEO: Master of The Stratosphere (1951)

A serial of 15 chapters; based on the original television series broadcast by the DuMont network in 1949 to 1955.

Directed by Spencer Bennet and Wallace Grissell
Produced by Sam Katzman
Writing Credits: Royal K. Cole, Sherman L. Lowe, Joseph F. Poland, and George H. Plympton;
based on characters from Captain Video and His Space Rangers
Cinematography by Fayte Browne
Film Editing by Earl Turner
Art Direction by Paul Palmentola
Set Decoration by Sidney Clifford
Special Effects by Jack Erickson
Music Department: Mischa Bakaleinikoff
Daniele Amfitheatrof composer - stock music (uncredited)
Mario Castelnuovo-Tedesco composer - stock music (uncredited)
Miklós Rózsa: composer - stock music (uncredited)
Moree Herring: set continuity

Cast:
Judd Holdren as Captain Video
Larry Stewart as Video Ranger
George Eldredge as Dr. Tobor
Gene Roth as Vultura
Don Harvey as Gallagher
William Fawcett as Alpha [Chs. 1-3, 7, 15]
Jack Ingram as Henchman Aker [Chs. 1, 7, 10-14]
I. Stanford Jolley as Zarol [Chs. 8-9]
Skelton Knaggs as Retner
Jimmy Stark as Ranger Rogers
Rusty Wescoatt as Henchman Beal [Chs. 1, 7, 11]
Zon Murray as Henchman Elko [Chs. 1, 7, 10-14]
Plus a cast of a few dozen uncredited actors
Stunts [uncredited]:
Eddie Parker
George Robotham
Wally West

Plot: Set in Earth's distant future, we see the adventures of a group of fighters for truth and justice known as The Video Rangers. They are led by Captain Video (no first name). The Video Rangers operate from a secret base on a mountaintop whose location is unspecified.

Captain Video has a teenage companion known only as The Video Ranger. The Captain receives his orders from "The Commissioner of Public Safety," (surname Carey) whose responsibilities range in the entire solar system as well as human colonies on planets around other stars. Captain Video is often aided by a scientist called Gallagher, who employs various machines and technologies to control the territory.

The Earth is threatened by a megamaniac from the planet Atoma named Vultura (Gene Roth), who is also at war with his neighboring planet called Afexa. His chief scientist, a man named Dr. Tobor (George Eldredge), is constantly at work finding ways to foil Captain Video and his rangers in order to help his boss conquer the universe, a plan which is doomed to fail.

Arrayed with a series of advanced technologies like a ray gun, a video detector, and other instruments, Captain Video embarks in a rocket to Afexa, where he meets with the leader of the resistance against Vultura called Alpha, of a race of men who are pacifists. They are not too stupid to reject the use of violence to extend their rebellion, however, and Video supplies them with several pieces of technology to help them. Along with his assistant Video Ranger, he also foils several schemes by Vultura and Dr. Tobor.

After a time, Dr. Tobor manages to infiltrate the secret lab and steals the codes to several devices while Gallagher is distracted by one of several emergencies. He takes the codes to Vultura, but the dictator is annoyed with how long it is taking to destroy Afexa. He threatens Tobor with annihilation while Tobor takes sides several times, baffling his enemies. He is at heart a survivalist. Loyalty is not his thing.

Meanwhile, Vultura marches out a protoype robot which lacks a proper control mechanism. His robot is crude, made of a man with tin sheet metal assembled in parts. It is meant to be virtually unstoppable. Vultura intends to build an army of robots to take over Afexa and the Earth. In an attempt to make the robots malfunction, Captain Video and Ranger are able to recode the controller. Apparently Dr. Gallagher has one which is a nifty shortcut. In a series of attacks, Tobor finally makes away with it.

31

Robbed of his robots, Vultura goes on a tear and decides to launch nuclear rockets to achieve his goal. Taking sides again, Tobor begs Video to spare him so they can together foil Vultura's plan.

Meanwhile, Alpha and his rebels take their planet back from Vultura. Forced to retreat, Vultura concentrates his rage on destroying Tobor for his betrayal, but his plan backfires. Yet there is no escape for the wicked. As Tobor escapes in the last remaining rocket, Captain Video fires on Vultura's lab and destroys it. END

Analysis and additional notes: I sat through all 15 chapters, but I did not like it. Not one bit. Aside from the seriously flawed robot, the sets were minimal and the "technologies" employed by Gallagher were incomprehensible and uniquely uniniteresting.

For example, their use of "video" (remote viewing) was marred by the cutting of shots among several angles in a viewing, impossible even for modern video. There would have to have been cameras set up all along the routes people used to even resemble something like surveillance.

Another example is the other machinery, which were set up in a blank room with toggles, switches, wheels and other doodads, which Gallagher himself used by means of several calculations which he entered into the machines. We don't even see any blinking lights. There is no actual effect but the occasional application of electricity here and there.

There is a twin engine rocket set up to travel from planet to planet, but once it leaves the atmosphere it should be relatively easy to get there. But no, it does not land so much as glides in with a crash.

The use of recycled costumes and props from other productions was heavy. The costumes were also minimalist. One could see pieces from *Buck Rogers* and also *Flash Gordon*. The pacifist rebels on Afexa were all dressed like Arab merchants, while Vultura himself was clad in an incomplete ensemble altogether, presenting the perfect picture of an overfed, self-absorbed autocrat.

Naturally, there are fistfights and gunfights galore among the wilds of the Santa Susana valley, which is recognizable from other productions. This area has been used so often that it is as popular a landmark as Vasquez Rocks, which had been used heavily in *Star Trek*. Sadly, that area is no longer available for production because of its use as the Santa Susana Field Laboratory, a testing facility for rocket engines and a small scope nuclear reactor. In 2006 it was discovered to be a radioactive field owing to a leak at the plant, and the Federal government directed the facility to clean it up. The plant was set up in 1949. Since 1980, production was halted on several films because of the risk. It's a pity, because the field is strewn with boulders bigger than a house, and the area was not conducive to development of residential housing. Since 2006, the area is considered off limits. But I digress.

This one had plot holes one could drive a semi truck through. The plot was boring and not engaging in any way, and Captain Video came off like a bad manager of a failing corporation. My recommendation is that you avoid this one like the plague. I give it 1 star out of 4 for the acting. IMdb gives it 5.8 out of 10, and Rotten Tomatoes has a page for it but no ratings.

Production: Captain Video was the first adventure hero explicitly designed by DuMont's "idea man" Larry Menkin for early live television. One of its most iconic episodes, widely written about in metropolitan New York newspapers, was titled "I TOBOR." The robot was an important recurring character, and represented the first appearance of a robot in live televised science fiction. Its original manufacturer's name was "ROBOT I," but the stencil with its name inadvertently was applied backward to create the enigmatic name. The robot was played by actor David Ballard, who stood 7-feet, 6-inches tall. But its design was crude in the extreme, and had to be (once again) remote controlled. The controller's range was such that one had to be in the same room to make it effective. So much for a robot army.

The *Captain Video* series was broadcast on television live 5 to 6 days a week, and was popular with children and adults. It even earned a special mention in the very first episode, *"TV or Not TV"*, of the phenomenally popular Jackie Gleason sitcom series *The Honeymooners* in which Ed Norton wore a space helmet while watching the show.

In the early days of the series, the show featured often incoherent scripts, along with jarring plot shifts to old cowboy movies. This led to derision of the show by the critics of the day, although it always was wildly popular with kids and many adults.

The quality of scripting improved after 1952, when the stories began to be written by such major science fiction writers as Damon Knight, James Blish, Jack Vance and Arthur C. Clarke. These later scripts displayed more intelligence, discipline and imagination than most of the other children's scripts of the era.

Other well known authors who occasionally wrote for the program included Isaac Asimov, Cyril M. Kornbluth, Milt Lesser, Walter M. Miller, Jr., Robert Sheckley, J. T. McIntosh and Robert S. Richardson. One of the more prolific writers for the show was Maurice C. Brachhausen—who wrote under the name M.C. Brock, and later had his own production company, Brock Video Productions.

Throughout the run of the series, it had a meager budget despite its success with the general public. in fact, according to most records, the show's "prop budget" was a miserly $25 per week. Few special effects were evident until the team of Russell and Haberstroh was hired in September of 1952. For the rest of the program's episodes, they provided effective model and effects work, prefilmed in 16 mm format and cut into the live broadcast as needed.

As a result of there being few surviving episodes, it is not clear what time period the series is set in, if it can be set in any concrete time frame at all. The Fawcett comic adventures are supposed to take place during the time of publication, in 1951. However, the stories in the surviving kinescopes could have taken place in 1950. The future is never defined or justified in the episodes.

The actors were paid so little they actually made more money from appearing in character at supermarket openings, county fairs and the like than they did from their acting salaries. Many actors were paid minimum scale and remained uncredited for the serial, which means they earned no royalties per showing.

The original star of *Captain Video*, Richard Coogan, left the show in 1950 partially because the show's producers refused to cut in the cast members for a percentage of the licensing dollars from the sale of Captain Video merchandise.

Bram Nossen, who played the villainous Dr. Pauli, dropped out in 1951 after suffering a nervous breakdown from the pressure of having to appear on TV 6 days a week. He was replaced by Hal Conklin, who we presume suffered the same fate, and in 1954 Stephen Elliott assumed the role. The jarring change in actors who looked nothing like each other was explained by saying that Dr. Pauli had undergone plastic surgery to outwit Captain Video.

A similar televisions series 14 years later, *Dr. Who*, went through several transformations of character faces but was explained as a natural state of the character once the actor was replaced. In 2018, the character changed genders. How about that?

Spin-offs: Six issues of a *Captain Video* comic book were published by Fawcett Comics in 1951.

And that's all they wrote.

THE DΛY THE EΛRTH STOOD STILL (1951)
Director: Robert Wise
Producer: Julian Blaustein
Original Music: Bernard Herrmann
Cinematography: Leo Tover (director of photography)
Music Dept: Bernard Herrmann, orchestrator (uncredited)
Samuel Hoffman and Paul Shure, musicia, theremin (uncredited)

Cast:
Michael Rennie as Klaatu
Patricia Neal as Helen Benson
Billy Gray as Bobby Benson Hugh Marlowe as Tom Stevens
Sam Jaffe as Professor Jacob Barnhardt
Frances Bavier as Mrs. Barley
Lock Martin as Gort
Frank Conroy as Mr. Harley
Tyler McVey as Brady (uncredited)
Well-known broadcast journalists of their time, H. V. Kaltenborn, Elmer Davis, Drew Pearson and Gabriel Heatter, appeared and/or were heard as themselves.

Plot: A flying saucer is tracked flying through the atmosphere at what is computed to be 4,000 miles an hour until it lands on the President's Park Ellipse in Washington, D.C., scattering park patrons and ball players alike. The local national guard quickly establishes a perimeter around the saucer, from which no sound, nor light, nor person, has emerged since its landing. Everyone is on pins and needles, waiting.

Then the saucer opens, and a man clad in a silver space suit and a helmet emerges announcing that he has come from outer space on a goodwill mission. When he takes out and opens a small device, a nervous soldier jumps the gun and shoots him. He goes down as the guard commander tells his men to stand down. The commander goes to help the strange astronaut, who is struggling to stay conscious.

Before anyone can move, a silver giant emerges from the craft, sizes up the situation quickly, and opens a dark slit in its featureless face. From that slit it produces a ray which overheats the soldiers' weaponry and disarms them quickly, then promptly melts a tank parked nearby. Before it can fire again, the astronaut orders the robot, called Gort, to stop its attack in a strange language which sounds like Latin (at that time, linguists were developing Esperanto. This may have been an example.). Gort's eye closes and it assumes a guard post next to the saucer.

The strange visitor then explains to the guard commander that the device was a gift for his President; that it would enable him to study the stars. But of course; now it is broken.

He is taken to Walter Reede Army Hospital, where he is found to be physically human, but stuns the doctors with the quickness of his healing and his age. He appears to be in his thirties but is way older than he looks. That probably his science is more advanced than theirs and he may even be immortal. As he puffs on a cigarette, one of them mutters that it makes him feel "like a third rate witch doctor."

Meanwhile the military tries to enter the space ship, finding it impregnable. Nothing can penetrate its hull. Gort stands by: mute, unmoved and unmoving. Frustrated, the military men decide to encase the robot in a new kind of plastic which it could not possibly break through [or so they think].

A man from the White House arrives to interview Earth's new visitor. He is the President's secretary, named Harley (Frank Conroy). The alien introduces himself as "Klaatu" and says that he bears a message so momentous and urgent that it must be revealed to all the world's leaders simultaneously. Harley informs him of the world situation and that politics prevent the possibility of getting all of the world leaders to meet; that some are at war with each other. Klaatu insists that he must try, and Harley reluctantly agrees to.

Later, Harley comes to Klaatu and reads him some of the responses to the effort to create such an assembly. It does not sound encouraging. Each government wants to either host the meeting or refuses to attend thanks to their enmity with other nations. Klaatu thinks about that, then says that perhaps if he gets to know the ordinary people on the street he might understand the source of their suspicions. Harley gently forbids this, and leaves Klaatu locked up under guard.

Of course, Klaatu is intelligent and resourceful, and easily manages his escape. By now the wound has healed entirely. He steals some luggage labeled "Maj. Carpenter" and, thus disguised, leaves the hospital undetected and wanders down the avenue. He listens to the radio through open apartment windows. Some broadcasts sound encouraging, some filled with political anticommunist hubris bordering on paranoia. (In fact, none were nearly as hysterical as some of the radio pundits we hear today.)

Able to read and speak English, no doubt learned from following Earth's radio and television signals, he stops at a window with a sign saying there is a room for rent. Acting on a hunch, he goes to the door and knocks on it.

The hostess is a bit fearful at first, but when he says he saw the sign, seems desperate to rent the extra room right away. (Maybe a mortgage default was looming.) He introduces himself, assuming the alias "Mr. Carpenter". She leads him on a tour of the house, describes the amenities, and introduces him to her other boarding guests. Among them are Helen Benson (Patricia Neal), a widow, and her son Bobby (Billy Gray).

At breakfast the next morning, while listening to some more alarming radio reports, Klaatu takes in his fellow boarders' suspicions and speculations about the alien visit and finds them amusing. Bobby is especially excitable and imaginative, making all kinds of speculations about the "space man". His mother is more sensible and tries to reign in his excitement by reminding him that he has to finish his homework and to remember to brush his teeth. Otherwise, she appears to tolerate his bouncy and inquisitive behavior.

While Helen and her boyfriend Tom Stephens (Hugh Marlowe) plan to go on a day trip together, Klaatu offers to babysit with Bobby and suggests that a tour of the city is in order. At first Helen is reluctant, but has a feeling her son will be in safe hands.

The boy eagerly shows him the sights, including a visit to his father's grave in Arlington National Cemetery, where Klaatu is dismayed to learn that most of those buried there were killed in wars. He explains to Bobby that where he comes from there are no wars; no povery or strife. Bobby takes that with some surprise: he has never lived in a time when there was no war.

They share some ice cream, then go to see the heavily guarded spaceship, where Klaatu realizes he can do nothing for now without attracting attention. A special fence has been set up so spectators can see the ship from a "safe" distance. A radio reporter is gayly asking what the tourists think of the great ship. He comes upon Klaatu and Bobby and asks Klaatu what he thinks it all means. Klaatu (as Carpenter) calmly states that he sees how much panic has been stirred up by wild speculation, and begins to outline his views when the reporter cuts him off, clearly not willing to engage in a long winded discussion. Thus deterred from his chance to convey his message to the world, Klaatu decides to bide his time.

The two then visit the Lincoln Memorial. Klaatu, impressed by the Gettysburg Address inscribed at the statue's base, gets an idea and asks Bobby who is the smartest person living in the world. Bobby suggests a leading American scientist, Professor Jacob Barnhardt (Sam Jaffe), who lives in the city. Bobby goes with Klaatu to Barnhardt's home but they find that the professor is absent. Klaatu looks through a window and spots a chalkboard covered with mathematical frustration, with the result a resounding "0! 00!! 000!!!" (Oddly enough, string theory appears to yield the same result.)

Klaatu enters through the side door and checks Barnhardt's work, then adds a key mathematical equation to the problem. The housekeeper comes in on him in mid stroke and asks what he is doing there. Klaatu then leaves his contact information with her. She begins to erase what he wrote but Klaatu warns her not to; that the professor might need it.

Then Klaatu takes Bobby to see a movie, giving him a pair of flawless diamonds in exchange for Bobby's two dollars to pay for the tickets. The boy is a budding opportunist who asks Klaatu not to tell his mother about the exchange; he does not want to be caught stealing.

Later, government agents arrive at the boarding house and escort Klaatu to see Prof. Barnhardt. Klaatu introduces himself and the scientist is completely amazed. He had not seen the arrival of Klaatu's ship but sees the event as monumentally historic. He asks about the equation. Apparently Klaatu has given him the solution to a problem he has been working on for years. Barnhardt asks him about its relative importance to the other terms. Klaatu tells him that it has enabled him to fly from one planet to another.

Klaatu then warns the professor that the people of "the other planets" have become concerned for their own safety after human beings had developed atomic power; and they are concerned that humankind will extend its aggression to the rest of the galaxy. Klaatu declares that if his message goes unheeded, "planet Earth will be eliminated." Barnhardt responds to this with some apprehension. Klaatu then adds his frustration with the political response to his efforts to warn the planet. Barnhardt suggests that he could arrange a meeting of scientists to convene at Klaatu's ship, and also suggests that Klaatu should arrange a demonstration of his power. Nothing big or destructive, but something which would attract everyone's attention to the seriousness of the matter.

That evening, Klaatu borrows a flashlight from Bobby, then returns to his spaceship to transmit a report to his authority and implement the idea, unaware that Bobby has followed him. When Bobby sees Klaatu speaking to his robot and entering the ship, he runs back to the lodging house.

When Helen and Tom have returned from their date, Bobby tells them what has happened, but Helen claims he is just letting his overactive imagination get the run of him again and sends him to bed. He retorts, "I never call you a liar." Helen then looks down and spots the mud on his sneakers. He says, "yeh. The grass was wet." Then he runs upstairs to his room.

By now Tom is deeply suspicious of Klaatu; he cautions Helen that Bobby has been hanging around with the strange man too much and it's giving him strange ideas.

He sneaks up to Klaatu's room and enters to have a look around. At first nothing seems out of place, but when he turns to leave he spots something glistening on the floor. It is one of the diamonds Klaatu has been using for money. He becomes excited about it as he shows her what he has found, but Helen is a little perturbed about Tom invading Carpenter's room; while Bobby switches his outlook to think that Carpenter is a also diamond smuggler.

Helen works as a secretary at the State Dept. and has frequent conversations with the switchboard operator, who declares she is completely spooked by the situation. The idea that there is an alien running freely around on Earth makes her feel terribly insecure.

Tom is apparently an insurance agent with big political ambitions. When Tom takes the diamond to be appraised, the jeweler informs him it is unlike any other diamond on Earth, and asks if Tom wants to sell it. Toms says no and returns to his office. He calls Helen to find out if she is free for lunch and arranges to meet her. When lunchtime comes, Helen takes her purse with her and goes to an elevator.

Klaatu intercepts her there and says he must talk to her about what happened the day before; that he wants to explain things about Bobby and what he might have seen. Helen says they can take another elevator which is less crowded.

While they are riding down, the elevator comes to a complete halt between floors. She looks down at her watch and sees that it is frozen exactly at noon. Klaatu then reveals his true identity and explains why he is there. At first Helen is skeptical but comes to the conclusion that Bobby was right and everything pointed to Klaatu.

We see a montage sequence showing that Klaatu has neutralized all electric power everywhere around the planet except in situations that would compromise human safety, such as hospitals and airplanes in flight. Cars will not start, blenders won't spin, laundry units contain wet wash, and so on. The whole world has stood still. Panic ensues as the world blames the space man for it.

Helen asks him why she was chosen to be approached. Klaatu says he needed a friend to help him, and that she is the most rational person he knows; that he was sure she would understand. Then Helen remembers what Tom had told her earlier about "writing his own ticket" and says that there would be nothing to stop him warning the military. She agrees to help Klaatu now that she understands the big picture.

After the blackout ends, the manhunt for Klaatu intensifies and Tom talks to her about his decision. Helen tries to convince him otherwise; doesn't he care about the rest of the world? He retorts that he doesn't, and that makes her very upset. She breaks off their relationship immediately. He has chosen poorly.

Later, Helen and Klaatu take a taxi to Barnhardt's home; there to join Barnhardt and go to the meeting of scientists. While they are en route, Klaatu instructs Helen that, should anything happen to him, she must tell Gort these words: "Klaatu barada nikto".

We see a citywide search by the military for Klaatu. Some people have seen the two in the taxi and sends them in that direction. When they are spotted, Klaatu leaves the taxi and tries to get away but is shot by military personnel.

In the ensuing mob to see the body, Helen is overlooked, slips away and heads to the spaceship on her own, while Klaatu's dead body is placed on a cot in a jail with a guard posted over it.

On some invisible cue, Gort awakens. It burns down the acrylic cage surrounding it and kills the guards before Helen arrives. Soon aftward, Helen enters the compound carefully but is confronted by the giant robot. Gort marches toward her, its terrible eye opening and powering up.

At first Helen is terrified and loses her nerve. She backs up and collides with some chairs stacked up in a corner, screaming her terror. Gort advances and looks down at her, preparing to fire. Helen finally finds her courage, looks up and utters the words once, then twice.

Gort closes its ray eye, then picks Helen up in its arms and takes her into the ship. The robot deposits her gently on the deck and seals her in. Helen tries to get out but does not know how.

Gort goes to the jail, burns a hole in the wall and retrieves Klaatu's body, then carries it back to the ship. It lays the body down on a table. It ignores Helen completely as it activates a control. As Helen watches, the machine powers up and resonates. Klaatu's body glows with energy until the process is complete.

Klaatu revives intact and healthy; rises and sees Helen. She is amazed, and asks if Gort has the power of life and death. Klaatu replies that that power is reserved for the "almighty spirit." He does not know how much longer he will live, but he is alive and must still carry out his mission.

Sometime later, the world assembly of scientists is gathered near the chairs set up for them, and they have been waiting for quite a while for the meeting to start. A commander of the military arrives, approaches Professor Barnhardt and advises him that Gort is still at large and that the group should disband for their own safety. Barnhardt is visibly disappointed with Klaatu's lateness, and tells the group that given the circumstances the meeting must be canceled.

A moment later, the ship opens. Helen disembarks and walks down the ramp to join the group, while Gort emerges and stands aside on guard. Then, Klaatu steps out of the spaceship dressed for flight and addresses the assembled scientists, explaining that humanity's penchant for violence and first steps into space have caused concern among other inhabitants of the universe, who have agreed to live together in peace. To enforce that peace, they created and empowered a race of robots like Gort to act immediately should such aggression occur. He adds that it's not the best way to police the galaxy but it is a system, and it works.

He then warns that if the people of Earth threaten to extend their violence into space, the Earth would be "reduced to a burned-out cinder", adding, "the decision rests with you." Then, waving a friendly thanks and goodbye to Helen, Klaatu enters the spaceship and departs to a flourish of alien music. END

Analysis and Additional Notes: This film is one of my favorites, and has influenced my science fiction writing ever since. It was crisp and clean in execution with almost Ansel Adams exactness. The plot flowed smoothly and told the story in the simplest terms. Above all, it showed that the world can get better, a positive message in a world riddled with political and scientific controversy. It takes science to elevate us above the primitive by presenting a hopeful vision of things to come instead of a constant apocalyptic pessimism.

The warning is that if we continue to make war on each other with ever escalating technologies of war, we will be destroyed. The choice is ours, in every breath, in every action. The decision rests with us.

For its masterful presentation and engaging plot and production values, I give it 4 stars out of 4. IMdb gives it 7.8 out of 10, and Rotten Tomatoes give it a 94% fresh rating, and 87% of their audience liked it. You can't go wrong with this one.

Production: In a 1995 interview, producer Julian Blaustein explained that Joseph Breen, the film's censor installed by the Motion Picture Association of America (MPAA) at Twentieth Century Fox studios, balked at Klaatu's resurrection scene as it was originally written. At his insistence a line was inserted into the film: when Helen asks Klaatu whether Gort has unlimited power over life and death, Klaatu explains that he has only been revived temporarily and "that power is reserved to the Almighty Spirit." Apparently the original form of the script never calls for it.

Technically (and actually) it is the machine Gort activates which has the power of life or death. That everyone seems to forget that is thanks to that misdirecting line inserted into the script. Gort itself appears to have no such power but its eye ray and its phenomenal strength, and a divine being of limitless power would have no need to send its servants to kill in the first place.

Of the "Christian" elements that he added to Klaatu's character, screenwriter Edmund North said, "*It was my private little joke. I never discussed this angle with Blaustein or Wise because I didn't want it expressed. I had originally hoped that the Christ comparison would be subliminal.*" The fact that the question even came up in an interview is proof enough that such comparisons did not remain subliminal, but they are subtle enough that it is not immediately obvious to all viewers which elements were intended to compare Klaatu to Christ.

For example, when Klaatu escapes from the hospital, he steals the clothing belonging to a "Maj. Carpenter;" carpentry being the profession Jesus (Joshua) bar Joseph learned from his father. These features are left to the audience to sort out once the whole film has been presented to them.

Blaustein set out to make a film that illustrated the fear and suspicion that characterized the early Cold War and Atomic Age. He reviewed over 200 science fiction short stories and novels in search of a storyline that could be used, since this film genre was well suited for a metaphorical discussion of such grave issues. Given the enormous success of other biblical stories, studio head Darryl F. Zanuck gave the go ahead for this project. Blaustein hired Edmund North to write the screenplay based on elements from Harry Bates's short story "Farewell to the Master". The revised final screenplay was completed on February 21, 1951.

The interior set of the ship was designed by Thomas Little and Claude Carpenter. They collaborated with noted architect Frank Lloyd Wright for the design of the whole spacecraft. Paul Laffoley has suggested that the futuristic interior was inspired by Wright's Johnson Wax Headquarters, completed in 1936. Laffoley quotes Wright and his attempt in designing the exterior: "*... to imitate an experimental substance that I have heard about which acts like living tissue. If cut, the rift would* *appear to heal like a wound, leaving a continuous surface with no scar."* The main hatch fully integrates with the hull without seam. However, during a scene showing an attempt to cut into the hull of the ship, a welding torch applied to its surface fails to burn it at all.

Principal outdoor photography for *The Day the Earth Stood Still* was shot on the 20th Century Fox sound stages and on its studio back lot (Century City, California), with a second unit shooting background plates and other scenes in Washington, D.C.. The primary actors never traveled to Washington for the making of the film.

The robot *Gort* was played by Lock Martin, who worked as an usher at Graumann's Chinese Theater and stood over 7 feet tall. He had to work carefully with the metallic suit as it had very little range of motion. The costume also had wires to operate the robot's eye. Director Wise decided that Gort's segments would be filmed at half hour intervals so Martin would not asphyxiate in the suit. [The latest viewing of the film showed air vents placed under the jawline of the suit.] The segments were edited into the film's final print. Martin also needed help to carry Ms. Neal to the ship. This part is cut so we do not see Gort actually picking her up, but moving behind a blind and then carrying her there with her already in his arms. My understanding is that the visible shots of him carrying Ms. Neal were interspersed with his carrying mannequins of both Rennie and Neal where they were needed.

The music score was composed by Bernard Herrmann in August 1951, and was the first score he composed after he moved from New York to Hollywood. Herrmann chose unusual instrumentation for the film: violin, cello, and bass (all three electric), two theremin (electronic instruments played by Dr. Samuel Hoffman and Paul Shure), two Hammond organs, a large studio electric organ, a piano, woodwinds and brass. Unusual overdubbing and tape reversal techniques were used as well to enhance the alien effects in the music.

The Day the Earth Stood Still was well received by critics and is widely regarded as one of the best films of 1951. The film was moderately successful when released, accruing $1,850,000 in distributors' domestic (U.S. and Canada) rentals, making it the year's 52nd biggest earner. The movie is ranked 7th on Arthur C. Clarke's list of the best science fiction films of all time, just above Stanley Kubrick's *2001: A Space Odyssey* (1968) which Clarke himself co-wrote.

In 1995, *The Day the Earth Stood Still* was selected for preservation in the United States National Film Registry as "culturally, historically, or aesthetically significant."

Since the release of the movie, the phrase "*Klaatu barada nikto*" has become popular in fiction and in popular culture. The Robot Hall of Fame described it as "one of the most famous commands in science fiction", while Frederick S. Clarke of <u>Cinefantastique</u> called it "the most famous phrase ever spoken by an extraterrestrial."

No translation was given in the film. Philosophy professor Aeon J. Skoble speculates that the famous phrase is a "safe-word"; that is, part of a fail-safe feature used during diplomatic missions such as the one Klaatu and Gort make to Earth. With the use of the safe-word, Gort's deadly force can be reprogrammed into a passive mode. Skoble observes that the theme has evolved into a "*staple of science fiction that the machines charged with protecting us from ourselves will misuse or abuse their power.*" In this interpretation, the phrase apparently tells Gort that Klaatu considers escalation unnecessary.

I have a different take on the translation. It may mean literally that "*Klaatu needs help.*" This may be the reason that Gort reacts the way it does. It knows that it must retrieve Klaatu in whatever his condition is or the mission will fail. It discards its defensive posture and goes proactive. The power of its ability to excercise stealth and quiet reserve despite its huge bulk is demonstrated when it manages to get Klaatu's body and carry it back to the ship with little to no opposition; helped by a citywide curfew announced when the military conducts its search for him. Therefore, it has no need to go into hostile mode.

General Colin Powell believed the film inspired President Ronald Reagan to discuss uniting against an alien invasion when meeting Mikhail Gorbachev in 1985. Two years later, Reagan told the United Nations, "*I occasionally think how quickly our differences worldwide would vanish if we were facing an alien threat from outside this world.*" Being an actor before he was president, Reagan was clearly a fan of this film.

In retrospect, the film had a tremendous impact on my own political education and appeared to be the first film to promote real pacifism in a world recovering from two world wars.

Robert Wise's attention to detail and the special effects of both the robot and the spaceship, along with the other amazing instrumentality in the ship, was clear and plausible. Any serious student of film should see it for the complete story as well as the effects. It was by far the most up to date and modern film of its time, with a message that rings clear to this day.

In addition to the clear presentation of the plot, the flying saucer that Klaatu rides in glows as it lands and takes off, with a strange machine-like sound which is reminiscent of reports of actual UFOs recorded in newspapers and magazine articles. This was a streamlined, no knobs craft which commanded respect.

Lastly, the character of Professor Barnhardt may have been developed to bring the opinions of a similar physicist, Dr. Albert Einstein, into focus. In 1921, Einstein's work on general and quantum relativity earned him a Nobel Prize. At that time he lived in Germany, but while on a visit to a university in the U.S. found himself exiled from his home country in 1933. Einstein's work got him a permanent position and a new home in the United States.

In 1939 Einstein wrote an impassioned plea to the government along with other scientists, warning that the Nazis were creating a weapon which could advance their ambitions of world domination and destroy millions. Though he was an avowed pacifist his suggestions actually galvanized the government to work toward achieving an atom bomb to act as a nuclear deterrent.

But when the two atomic bombs leveled Hiroshima and Nagasaki in 1945, Einstein became entirely antinuclear, and joined with Bertrand Russell in issuing a manifesto toward nuclear disarmament a few months before his death in 1955.

FLIGHT TO MARS (1951)

Directed by Lesley Selander
Produced by Walter Mirisch
Screenplay by Arthur Strawn
Music by Marlin Skiles
Cinematography by Harry Neumann
Edited by Richard V. Heermance
Production company: Monogram Productions, Inc.
Distributed by Monogram Distributing Corp.; release date November 11, 1951; running time: 72 minutes

Cast:
Marguerite Chapman as Alita
Cameron Mitchell as Steve Abbott
Arthur Franz as Dr. Jim Barker
Virginia Huston as Carol Stafford
John Litel as Dr. Lane
Morris Ankrum as Ikron
Richard Gaines as Professor Jackson
Lucille Barkley as Terris
Robert Barrat as Tillamar
Wilbur Back as Councilman
William Bailey as Councilman
Trevor Bardette as Alzar
Stanley Blystone as Councilman
David Bond as Ramay
Raymond Bond as Astronomer #2

Plot: The first expedition to Mars, led by physicist Dr. Lane (John Litel), includes Professor Jackson (Richard Gaines), engineer Jim Barker (Arthur Franz), and his assistant Carol Stadwick (Virginia Huston). Journalist Steve Abbott (Cameron Mitchell) is also aboard to cover the historic mission.

A final interview with his crew mates before launch makes Dr. Lane to realize that there are grave risks for them all. He takes it all in stride, realizing that he is lucky to even be there.

The launch is successful. The control cabin is cramped but comfortable, as the crew lie strapped down in cots. The pressure of acceleration pulls them down while the instruments read the progress of the flight. Once they are out of Earth's atmosphere, weightlessness allows them to unstrap and begin their observations. They are able to see out of a single porthole, and are eyewitnesses to the sight of Earth receding in the distance. Dr. Lane relays their observations to Earth.

They lose contact with Earth when a meteor storm disables both their landing gear and radio. The crew is forced to decide whether to crash land on Mars or turn back for Earth. Professor Jackson makes the case that the purpose of their expedition is to collect data, data which they can send back to Earth using self-propelled space cylinders equipped with homing devices. They decide to proceed with the mission, knowing they can never return.

After the ship safely crash lands in a little valley on Mars, the crew disembark and explore the surface for a bit when they see what looks like a structure some distance away. They go toward it. There, they are met by five Martians who appear to be human and are friendly. They are also able to communicate in English. They invite the astronauts to join them beneath the surface.

The astronauts are escorted down an elevator to an underground city, where they are given shelter and food.

After some rest, the five astronauts are introduced to the planetary council, where the Martian leader, called Ikron (Morris Ankrum), explains that they have been receiving Earth's broadcasts and learned Earth's languages, but were unable to communicate with Earth. Their transmissions were too weak, possibly through interference by Earth's ionosphere. Ikron suggests that his people may be able to repair the rocket ship and help them to return to Earth.

Armed with this news, the astronauts are encouraged to explore the city and learn about Mars. The expedition members are amazed at the high level of Martian technology around them. They soon learn that the city is sustained by a life support system powered by a mineral called Corium.

The crew meet Tillamar (Robert Barrat), a past president and now a trusted council advisor, who gives them the lay of the land. A woman called Terris (Lucille Barkley) shows them to their quarters and serves the group automated meals. While the astronauts reside in relative luxury, the council meets once again.

In this meeting, Ikron reveals that their Corium supply is nearly depleted. He recommends that the Earthmen's spaceship be reproduced, once repaired, to create a fleet of ships that can evacuate the Martians to Earth. The council votes to adopt Ikron's plan, while also deciding to hold the Earthmen captive during the repair process. Ikorn keeps himself informed of the progress by using Terris as a spy.

Alita (Marguerite Chapman), a leading Martian scientist and daughter of Tillamar, is placed in charge of the repairs to the spaceship. When she meets with Dr. Barker, she reveals her thorough understanding of science and the engineering necessary to make the repairs go more smoothly. She is no ordinary woman, as Dr. Barker observes to his mates.

But, Dr. Barker begins to suspect the Martians' motives and fakes an explosion aboard, slowing the ship's repairs down. This seems to be a problem, but Barker explains to the others, and warns them to be on their guard. During the repair project, he and Alita begin to fall in love. She does not appear to be cognizant of her council's decisions.

When he announces their return to Earth is set for the next day, instead of months later, Barker surprises everyone with the additional news that Tillamar and Alita will be joining them. Tillamar explains that he and his people are tired of Ikron's aggressive leadership and his plan to take over the Earth. They are asking for asylum. Together, they and the astonauts hasten their repairs to the ship.

Terris reports the suspicious behavior around the ship, leading to Ikron detaining Tillamar and Alita, but Dr. Barker foils Ikron's plan to seize the repaired Earthship after freeing both of them. The other astronauts are already aboard awaiting him and their new friends.

After a brief confrontation with Martian guards at the spaceship's gangway, the three make it aboard safely, and the ship is able to blast off for Earth. The Martian colony will not survive, but the best of both worlds are on their way home. END.

Analysis and additional notes: I must admit I did not expect this one to be that good. The script was sound and the science was almost as good as one would expect. There were few scientific inconsistencies, except that no one ever talked about how cold it would have been on Mars. The astronauts wore little more than coveralls and gas masks. Knowing what I do about Mars, I would have expected them to freeze into sticks in about 5 seconds.

For once, we see a female scientist who is able to hold her own against the usual male superiority complex. Dr. Barker does not disparage, nor does he dismiss her out of turn. In fact, he finds it refreshing to be able to carry on a scientific discussion with an equal. This in itself is a sign the story would proceed in a normal and mature manner. Alita was not a token female. She was a sign of things to come.

However, we are not permitted to see how the Martians actually lived. There was no caste system but the only sign of democracy was the council voting, up or down. Rarely down, since Ikron was something of a dictator. Clearly, he had deposed Tillamar and made sure that his orders were carried out with little dissent. Yet, there are members of the council who disagree with his approach. Such rancor usually leads to revolt, and we don't get to see what happened with Ikron once he failed to secure the space ship.

Once the facts are revealed, we see a civilization in decline. With the Corium petering out, the life support system would fail and every Martian would die. Even if Ikron succeeded in reproducing the Earth ship, it would take time the Martians did not have. So, not a happy ending for the Martians after all.

The only one I could see would be if, once the astronauts told their story, a world council would call for ships to be built to return to Mars and rescue the Martians. But as usual the movie ended too soon.

For its smooth pacing and credible script I give it 3 stars out of 4. But IMdb only gives it 5.2 out of 10, and Rotten Tomatoes gives it no rating, but only 27% of the audience liked it.

Production: *Flight To Mars* was a low-budget "quickie" shot in just five days. The film's principal photography took place in Death Valley, California from May 11 through late May 1951.

Except for some of the flight instruments, *Flight To Mars* reuses the interior flight deck sets and other interior props from Lippert Pictures' 1950 science fiction feature *Rocketship X-M*. Even that earlier film's spaceflight sound effects are reused, as are the concepts of space flight outlined in RX-M's screenplay. The main difference is this film was shot in color, not black-and-white, and the flight to Mars was planned; the earlier Lippert film concerns an accidental journey to the Red Planet, which happens during a planned expedition to the Moon.

Flight To Mars postulates a humanoid species which is superior, in many ways, to humanity, and could possibly pose a strategic threat.

In the Lippert film, however, the Martians are a throw-back, a consequence of a long ago nuclear holocaust, which occurred millennia earlier. Those Martians pose only an immediate, tactical threat to the RX-M's crew.

A sequel titled *Voyage To Venus* was proposed but never made.

Flight To Mars is not in the public domain. The copyright was renewed under Certificate # RE-26-731/RE-37-81 from the Copyright Office, Library of Congress. Rights were assigned to Wade Williams.

Reception: The <u>New York Times</u> film review notes: "Flight to Mars is the second American film of the postwar era (after the previous year's Rocketship X-M) to depict a manned space trip to the Red Planet." Critical reaction to *Flight To Mars* was not positive. Film reviewer Glenn Erickson characterized the film as derivative. "Of all the early space movies, none is so disappointing as Flight To Mars. Destination Moon was scientifically accurate, and Rocketship XM had a gripping dramatic script. This copycat production has neither." He further described the shoddy production values as, "Producer Walter Mirisch put the show together from found items – the ship interior is from Rocketship XM, and the Martian suits from Destination Moon."

I disagree. Thought the science was sketchy, the story was socially more interesting than *Rocketship XM*. Not to mention that the ending was more positive than the previous film.

LOST CONTINENT (1951)

Directed by Sam Newfield
Produced by Jack Leewood, Robert L. Lippert, and Sigmund Neufeld
Written by Orville H. Hampton and Richard H. Landau; story by Carroll Young
Music by Paul Dunlap
Cinematography by Jack Greenhalgh
Edited by Philip Cahn
Distributed by Lippert Pictures Inc.; release date: August 17, 1951
Running time: 83 min

Cast:
Cesar Romero as Maj. Joe Nolan
Hillary Brooke as Marla Stevens
Chick Chandler as Lt. Danny Wilson

John Hoyt as Michael Rostov
Acquanetta as Native girl
Sid Melton as Sgt. William Tatlow
Whit Bissell as Stanley Briggs
Hugh Beaumont as Robert Phillips
Murray Alper as Air Police Sergeant

Plot: Major Joe Nolan (Cesar Romero) is the head of an expedition to the South Pacific to retrieve an atomic powered rocket that vanished without a trace. He had previously lived in a South American jungle, as has fellow serviceman and pilot Lt. Danny Wilson (Chick Chandler), who is also on the expedition. Aircraft mechanic Sgt. William Tatlow (Sid Melton) is also recruited for the expedition, which includes the three scientists who helped build the rocket.

The three scientists are: Michael Rostov (John Hoyt), Marla Stevens (Hillary Brooke), and Stanley Briggs (Whit Bissell).

Their transport aircraft encounters an anomalous weather system and crash lands on a remote, unknown tropical island in the area where the rocket was lost on radar. They find only two occupants left on the island, a native woman (Acquanetta) and her young brother. The woman tells them that something fell from the sky atop the forbidding, cloud shrouded plateau that dominates part of the island. The rocket's fiery arrival caused the rest of the native population to abandon the island.

The expedition team finds that the only way to the plateau is up. They begin a long and perilous climb up the escarpment. It is slow going, but Briggs somehow loses his footing and falls to his death. After long stretches of tedious rock climbing, the expedition finally arrives on the top.

Emerging from what turns out to be a toxic gas cloud cover, they discover a lush, prehistoric jungle inhabited by various dinosaurs and a large deposit of uranium, which disables their electronic tracking equipment.

The group comes upon a brontosaurus, which then attacks Robert Phillips (Hugh Beaumont) as he quickly retreats up a tree. This results in Nolan and Wilson shooting at it, but they quickly discover that the dinosaur's thick hide absorbs bullets with little effect. Eventually, the dinosaur retreats.

Later that night they set up camp. When Nolan wakes up in the morning, he finds Phillips and Russian scientist Michael Rostov (John Hoyt) are gone. He soon discovers that Rostov got himself stuck in a large rock crevice near a triceratops. He accuses Rostov of arranging the accident on purpose, but Rostov insists that he tried to help Phillips escape. The triceratops nearly attacks the group, but another makes a challenge and the two dinosaurs fight to the death while the group make their escape.

Nolan suspects that Rostov is up to no good because he also appeared able to save Stanley Briggs on their climb up but did not. Eventually Rostov reveals himself to be a victim of the Holocaust in which he lost his wife and unborn child. That is still no excuse, as far as Nolan is concerned. But then Rostov reveals that because of his tortures he cannot lift his arms, so he could do nothing to help Briggs.

A pterosaur is later shot for food by Wilson near the rocket's landing site. They soon discover that the rocket is surrounded by a brontosaurus and a pair of triceratops, but Nolan devises a strategy to scare off the dinosaurs using the weapons.

Rostov and Phillips retrieve the needed data from the rocket. With his back turned, Tatlow is gored to death by an angry triceratops, just as it is shot by Nolan and Wilson. The team digs a grave and makes a cross marker for Tatlow. When violent earthquake tremors begin, the team makes a hasty retreat down the side of the plateau.

The four surviving members manage to successfully return to the island's valley with the rocket's critical component, just in time to escape the island using a native outrigger canoe. Then, the survivors watch from a distance as the island is first rocked by more violent earthquakes and then the catastrophic eruption of the island's volcano, which finally destroys everything. END

Analysis and additional notes: Okay, this one was a stinker from beginning to end. Not only was there not enough science to call it science fiction, the dinosaurs were made up of stock footage from prior dinosaur films like *The Lost World* (1925), blended with puppets led along with strings and stop animation.

There is little exposition to explain what the rocket was for. What happened to the native girl and her brother when the volcano erupted? The earthquake sequences were also stock footage from prior films.

Finally, the surviving explorers get off the island in an outrigger canoe, but the island is suddenly reduced to a series of explosions and no tsunami ensues. The film ends with no actual resolution, as the men are left out in the canoe. Blechhh. Above all, this story was as low budget as could be.

For its plodding script and cliffhangers, I give it 1 star out of 4. IMdb gives it 3/10, and Rotten Tomatoes gives it no rating, and only 4% of the audience liked it.

Production: Lost Continent was a low budget film shot in just 11 days from April 13 to late April 1951 at Goldwyn Studios back lot.

Black and white footage set atop the prehistoric escarpment was tinted a mint green color on all theatrical release prints, to produce an eerie, other worldly effect. The general plotline of the film strongly resembles that of Sir Arthur Conan Doyle's novel, *The Lost World*. Only less people survived this one, and the dinosaurs were stolen from that and other films.

Reception: Lost Continent was not able to overcome its low quality despite having Cesar Romero (a popular screen idol at the time) in a leading role. A later review clearly identified the main issue: "... a good third of the movie is spent showing our characters climbing the same styrofoam set prop from different angles... The pacing is pretty slow: the first twenty minutes is spent introducing the characters; the next 20 is spent having them climb up a mountain, and then jamming what little action there is into the remaining run time—all of which you would have seen in the trailer".

About Cesar Romero: Cesar Julio Romero, Jr. (February 15, 1907 – January 1, 1994) was an American actor, singer, dancer and vocal artist. He was active in film, radio, and television for almost 60 years. His wide range of screen roles included Latin lovers, historical figures in costume dramas, characters in light domestic comedies, and the Joker on the *Batman* television series, who was included in TV Guide's 2013 list of The 60 Nastiest Villains of All Time. I don't know why, but when I was a very young girl I had a crush on him. I grew out of it.

Lost Continent was featured in a Season 2 episode of *Mystery Science Theater 3000*. Dr. Forrester and TV's Frank taunted Joel Robinson before the film and began with the words "Rock Climbing." In a host segment Michael J. Nelson portrayed actor Hugh Beaumont as a member of the Four Horsemen of the Apocalypse.

The *Lost Continent* episode of MST3K was released by Shout! Factory as part of their Volume XVIII series DVD boxed set.

No further notes are available.

THE MAN FROM PLANET X (1951)

Directed by Edgar G. Ulmer
Produced by Jack Pollexfen and Aubrey Wisberg
Written by Aubrey Wisberg and Jack Pollexfen
Music by Charles Koff
Cinematography by John L. Russell
Edited by Fred R. Feitshans, Jr.
Distributed by United Artists; release date: March 9, 1951
Running time: 70 minutes
Budget: $51,000 (est.); box office: $1.2 million

Cast:
Robert Clarke as John Lawrence
Margaret Field as Enid Elliot
Raymond Bond as Professor Elliot
William Schallert as Dr. Mears
Roy Engel as Tommy the Constable
Charles Davis as Georgie, man at dock
Gilbert Fallman as Dr. Robert Blane
David Ormont as Inspector Porter
June Jeffery as Wife of missing man
Franklyn Farnum as Sgt. Ferris, Porter's assistant (uncredited)

Cast notes: Actor Pat Goldin and dwarf actor Billy Curtis have both been rumored to be the unknown actor who played the role of the alien space visitor in the film. However, Robert Clarke, who is frequently named as the source of the Pat Goldin rumor, never actually knew the name of the actor who played the role of the alien, nor did the other cast members, including Margaret Field and William Schallert. Clarke recalls only that he was of Jewish origin, stood about five feet tall, and was once part of an acrobatic vaudeville act. Margaret Field and producer Jack Pollexfen later recalled only that the actor had complained about his uncomfortable costume and his low pay, while William Schallert remembered him only as a very small, middle aged man who wasn't much of an actor.

Plot: At an observatory operated by Professor Elliot (Raymond Bond), he discovers that a rogue planet has entered the solar system and will pass by close to Earth. He passes on his observations to the world council on science. This brings his American friend, a reporter named John Lawrence (Robert Clarke), to his castle on the Scottish moors to report on the discovery.

The village nearby is small and folked by an insular and superstitious lot. There, Lawrence meets with Elliot's daughter Enid (Margaret Field), who drives him from there to the castle. They share reminiscences as they go. She makes the comment that it has been years since Elliot has had any visitors.

Once there, Lawrence meets with Elliot and his colleague Dr. Mears (William Schallert), whom he knows from a recent scandal. Elliot claims that Mears had served his time and has repented his prior misdeeds, and has proven a good friend as well.

Lawrence is offered a spare room to stay in, that the village is too far away to make the journey back and forth. At first Lawrence refuses; he has already imposed on the hospitality. But then a storm breaks out and he is forced to stay the first night. As he looks out the window, he sees a streak of light looking too much like a meteorite than a thunderbolt. But then he dismisses it all as an illusion, a trick of the light, and goes to bed.

The next morning, Enid drives him down into the village, where he takes a room at the inn. On the way back to the castle, the car gets a flat tire, and Enid is forced to walk all the way back to the castle.

Later, Lawrence borrows a bicycle to ride to the castle, and on the way finds the car mired in the road. He starts to get out the jack when he is met by a police constable named Tommy (Roy Engel), who gives him the lowdown about the village. Then he offers to help Lawrence replace the tire. After that, Lawrence loads the bicycle on the car and takes it to the castle.

Based on Dr. Elliot's observations, the rogue planet is closer than ever. He and Lawrence are discussing the situation when they see a mysterious light out on the moor. Perhaps it is a man in trouble.

Enid has seen it also, and goes out to investigate on her own. When she arrives, she sees what looks like a space ship, and looks around it, then in through the window. Suddenly, she sees a face peering back at her. It is a strange face. Enid nearly drops her torch and screams, then runs back to the castle.

Elliot and Lawrence are instantly intrigued and curious. Warning Enid to stay home, they venture out on the moor and find the space ship. At first they see no one there. Then, they discover a misshapen man lying on the ground near the craft, clearly in distress. He is trying to adjust something on his suit. Lawrence realizes that he is trying to regulate his air mix, and reaches out to turn a valve. That seems to calm the alien visitor.

Elliot is excited about this discovery. He tries to talk to the visitor, but no headway can be made. He and Lawrence abandon the visitor and start back to the castle. The visitor gets to his feet and follows them. When they arrive, they coax the visitor to enter the front and lead him to a room, where they sit him down to rest.

Dr. Mears is instructed to supervise their alien visitor and to make sure he is comfortable while they retire to eat supper.

Dr. Mears works hard to learn the visitor's language and discovers that the humanoid speaks in musical tones (a humming sound). He tries to force it to disclose the metal formula for its spaceship. He shuts off its breathing apparatus and leaves the spaceman for dead, telling the professor that communication was hopeless.

Meanwhile, Dr. Elliot comes down with what looks like the flu. He is too ill to manage his own affairs, and Enid has gone missing. Instructed to go to the chemist (drug store, in Scot parlance) for medicine, Lawrence goes into town and is waylaid by the villagers, who have loved ones gone missing also.

Lawrence manages to get away with Tommy's help and returns to the castle, but now Elliot is also gone.

With more villagers now missing, including Mears, and with the phone lines suddenly dead and the village in a panic, Lawrence and Tommy are finally able to get word to Scotland Yard by using a heliograph to contact a passing freighter just off the coast.

When a Detective Inspector (David Ormont) and a sergeant fly in and are briefed on the situation, the Inspector decides that the military must destroy the spaceship. Lawrence objects that doing so will also kill the people who are now under the alien's control.

With the planet due to reach its closest approach to Earth at midnight, Lawrence is given until 11:00 pm to rescue them. He sneaks up to the alien ship and finds that the villagers are all digging around it to free it from the mud. Elliot is lying nearby, too ill to help, and Lawrence finds Mears nearby. He learns from Mears that the spaceman intends to use its ship as a wireless relay station in advance of an invasion coming from the approaching planet, which we also learn is a dying world.

Lawrence orders the enthralled villagers to leave and attacks the alien, shutting off its breathing apparatus, then escapes with Enid and the professor. Mears, however, returns to the spaceship and is killed when the military opens fire and destroys it. No invasion happens and the mysterious Planet X slowly exits the solar system, headed for deep space. END

Analysis and additional notes: I remember seeing the alien's face a long, long time ago in a brief flash of channel surfing. I did not see it again until just recently. Now that I had seen the film in its entirety, I could see why this was a prime example of science fiction, both in its scope and in its storyline. First contact is always imagined as the best of science fiction, and for once there is no gung-ho hostility toward the alien except in the very end, which could have been avoided had the authorities been more empathetic.

While the cast note indicates that we never learned the name of the actor who played the alien, there is some acting. His struggles with his oxygen regulator, his pitiful cries as Mears threatens to turn off his air supply, all signal some acting. Yet, his "featureless" face shows nothing. We can only left to imagine again.

There were also hints that the alien visitor was not alone, but we see no others.

The space craft's design was different from the usual flying saucer mockup. It was at once bulbous and pointy. One would not expect a ship's design to present us with an "alien" aspect but this one did. It was at once weird and curious.

It is only by Lawrence's observations that we learn there is to be an invasion from an alien world. Up to now, the rogue planet was presumed to be uninhabitable. And it would be. There would be no tidal forces to drive its seas, if it had any; and no civilization would be able to be formed if the planet was passing through deep space and invading solar systems, only to pass on. So I think the alien came from somewhere else and just happened to land on Earth at the perigee of the planet's approach.

Here's another thing which I think was omitted from the film. If there was a rogue planet approaching Earth, there would be tidal waves, earthquakes, volcanic eruptions, and other physical disturbances to signal the planet's gravitational disruptions. There were none.

For its weird aspect and approach to alien visitations, I give it 2 stars out of 4. IMdb gives it 5.2/10, and Rotten Tomatoes gives it a whopping 100% fresh, with 38% of their audience liking it.

Production: The film went into production on December 13, 1950, at Hal Roach Studios in Culver City, California, and wrapped principal photography 6 days later. In order to save money, the film was shot on sets for the 1948 Ingrid Bergman film *Joan of Arc*, using artificial fog to change moods, plot locations, and to hide the lack of backdrops and staged landscapes for the outdoor scenes.

Popular culture: Invaders From Mars, The War of the Worlds, both released in 1953, and *The Thing from Another World* (1951), all began production around the same time this film was made. *The Day The Earth Stood Still* finished production six months before, in the summer of 1951. At that time, there was a virtual race to produce science fiction films, each studio trying their best to capture theatrical revenues.

The alien can communicate using only modulated musical sounds, a concept used three decades later in Steven Spielberg's *Close Encounters of The Third Kind.* The alien appears alongside other film monsters in the 2003 film *Looney Tunes: Back in Action,* in the scene that occurs at "Area 52".

THE MAN IN THE WHITE SUIT (1951) UK

Directed by Alexander Mackendrick
Produced by Michael Balcon
Written by John Dighton, Roger MacDougall, and Alexander Mackendrick
Music by Benjamin Frankel
Cinematography by Douglas Slocombe
Edited by Bernard Gribble
Production company: Ealing Studios
Distributed by General Film Distributors; release date August 7, 1951

Running time: 85 minutes

Cast:
Alec Guinness as Sidney Stratton
Joan Greenwood as Daphne Birnley
Cecil Parker as Alan Birnley
Michael Gough as Michael Corland
Ernest Thesiger as Sir John Kierlaw
Howard Marion-Crawford as Cranford
Henry Mollison as Hoskins
Vida Hope as Bertha
Patric Doonan as Frank
Duncan Lamont as Harry
Harold Goodwin as Wilkins
Colin Gordon as Hill
Joan Harben as Miss Johnson
Arthur Howard as Roberts
Roddy Hughes as Green
Stuart Latham as Harrison
Miles Malleson as the Tailor
Edie Martin as Mrs. Watson
Mandy Miller as Gladdie
Charlotte Mitchell as Mill Girl
Olaf Olsen as Knudsen
Desmond Roberts as Mannering
Ewan Roberts as Fotheringay
John Rudling as Wilson
Charles Saynor as Pete
Russell Waters as Davidson
Brian Worth as King
George Benson as the Lodger
Frank Atkinson as the Baker
Charles Cullum as 1st Company Director
F.B.J. Sharp as 2nd Company Director
Scott Harold as Express Reporter
Jack Howarth as Receptionist at Corland Mill
Jack McNaughton as Taxi Driver
Judith Furse as Nurse Gamage

Plot: Sidney Stratton (Alec Guinness), a brilliant young research chemist and former Cambridge scholarship recipient, has been dismissed from jobs at several textile mills in the north of England because of his demands for expensive facilities, and his obsession with inventing a cloth fiber which will revolutionize the textile industry.

While working at the Birnley Mill, he accidentally becomes an unpaid researcher and invents an incredibly strong fiber which repels dirt and never wears out. From this fabric, a suit is made for him—which is brilliant white because it cannot absorb dye, and slightly luminous because it contains radioactive elements.

Stratton is lauded as a genius until both management and the trade unions realize the long term consequence of his invention: once consumers have purchased enough of the cloth, demand will drop precipitously and put the textile industry out of business. The managers try to trick and bribe Stratton into signing away the rights to his invention but he refuses. Managers and workers each try to shut him away, but he escapes, only to turn up later.

The climax sees Stratton running through the streets at night in his glowing white suit, pursued by both the managers and their employees. As the crowd advances, his suit begins to fall apart as the chemical structure of the fiber is found to break down with time. The mob, seeing the flaw in his process, rip pieces off his suit in triumph, until he is left standing only in his underwear.

Only Daphne Birnley, the mill owner's daughter, and Bertha, a works laborer, have any sympathy for his disappointment.

The next day, Stratton is dismissed from his job. As he departs with his carton of things, he consults his chemistry notes. A thought hits him and he exclaims, "I see!" With that he strides off, perhaps to try again elsewhere. END

Analysis and additional notes: This was labeled "satire" but I can't see it. It is funny to be sure, but it is also tragic in its own way. Most inventors and researchers are ignored until they document their processes and also provide proof their work. In this case, Stratton did not do his due diligence and test the fabric before he designed the suit. Still, the story of his difficulties, his rise to fame and ultimate downfall (which is rendered doubtful in the last scene) is an object lesson in what happens when one embarks on an experiment which is untested and also fails.

I don't know what anyone thought about the idea that the suit is radioactive (radium rears its ugly head once again), but the fact that the fiber has a short shelf life is more important than that. One could get radiation sickness (Stratton did not) and also be embarassed at the same time. So, comedy/science fiction, yes, but satire it is not.

For its engaging plotline and Alex Guinness's acting ability, I give it 3 stars out of 4. IMdb give it 7.4/10, and Rotten Tomatoes gives it a rating of 100% fresh, while 82% of their audience liked it.

Production: Sound: Whenever Sidney Stratton's apparatus is bubbling, or whenever he is thinking about his stainless fiber, the musical accompaniment to *The Man In The White Suit* is a samba created from a series of recorded bubbles, gurgles, woofs, and squirts. These sounds were not made using traditional musical instruments but actual laboratory equipment.

According to promotional material at the British Film Institute, London, the music was a collaboration of director Alexander Mackendrick and sound editor Mary Habberfield. The bubble sound was obtained by blowing through a glass tube into a viscous glycerin solution. The two drip sounds were obtained by smacking two pieces of brass and glass tubes against the palm of the hand. The draining sound was created by air blowing through a tube into water and then amplifying the bubble sound through a metal tube. After Habberfield captured each sound effect, she mixed them in different combinations by trial and error until she found the leitmotif of Sidney Stratton and his bubbling apparatus in the film.

Reception: It was one of the most popular films of the year in Britain. The British Film Institute named it the 58th greatest British film of all time. In 2014 The Guardian included it on their list as one of the 20 best British science fiction films.

SUPERMAN AND THE MOLE MEN (1951)

Directed by Lee Sholem
Produced by Barney A. Sarecky
Written by Richard Fielding; based on characters by Jerry Siegel and Joe Shuster
Music by Darrell Calker and Walter Greene
Cinematography by Clark Ramsey
Edited by Albrecht Joseph
Production company: Lippert Pictures
Distributed by Lippert Pictures; release date November 23, 1951
Running time: 58 minutes

Cast:
George Reeves as Clark Kent / Superman
Phyllis Coates as Lois Lane
Jeff Corey as Luke Benson
Walter Reed as Bill Corrigan
J. Farrell MacDonald as Pop Shannon
Stanley Andrews as The Sheriff
Ray Walker as John Craig
Hal K. Dawson as Chuck Weber
Phil Warren as Deputy Jim
Frank Reicher as Hospital Superintendent
Beverly Washburn as Child
Billy Curtis as a Mole-Man
Jerry Maren as a Mole-Man
John T. Bambury as Mole-Man (uncredited)

Plot: Mild-mannered reporter Clark Kent (George Reeves) and Lois Lane (Phyllis Coates) are sent to the small town of Silsby for the close of the world's deepest oil well. No explanation has been given for its closure, and the well workers are nervous and agitated, believing that the well is cursed. Strange things have been going on in the middle of the night. The townspeople are all shocked and angry that their livelihoods are being threatened by the closure, but there is little anyone can do about it. Clark and Lois decide to come back to the well later to determine if the tale is true.

That evening, the lid to an adjunct well opens, and two small bald headed humans emerge to explore the well. They are clad in black and have very pale faces. They are about to look at the actual well tower when an elderly night watchman comes upon them and suffers a heart attack. The two little men return to their hatch and disappear.

Lois Lane and Clark Kent arrive at the oil well later and find the dead watchman. They find the foreman of the well works, a man named Corrigan (Walter Reed) and tell him what has happened. Clark and the foreman are exploring the surrounding area for signs of intruders when Lois sees one of the creatures and screams. But no one believes her when she tells them what she saw.

The medical examiner is summoned, and he later leaves with Lois. Clark stays behind to confront the foreman, who confesses that the well was closed for fear that they had struck radium and not oil. The foreman proceeds to show Clark ore samples that were collected during different stages of drilling. All of them glow brightly.

The townspeople become afraid of the little mole men because of their peculiar appearance and because everything that they touch glows in the dark. They form an angry mob in order to kill the "monsters", directed by the violent and incalcitrant Luke Benson (Jeff Corey). They are admonished not to resort to violence by the Sheriff (Stanley Andrews) but Benson has his own ideas.

Superman is the only one able to resolve the conflict, stopping Benson and the mob by enduring their bullets. Yet Benson is offended by this, declaring that Superman cannot tell him what to do. The Sheriff intervenes and says again that if Benson does not keep to the law, the law will determine his fate.

Later, Superman saves one of the mole men after he has been shot and flies him to the hospital. The second mole man returns to the well head and disappears down its shaft.

Later, a doctor (John Craig) reveals that the injured creature will die unless he has surgery to remove the bullet. Clark Kent is forced to assist when the nurse refuses to do so out of fear. It turns out that the mole men are as human as we are, and the glow is actually harmless phosphorescence. Though they lack the faculty of speech (or perhaps they are telepathic), they have done no harm to anyone, and were exploring out of curiosity about the world of the surface.

Soon afterward, Benson's mob arrives at the hospital demanding that the creature be given to them, causing Superman to stand guard outside the hospital. Lois Lane stands at Superman's side, until a shot is fired from the mob, narrowly missing her. Superman sends Lois inside the hospital for her safety, and begins to relieve the mob of their rifles and pistols. He warns Benson not to try anything, because "these men have as much right to live as you do."

Later, three more mole men emerge from the drill shaft, this time bearing a strange weapon with them, and make their way to the hospital. Benson and his mob see them, but Benson goes after them alone. When the mole men see him, they fire their laser weapon at him. Superman sees this and jumps quickly in front of the pulsating ray, saving Benson's life.

A grateful Benson thanks him, at which Superman says "it is more than you deserve!"

Superman fetches the wounded mole man from the hospital and returns him and his companions to the well head. Soon afterward, from deep underground, the mole men destroy the drill shaft, making certain that no one can ever use it again. All that is seen of this action is a small explosion.

Lois observes, "It's almost as if they were saying, 'You live your lives ... and we'll live ours'". Clark smiles. END

Analysis and additional notes: Meant to be a feature film for a theater audience, *Superman And The Mole Men* proved to be a riveting thrill ride. Not only did Superman rule the day (as he always does), it provided a story which was sympathetic toward the "villains" for a change. The mole men in the story lived in a cavern thousands of miles down from the surface, and were curious when the drill penetrated its roof. We see that they are merely curious, and explore the area only at night when everyone is away. The younger one of the first two follows his companion's lead, but is not swift enough to avoid a bullet. We see him examine a flower by the road. They are innocuous as can be.

Contrast that with the villainous and violent Benson, who does not recognize authority and who nearly meets his death if it were not for Superman. Benson represents the worst of us: bigoted, selfish, and criminally bent. He demonstrates his prejudice immediately, even to the Sheriff, who could arrest him for inciting a riot but charitably does not. In the end, Benson is grateful to Superman but the man of steel does not accept it. He has already lost patience with Benson. It's hard not to.

The relationship between Lois and Clark becomes a bit strained when Lois berates him for his "cowardice". Clark swears to her that one day... and then he stops. He cannot reveal himself to Lois, so he has to bite his remark. We all know that it is vital for someone leading a double life to conceal the truth. It is about the only flaw in Superman's persona. But we hope that one day he will tell her.

This film formed the pilot for the *Superman* television series.

For its engaging plotline and superior acting, I give *Superman and The Mole Men* 3 stars out of 4. IMdb gives it 5.9/10, and Rotten Tomatoes gives it no rating as yet, but only 34% liked it. I don't understand why this one did not catch on. Oh, well.

A word about phosphorescence: It is a type of photoluminescence related to fluorescence. Unlike fluorescence, a phosphorescent material does not immediately emit the radiation it absorbs, like light.

Everyday examples of phosphorescent materials are glow-in-the-dark toys, stickers, paint, and clock dials that glow after being charged with a bright light or room light. Typically, the glow slowly fades out, sometimes within a few minutes or up to a few hours in a dark room.

The study of phosphorescent materials led to the discovery of radioactivity in 1896.

Production: Superman and The Mole Men was the first theatrical feature film based on any DC Comics character. Two live action, multiple chapter movie serials from Columbia Pictures Inc., based on the *Superman* comics feature and radio program, featured Kirk Alyn as Superman and Noel Neill as Lois Lane, and had been shown in weekly installments in movie theaters. Prior to these, there was a Superman animated cartoon series produced during World War II for theater goers. In fact, Superman was the only superhero so popular that he went beyond the comic books soon after his invention in 1941.

A close comparison occurred with Batman (Then called The Batman) after his premier in Detective Comics in 1939. But a film series was not produced until 1943.

The image of actors Reeves and Coates on the theatrical release poster is a painting derived by reversing ("flopping") a publicity photograph image of the two actors, with Superman's "S shield" emblem then reversed in order for it to read correctly.

The original screenplay was by "Richard Fielding", a pseudonym for Robert Maxwell and Whitney Ellsworth.

Superman And The Mole Men was filmed in a little more than 12 days on a studio back lot and runs just 58 minutes. It originally served as a trial balloon release for the syndicated *Adventures of Superman* TV series, for which it became the only two part episode, "The Unknown People". Some elements of the original film were trimmed when converted for television, including some portions of a lengthy chase scene and all references to "Mole Men".

The theme music used for the film had a generic "science fiction sound", with nothing suggesting a specific Superman theme. The title cards used were similarly generic, with low grade animation of comets sailing by Saturn-like ringed planets.

The film's original film score by Darrell Calker was removed when *Superman And The Mole Men* was cut into the two part *Superman* TV episode. It was replaced with "canned" production library music used in the first season of the *Superman* television series.

The weapon of the mole men, which they retrieve from their subterranean home in order to defend themselves and rescue their injured comrade, was a prop made by adding metal shoulder braces to one end of an Electrolux vacuum cleaner body; for the ray's "gun barrel" a standard metal funnel was attached to the other.

Home video releases: *Superman And The Mole Men* was first released on VHS and LaserDisc by Warner Home Video on July 22, 1988, coinciding with the 50th anniversary celebrations of the Superman character that year. Both the two part TV episode and the full feature are on the 2005 first season DVD release for *Adventures of Superman*. During 2006, the film was released as a bonus feature on the DVD 4-Disc Special Edition of *Superman: The Movie*. Later, *Superman and The Mole Men* was repackaged for its 2011 Blu-Ray box set release, then released on DVD in 2017 by Cheezy Movies.

THE THING FROM ANOTHER WORLD (1951)

Directed by Christian Nyby
Produced by Edward Lasker
Screenplay by Charles Lederer; uncredited: Howard Hawks and Ben Hecht
Based on *Who Goes There?* a 1938 novella by John W. Campbell, Jr.
Music by Dimitri Tiomkin
Cinematography by Russell Harlan, ASC

Edited by Roland Gross
Production company: Winchester Pictures Corporation
(yes, the gun mfr.)
Distributed by RKO Radio Pictures; release date: April 27, 1951
Running time: 87 minutes
Box office: $1.95 million (in US rentals)

Cast:
Kenneth Tobey as Captain Patrick Hendry
Margaret Sheridan as Nikki Nicholson
Robert Cornthwaite as Dr. Arthur Carrington
Douglas Spencer as Ned Scott (Scotty)
James Young as Lt. Eddie Dykes
Dewey Martin as Bob (Crew Chief)
Robert Nichols as Lt. Ken MacPherson
William Self as Corporal Barnes
Eduard Franz as Dr. Stern
Sally Creighton as Mrs. Chapman
James Arness as 'The Thing'
Uncredited:
Paul Frees as Dr. Voorhees
John Dierkes as Dr. Chapman
George Fenneman as Dr. Redding
Everett Glass as Dr. Wilson
Edmund Breon as Dr. Ambrose
Norbert Schiller as Dr. Laurence
Nicholas Byron as Tex Richards
David McMahon as General Fogerty

Plot: A United States Air Force crew is dispatched from Anchorage, Alaska at the request of Dr. Carrington (Robert Cornthwaite), the chief scientist of a north pole scientific outpost. They have radiometric evidence that an unknown flying craft has crashed in their vicinity, so reporter Ned Scott (Douglas Spencer) tags along for the story.

Dr. Carrington later briefs Captain Hendry (Kenneth Tobey) and his airmen, and Dr. Redding (George Fenneman) shows photos of a flying object moving erratically before crashing—not the usual movements of a meteorite.

Following erratic magnetic pole anomalies, the crew and scientists fly to the crash site where the mysterious craft lies buried beneath refrozen ice. As they spread out to outline the craft's general shape, the men realize they are standing in a circle. They have discovered a crashed flying saucer.

They try de-icing the buried craft with thermite heat bombs, but only ignite its metal alloy, causing an explosion that destroys the saucer. Their Geiger counter then points to a slightly radioactive frozen shape buried nearby in the ice. It appears that the shape is a man, probably having escaped the explosion only to freeze.

They excavate a large block of ice around the tall body and fly it to the research outpost, just as a major storm moves in, cutting off their communications with Anchorage.

Some of the scientists want to thaw out the body, but Captain Hendry insists on waiting until he receives further instructions from the Air Force. Later, Corporal Barnes (William Self) takes the second watch over the ice block and to avoid looking at the body within, covers it with an electric blanket that the previous guard had left turned on. As the ice slowly melts, the Thing inside revives.

Barnes panics and shoots at it with his sidearm, but the alien escapes into the raging storm. The Thing is attacked by sled dogs but kills them. The airmen recover a severed arm. Thinking that the alien cannot get far in his condition, they take the arm to Carrington for examination.

A microscopic examination of a tissue sample reveals that the arm is vegetable rather than animal matter, demonstrating that the alien is some very advanced form of plant life. As the arm warms to ambient temperature, it ingests some of the dogs' blood covering it, and the hand begins moving. Seed pods are discovered in the palm.

The Air Force personnel believe the creature is a danger to all of them, but Dr. Carrington is convinced that it can be reasoned with and has much to teach them. Carrington deduces their visitor requires blood to survive and reproduce. He later discovers the body of a dead sled dog hidden in the outpost's greenhouse. Carrington has Dr. Voorhees (Paul Frees), Dr. Olsen (William Neff) and Dr. Auerbach stand guard overnight, waiting for the Thing to return. Carrington secretly uses blood plasma from the infirmary to incubate seedlings grown from the alien seed pods.

Later, the bodies of Olsen and Auerbach are discovered strung up in the greenhouse, both drained of blood. Dr. Stern is almost killed by the Thing but escapes. Hendry rushes to the greenhouse after hearing about the bodies, and is attacked by the alien. Hendry slams the door on the Thing's regenerated arm as it tries to grab him. The alien then escapes through the greenhouse's exterior door, breaking into another building in the compound. Through all of this, Scott tries to take a picture or two, but is unable to.

Nikki Nicholson (Margaret Sheridan), Carrington's secretary, reluctantly updates Hendry when he asks about missing plasma, and Hendry confronts Carrington in his lab, where he discovers the alien seeds have grown at an alarming rate. It's bad enough that Carrington is infatuated with the alien being, but now the presence of the plants suggests that if they are allowed to reach maturity there will be more aliens running around loose.

Following Nicholson's suggestion, Hendry and his men lay a trap in a nearby sleeping room: after dousing the alien with buckets of kerosene, they set it ablaze with a flare gun, forcing it to jump through a closed window into the Arctic storm. Nicholson is almost burned but the mattress she uses as a shield protects her. A couple of the men sustain some serious burns.

Later, Nicholson notices that the temperature inside the station is falling. She alerts the others by asking them to see their breath, as they are all dressed in layers of clothing. A heating fuel line has been sabotaged by the alien. The cold forces everyone to make a final stand near the generator room. They rig an electrical "fly trap", hoping to electrocute their visitor. Again, Scott wants to take some pictures, but is drafted into helping out.

As the Thing advances, Carrington shuts off the power to the trap and tries to reason with it, but is brutally knocked aside. The alien is both angry and hungry. On Hendry's direct order that nothing of the Thing should remain, the alien is reduced by arcs of electricity to a smoldering pile of ash; Dr. Carrington's growing seed pods and the Thing's severed arm are destroyed by fire as well.

When the weather clears, Scott files his "story of a lifetime" by radio to a roomful of reporters in Anchorage. Scott begins his broadcast with a warning: "Tell the world. Tell this to everybody, wherever they are. Watch the skies everywhere. Keep looking. Keep watching the skies." END

Analysis and additional notes: This one was long ago relegated to the monster list, but has since been restored to the science fiction list. Why? Because it is more science fiction than monster thriller. We even have one scientist go mad right in front of us.

There is a particularly scientific scene when the scientists discuss the composition of the alien arm; there is some fear that the alien has everyone trapped in the compound quarters, ostensibly to use them as feeding stock. Even more interesting is that the word "vampire" does not come up even once, even as everyone discovers that the alien drinks blood.

A scientist mentions that there are carnivorous plants on Earth that drink blood, insects, whatever they can grab hold of. He mentions the century plant (Agave Americana), but he is wrong. The century plant does not survive on anything but rain, and is a succulent used to manufacture Tequila. That is the extent of it.

Some of the sled dogs were killed by the Thing, but we don't know what happened to the rest. I would have thought that they would be housed with their human masters, but no mention is made after the death scene. That is one point of continuity which bothered me.

The other is Dr. Carrington and his insistence that everyone treat the alien with kid gloves. I'm sorry, but science or not, if I knew that an alien being was after me I'd run, not walk, to the nearest shelter. For a scientist of his calibre to suddenly go weak at the knees is not characteristic and not credible. Plus, his lack of empathy for his fellow scientists, dead or not, would brand him a pariah of the first water. No, I don't care about the scientific method. Most scientists are human beings first and scientists second. They know the difference.

As for the Thing himself (he is easily recognizable as male), we see that he is angry about his space ship being blown up and he is always hungry. Part of that may have something to do with the cold of the Arctic ice. His plan is to keep the team under one roof so he can feed at his leizure. Then he would probably move on to warmer climes, and menace other populations, until he was killed more violently than by electrocution. When I saw the team laying the trap, the words that

71

came to mind were "bug zapper". Had they not succeeded, they would have been doomed. So, end of story.

For its chilling mystery and scientific methods employed, I give it 3 stars out of 4. IMdb gives it 7.2/10. Rotten Tomatoes gives it an 88% fresh, and 73% of their audience liked it.

Production: No actors are named during the film's dramatic "slow burning letters through background" opening title sequence, while the cast credits appear at the end of the film. No performers are named in the film's advertising graphics. Many cast members with significant speaking parts are not credited at all. Appearing in a small role was George Fenneman, who at the time was gaining fame as Groucho Marx's announcer on the popular quiz show *You Bet Your Life.*

Fenneman later said he had difficulty with the overlapping dialogue in the film. It is true that the dialogue was fast and clippy, with actors sometimes overlapping each other. Something to do with the pacing of the director's vision, but mostly with the fact that people do talk over each other at times in real life; especially if they are excited about something. This made the dialogue more credible to me than the usual stage pacing expected in a film.

The film was partly shot in Glacier National Park and interior sets built at a Los Angeles ice storage plant. This accounts for the actors always being clad in layers of clothing and wearing their fur jackets. It lent a great deal to the idea of the story taking place in the Arctic.

The film took full advantage of the national sentiment of the time to help enhance the horror elements of the story. The film reflected a post-Hiroshima skepticism about science and negative views of scientists who meddle with things better left alone. In the end it is American servicemen and several sensible scientists who win the day over the alien invader, with a practicality which is not seen an many films of the day.

Screenplay: The film was loosely adapted by Charles Lederer, with uncredited rewrites from Howard Hawks and Ben Hecht, from the 1938 novella *Who Goes There?* by John W. Campbell, Jr.. The story was first published in Astounding Science Fiction under Campbell's pseudonym Don A. Stuart (Campbell had just become Astounding's managing editor when his novella appeared in its pages).

The film's screenplay changes the fundamental nature of the alien as presented in Campbell's 1938 novella: Lederer's "Thing" is a

72

humanoid life form whose cellular structure is closer to vegetation, although it must feed on blood to survive. Reporter Scott even refers to it in the film as a "super carrot." The internal, plant-like structure of the creature makes it impervious to bullets (but not to other destructive forces). Campbell's "Thing" is a life form capable of assuming the physical and mental characteristics of any living thing it encounters; this characteristic was later realized in John Carpenter's adaptation of the novella, the 1982 film *The Thing*. We do not see any shapeshifting in the 1951 film. It is merely suggested.

Director: There is debate as to whether the film was directed by Hawks with Christian Nyby receiving the credit so that Nyby could obtain his Director's Guild membership; or whether Nyby directed it with considerable input in both screenplay and advice in directing from producer Hawks for Hawks' Winchester Pictures, which released it through RKO Radio Pictures Inc.. Hawks gave Nyby only $5,460 of the $50,000 director's fee that RKO paid and kept the rest, but Hawks denied that he directed the film.

Cast members disagree on Hawks' and Nyby's contributions. Tobey said that "Hawks directed it, all except one scene", while on the other hand, Fenneman said that "Hawks would once in a while direct, if he had an idea, but it was Chris' show." Cornthwaite said that "Chris always deferred to Hawks... Maybe because he did defer to him, people misinterpreted it."

Although William Self said that "Hawks was directing the picture from the sidelines", he also said that "Chris would stage each scene, how to play it. But then he would go over to Howard and ask him for advice, which the actors did not hear ... Even though I was there every day, I don't think any of us can answer the question. Only Chris and Howard can answer the question." Self later became President of 20th Century Fox Television. On describing the production, Self said, "Chris was the director in our eyes, but Howard was the boss in our eyes."

At a reunion of *The Thing* cast and crew members in 1982, Nyby said: "Did Hawks direct it? That's one of the most inane and ridiculous questions I've ever heard, and people keep asking. That it was Hawks' style. Of course it was. This is a man I studied and wanted to be like. You would certainly emulate and copy the master you're sitting under, which I did. Anyway, if you're taking painting lessons from Rembrandt, you don't take the brush out of the master's hands."

Reception: *Critical and box office reception*: *The Thing From Another World* was released in April 1951. By the end of that year, the film had accrued $1,950,000 in distributors' domestic (U. S. and Canada) rentals, making it the year's 46th biggest earner, beating all other science fiction films released that year including *The Day The Earth Stood Still* and *When Worlds Collide*.

Bosley Crowther in <u>The New York Times</u> observed, "Taking a fantastic notion (or is it, really?), Mr. Hawks has developed a movie that is generous with thrills and chills...Adults and children can have a lot of old-fashioned movie fun at 'The Thing', but parents should understand their children and think twice before letting them see this film if their emotions are not properly conditioned."

"Gene" in <u>Variety</u> complained that the film "lacks genuine entertainment values." More than 20 years after its theatrical release, science fiction editor and publisher Lester del Rey compared the film unfavorably to the source material, John W. Campbell's *Who Goes There?*, calling it "just another monster epic, totally lacking in the force and tension of the original story."

The Thing is now considered by many to be one of the best films of 1951. The consensus is that the film "is better than most flying saucer movies, thanks to well-drawn characters and concise, tense plotting."

In 2001, the United States Library of Congress deemed the film "culturally significant" and selected it for preservation in the National Film Registry. Also, <u>Time</u> magazine named *The Thing From Another World* "the greatest 1950s sci-fi movie."

Legacy: *The Thing From Another World* is now considered to be one of the great science fiction films of the 1950s.

Related productions: In 1980, <u>Fantasy Newsletter</u> reported that Wilbur Stark had bought the rights to several old RKO Pictures fantasy films, intending to remake them, and suggested the most significant of these purchases was *The Thing From Another World*. This soon led to the making of a more faithful adaptation of Campbell's story, directed by John Carpenter and released in 1982 under the title *The Thing*, with Stark as executive producer. It paid homage to the 1951 film by using the same "slow burning letters through background" opening title sequence.

Matthijs van Heijningen Jr. made a 2011 prequel to John Carpenter's 1982 film using the same title, *The Thing*.

A colorized version of the original film was released in 1989 on VHS by Turner Home Entertainment; it was billed as an "RKO Color Classic".

UNKNOWN WORLD (1951)

Directed by Terry O. Morse
Produced by Irving A. Block, Jack Rabin, and Robert L. Lippert
Written by Millard Kaufman
Music by Ernest Gold
Cinematography by Henry Freulich and Allen G. Siegler
Edited by Terry O. Morse
Distributed by Lippert Pictures Inc.; release date October 26, 1951
Running time: 74 minutes

Cast:
Victor Kilian as Dr. Jeremiah Morley
Marilyn Nash as Joan Lindsey
Bruce Kellogg as Wright Thompson
Otto Waldis as Dr. Max A. Bauer
Tom Handley as Dr. James Paxton
Dick Cogan as Dr. George Coleman
Jim Bannon as Andy

Plot: Dr. Jeremiah Morley (Victor Kilian) is concerned about an imminent nuclear war. He presents his arguments to an assembly of world scientists and tries to end nuclear war, but is unsuccessful. He uses his own funds to organize an expedition of scientists to explore the Earth beneath the surface and look for a safe place to harbor humanity in the event the surface is no longer viable for survival.

Morley has developed a large atomic powered mining machine, called the Cyclotram, for this purpose. The expedition members consist of Andy (Jim Bannon), Joan Lindsey (Marilyn Nash), Dr. Max A. Bauer (Otto Waldis), Dr. James Paxton (Tom Handley), and Dr. George Coleman (Dick Cogan).

The expedition begins after government funding has fallen through and they are bailed out at the last minute by private funding

75

from a rakish newspaper heir named Wright Thompson (Bruce Kellogg), who insists on going with them for a lark.

After drilling down several thousand feet, the Cyclotram emerges in a series of caverns, all of which are large but have no potable water or springs nearby. There is no choice but to go on, Morley says.

The Cyclotram drills down several more thousand feet when it stops in another cavern. Everyone wants to stretch their legs, but they discover that there is nothing there to see, so they move on.

A romantic rivalry soon develops between Andy and Thompson for Joan, but she's not having any of it. She is too busy caring for a brace of rabbits brought to test the living conditions underground.

In yet another cavern the instruments show that there is something wrong. Two of the team volunteer to go outside and test the environment. They do not return. Eventually, Morley and the others use their wits and go outside wearing gas masks. They discover the two lying dead, having been overcome by methane or some other gas.

There is an argument about whether to turn back. They had already found a cavern with water, but Morely is insistent that they go on. When the Cyclotram drills down further still, it comes out in an enormous underground expanse with a plentiful air supply, its own large ocean, and phosphorescent light.

However, Joan discovers that all the lab rabbits brought with them have given birth to dead offspring. Through necropsies, she discovers that this strange underground world has somehow rendered the rabbits, and hence any other life form, sterile. Dr. Morley is deeply depressed by this news.

Then, when an underground volcano suddenly erupts, he fails to enter the safety of the Cyclotram with the others and quickly perishes.

The remaining survivors discover another exit through the underground ocean to avoid the eruption, and find themselves rising toward the surface of the upper world in a strong, upward moving ocean current. The Cycotram eventually breaks the surface near an unknown tropical island. END

Analysis and additional notes: I don't know about you, but apart from the adventures in the caverns, this film was about as pessimistic as it gets. First of all, Dr. Morley is of the opinion that the only place to go is down instead of up, in case of a nuclear war. Second, the whole expedition was more of a futile gamble.

In the film, we are not shown a whole lot. Most of the scenes involved seeing the scientists seated in what was apparently a moving cabin. We see a mere glimpse of the actual Cyclotram in action from time to time. The expedition halts long enough for the team to explore some beautiful caverns which go nowhere. Some have running water, some don't.

In the end, the only cavern Morely likes is the one least likely to have any redeeming value. Yes, there is light, and yes, there is water. But nothing grows there, there is nothing alive. Only when Joan reaches her conclusions is Morely finally convinced that his effort was worthless.

We are also expected to accept that the Cyclotram will not have any mechanical problems. I don't know that much about drilling down into the earth but I do know that eventually drill bits do wear out, and also other parts of a machine. Yet it crunches through the most durable rock as if it is styrofoam. This inconsistency cannot stand.

As for their escape from the eruption, I cannot believe in a siphon of water which travels in a straight line all the way to the surface from thousands of feet down. The Earth simply does not work that way. Sooner or later, the Cyclotram should have encountered a blockade, and the expedition team should have tried to decompress on the way up. But there is no exposition for this.

And, there is no satisfactory ending. There is no further discussion of what happens afterward. What did the scientists say? Where are the crowds of reporters wanting to hear their story? It simply ends when the Cyclotram reaches the surface of the ocean.

That is what I call a cheat.

For its plodding pacing and dull stretches of cabin moving, I give this one 1.5 stars out of 4. IMdb gives it 3.9/10, and Rotten Tomatoes gives it no rating, but only 8% of their audience liked it.

Production: Portions of *Unknown World* were filmed in Carlsbad Caverns, Bronson Caves, Nichols Canyon, and at Pismo Beach. I should point out here that Bronson Caves is a couple of holes in the side of a mountain, that are barely more than 30 yards long and have exits. They are good for shooting emerging scenes, such as the Batmobile in the *Batman* TV series of the 1960s, but not much else.

Unknown World was put together by two Hollywood special effects men, Jack Rabin and Irving Block, who are two of the film's three producers. Some of the plot elements of *Unknown World* were reused years later in the big studio science fiction film *The Core* (2003).

Reception: The B-Movie Review site Million Monkey Theater found that the "production crew try hard, and it really seems like they have an important message to tell, but the execution and polish are lacking"

Imitation: DC Comics had a comic book called *Cave Carson* that was similar.

WHEN WORLDS COLLIDE (1951)

Directed by Rudolph Maté
Writing credits: Edwin Balmer (novel); Sydney Boehm, Philip Wylie (novel)
Produced by George Pal; Cecil B. DeMille executive producer (uncredited)
Music by Leith Stevens
Cinematography by W. Howard Greene and John F. Seitz

Cast:
Richard Derr as David Randall
Barbara Rush as Joyce Hendron
Peter Hansen as Dr. Tony Drake
John Hoyt as Sydney Stanton
Larry Keating as Dr. Cole Hendron
Rachel Ames as Julie Cummings (as Judith Ames)
Stephen Chase as Dr. George Frye
Frank Cady as Harold Ferris
Hayden Rorke as Dr. Emery Bronson
Sandro Giglio as Dr. Ottinger
More cast listed alphabetically:
Kirk Alyn as Rioter Bringing Guns (uncredited)
[Kirk Alyn starred in the *Superman* series of short films]
Gertrude Astor as Traveler (uncredited)
Paul Frees as Narrator / U.S. President (voice) (uncredited)

Gay Nelson as Leda (uncredited)
Keith Richards as Stanley - Dr. Bronson's Assistant (uncredited)
Harry Stanton as Dr. Zenta, Astronomer (uncredited)

Plot: David Randall (Richard Derr) is a skilled pilot who is paid to deliver photographs from one eminent astronomer to another. The recipient, Dr. Cole Hendron (Larry Keating), tears open the packet and confirms the awful findings: a star is tearing through the solar system and will pass by Earth fairly soon. Its only planet, called Zyra, will collide with Earth and destroy it.

When he presents his conclusions at a meeting of the World Science Council, the situation is viewed with skepticism and even denial by other scientists. But Dr. Hendron is adamant that preparations should be made to evacuate Earth and immediately as possible. He proposes that rocket ships could be built to transport a good sample of the human population, animals and other foodstuffs, and equipment, to Zyra. He discusses the difficulties of transporting everyone. He also points out that Zyra may not be habitable, but that it is the only hope there is of preserving the human race in the face of this terrible and unavoidable catastrophe, or the human race will become extinct.

A huge argument erupts. Heckling and accusations ensue. One of the scientists suggests that this is similar to a eugenics project, and who is Hendron to decide who lives and who dies? Hendron replies that a worldwide lottery must be established, and that each nation must select by that system alone and build their own ships, and also that no nation should declare Zyra its sovereign territory. He says that he will submit his own name to the pot if it will hasten the council's decision. He argues desperately that there is no time to waste in debate over this. The need is to act now.

When the council meeting is over, two notable philanthropists give Dr. Hendron some of the money he needs to build the rocket ship for the United States, and a colleague, Dr. George Frye, offers his help as ship designer and project manager.

The rest of the money will come from Sydney Stanton, a wheelchair-bound industrialist with a personal stake. He insists that he must be allowed to come along on the ship in return for his money, no matter what the results of the lottery will be. Hendron tells Stanton that he cannot place himself above the rules, and that his money will be well spent but that Stanton must be willing to do it for the preservation of humanity alone, not for personal gain. Stanton reluctantly goes along. For once he is not able to call all the shots or have things his way. Fuming with exasperation, he orders his assistant to give Hendron everything he needs.

Randall has been by Hendron's side all along as a new friend and colleague, and his support so far has been of tremendous value already. He tells Dr. Hendron that he does not know how he fits in to all of this. He's a pilot, nothing more, and he feels he will not have a place in the new world. Hendron assures him that he is more valuable than ever when he reminds Randall that every little bit he has done so far has already earned him a place on the ship.

Randall takes Hendron's advice to heart and volunteers to help out wherever he can on the American project (At this point, all focus is on this particular project with the international effort falling into the background). Soon he sheds his carefree attitude in the face of this monumental threat to existence and finds himself busier than he has ever been before, flying in supplies and working with the transportation side of things.

Joyce Hendron, Dr. Hendron's daughter, is in charge of organizing and cataloging, solving problems, and in other ways helping to hurry things along. Soon, Randall's admiration for her turns to love.

We see the ship being built, slowly, one beam and part at a time, but with a distinct sense of haste. Dr. Frye has conceived of a ramp launching system, where the ship (a Willy Ley rocket!) launches like a jet but uses the elevated ramp to boost it upward. From there, he claims the ship will fire its rockets and exit to space. His design calls for Zyra being close by but they must go into space until the collision debris has cleared. Then they could land safely on the alien planet. (On a planetary scale this is practically impossible, but since no physicist was consulted about this we can suspend our disbelief in favor of the plotline. The actual effects are too complex to go into here.)

While this is going on, those not busy on the assembly line are lined up at the pot and pulling lottery slips. Some smile at the results; others look distinctly crestfallen but resume their work nevertheless. There is a side romance introduced where two young grad students in love are caught in a terrible twist of fate. The young man has won his place on the ship in the lottery, whereas his girlfriend has not. The two are devastated and will not leave each other behind. Sometime later, the young man delivers his ticket to Hendron and declares that he would rather stay behind and die with his lover than live without her.

Stanton, who was not selected after all, immediately demands the ticket and says that in this way he is still assured a seat on that ship. Hendron reluctantly hands the ticket over. Stanton's assistant remains silent but his face speaks volumes of his hatred for Stanton.

Meanwhile, Randall and Joyce's fiance' (Dr. Tony Drake) find common ground over Joyce's future. Randall declares that he loves Joyce but will not do anything to jeopardize her happiness. Drake, feeling as if he has the upper hand, says that if there was anyone he could trust with Joyce it would be Randall. They come to the mutual agreement that Joyce is *their* girl, and that each would be prepared to support her should something happen to the other.

Joyce comes upon them talking and says that she is pleased with their acceptance of each other as friends instead of enemies, but now it's time to get back to work. (She does not talk about it, but something in her body language hints that she has known about Randall's affection for her for some time. There just has been no time for her to dwell on it.)

Interspersed with these touching scenes is a brief montage of other projects going on over the world, their successes and failures, and even small wars breaking out. In this way we are shown the way humankind deals with total extinction, whether for good or bad.

As the time draws near to collision the scientists are studying the rogue star's effect on Earth. They discover that it will be close but that the star is far enough away to pass without more than a minor disruption to Earth's orbit.

Everyone hunkers down close as earthquakes caused by the star's passing rock the planet. Buildings fall, cracks open in the surface, fires and burst dams devastate the landscape. Millions of people die. This time, however, resources are turned to restoring the evacuation ships to flight condition. But some ships will never fly.

As luck would have it, the American ship has managed to escape destruction, but the launching ramp must be repaired. The project team redoubles their efforts, as Zyra is now closer than ever and there is no time to rest. Everything is, "hurry! Hurry!" But there is dissatisfaction among those who were denied a seat on the ship. Sooner or later, this grumbling will lead to violence. Hendron and the other project scientists know this but cannot do anything about it.

At last, the day is at hand. Zyra is now so close to Earth it is visibly larger than the moon. Earth begins to rock with earthquakes again as the final preparations are made to launch the ship.

As the last of the animals are loaded aboard, a boy who was selected finds a stray puppy and smuggles him aboard. Before long he is caught. Flightload is now critical, but the boy says the pup only weighs a few extra pounds. At the last second, Dr. Frye makes a decision and allows the puppy to stay. Then he climbs into the cockpit and straps himself in next to Randall, who was convinced by Dr. Hendron earlier that he must take over if something should happen to Frye. The countdown begins.

Those who were abandoned are now thoroughly angry and arm theselves, meaning to break through the gates of the compound and take over the ship. A shootout ensues between the guards and the rioters, even as it is far too late.

Dr. Hendron and his colleague Dr. Bronson are standing on the launch pier with Stanton and his assistant. The winds are whipping up into a frenzy as Zyra draws ever closer. Hendron and Dr. Bronson had discovered that Bronson is critically ill and will not survive the journey. Hendron says goodbye to Bronson and boards the ship.

At the last second, Bronson hands his ticket over to Stanton's assistant and says, "I'll take care of things here."

The assistant shakes his hand with a smile and starts to leave Stanton behind, running for the ship, when Stanton pulls out a revolver and shoots him in the back. Then, Stanton finds that Bronson has not started pushing his chair forward. He asks, "well, what are you waiting for?"

Bronson says, "you and I are going to stay here. The future has no need for us."

Shocked, Stanton yells something incomprehensible into the furious wind as the ship powers up. Then slowly he rises from the chair and takes a few steps forward. But it is too late.

The ship launches, destroying the pier as it does so. We see it push upward into a sky already dark with Zyra's huge bulk. Randall and the passengers are pressed into their seats by gravity until they pass out.

We are treated to a great scene of the two planets colliding. Whole chunks of Earth are sheared off and break into fragments while Zyra plows on like a juggernaut through it.

Randall revives and finds himself still strapped in, a calm and quite healthy Dr. Frye sitting next to him and working at the controls. Feeling somewhat cheated, he says, "Doctor Hendron lied to me."

Frye replies, "that's all right. It might have happened anyway."

The ship finally lands. At first, the passengers are uncertain of the situation. Dr. Frye reports that the atmosphere seems to be similar to Earth's, but now there was only one way to find out. He opens the hatch and sniffs. Nothing happens. Slowly, the new colonists emerge from the ship and stand on the outer hatch. A panorama of a flat plain dotted with what look like ancient buildings and a sky bright with the sun rising greets them. Whatever happens now, mankind has survived against the odds. END

Analysis and additional notes: When I first saw this movie years ago it was shown on a black and white television, and I had no idea it was in color. I also was not cognizant of its social importance until I was well into my teens, as at the time it was marketed as a "B" movie. Despite its somewhat primitive special effects for the time, it was still a very exciting film. As I have noted before, the actual physics of a pair of planets in collision were overlooked in favor of the relevence of the plot. And what a plot it is: how mankind can preserve itself and survive the total destruction of the homeworld.

Much of it is fairly self-explanatory. We know that the fight to survive, the quest for resources, the basic need for air, food, water, shelter, companionship, and the imperative to reproduce as a species are all there. We see a brief brush with politics and capitalism; and even the pushback against the selfish motivations of those who crave power in order to create a new progressive order where greed and power mean nothing. The science is kind of injected as an afterthought but forms a powerful background for a film about the human condition.

The end of the film, however, is what bothers me; like a chord played off key in an almost perfect etude. It was short and punctual. It was almost as if the money to make the film had run out at the last minute, and what we are left with is a stark future with a dark and unsatisfying outcome. It seems that there should have been more room for discussion, but the story ended there.

I mean, what is Zyra's condition now that it has collided with another planet? What were those buildings? What people are already there, and did any of their civilization survive? Would they welcome the colonists or reject them? How many other ships landed? What kind of world would humankind make of it? And as Zyra is captured by the sun, will it also simply spiral in and be destroyed? These questions were not answered nor even hinted at.

Here was the potential for making a sequel, or even a series, about the new world on Zyra. What we know about human history is that, no matter what we do the same old habits go with us. I hope that the film taught viewers more than that.

This film was one of of George Pal's raft of amazing and highly intelligent science fiction films. The next one would make history.

Production: A feature film, based on the original novels *When Worlds Collide* and its sequel *After Worlds Collide*, was first serialized in Blue Book magazine in 1932, and was considered by producer/director Cecil B. DeMille. When George Pal began his version years later, he wanted a more lavish production with a larger budget, but he wound up being forced to scale back his plans.

Douglas Fairbanks Jr. was first considered for the role of Dave Randall, but Richard Derr was finally hired for the part.

Chesley Bonestell is credited with the artwork used for the film, and he created the design for the space ark that was constructed. The final scene in the film, the sunrise landscape on Zyra, was taken from a Bonestell sketch. Because of budget constraints, the director was forced to use this color sketch rather than a finished matte painting. A poor quality still image showing a drowned New York City is often attributed to Bonestell, but it was not actually drawn by him.

UCLA's differential analyzer is shown briefly near the beginning of the film. It verifies the hand made calculations confirming the coming destruction of the Earth. "There is no error."

Producer George Pal had thought about making a sequel based on the second novel, *After Worlds Collide*, but the box office failure of his 1955 *Conquest of Space* made that impossible.

Reception: *When Worlds Collide* was reviewed by Bosley Crowther of <u>The New York Times</u>, who noted that George Pal had followed up on his other prophetic epic, *Destination Moon*: "... this time the science soothsayer, whose forecasts have the virtue, at least, of being represented in provocative visual terms, offers rather cold comfort for those scholars who would string along with him. One of the worlds which he arranged to have collide is ours." He reported that "Except for a rustle of applause to salute a perfect pancake landing, the drowsy audience at the Globe, where the film opened yesterday, showed slight interest. It appeared skeptical and even bored. Mr. Pal barely gets us out there, but this time he doesn't bring us back."

Freelance writer Melvin E. Matthews called the film a "doomsday parable for the nuclear age of the '50s." Emory University physics professor Sidney Perkowitz notes that *When Worlds Collide* is the first in a long list of films where "science wielded by a heroic scientist confronts a catastrophe." He called the special effects exceptional.

Librarian and filmographer Charles P. Mitchell was critical of the "... scientific gaffes that dilute the storyline" and a "failure to provide consistent first-class effects". He stated that there were inconsistencies in the script, citing (incorrectly), the disappearance of Dr. Bronson in the second half of the film. He summarized that "the large number of plot defects are annoying and prevent this admirable effort from achieving top-drawer status."

Awards: When Worlds Collide won the 1951 Academy Award for special effects. It was also nominated for Best Cinematography - Color.

Comic book adaptation: The film was adapted into a comic book by George Evans.

Popular culture: When Worlds Collide is one of the many classic films referenced in the opening theme ("Science Fiction/Double Feature") of both the stage musical *The Rocky Horror Show* (1973) and its cinematic counterpart, *The Rocky Horror Picture Show* (1976).

In the feature film *Star Trek II: The Wrath of Khan* (1982), two cargo containers can be seen labeled "Bellus" and "Zyra" in the Genesis Cave. (Bellus was the name of the rogue star which swept through the solar system, but did not destroy Earth.)

In the film adaptation of *L.A. Confidential* (1997), tabloid writer Sid Hudgens arranges for the publicity loving Jack Vincennes to arrest a young actor on the night of the premiere of *When Worlds Collide*, resulting in photos of the arrest with the theater marquee in the background, accompanied by the headline "Movie Premiere Pot Bust". The scene is shown as taking place in 1953, long after the actual 1951 premiere of *When Worlds Collide*. Perhaps it was a metaphor, but we'll never know.

When Worlds Collide is the title of a 1975 album (the related single is "Did Worlds Collide?") by Richard Hudson and John Ford, their third release after leaving Strawbs.

"When Worlds Collide" is the title of a single by the heavy metal band Powerman 5000 from the 1999 album *Tonight The Stars Revolt!*.

Remake: The 1998 film *Deep Impact* originated as a joint remake of *When Worlds Collide* and an adaptation of the 1993 Arthur C. Clarke novel *The Hammer of God*, and the project was acknowledged as such at first, although the finished film did not acknowledge any of its sources since it was judged as being different enough to not require any.

Paramount Pictures began preproduction on a remake of *When Worlds Collide* around 2013. As of August 25, 2015, no release date had been announced. Recently, SciFi.com stated that Steven Spielberg was planning a remake as late as 2015. To date there have been no further updates.

ALRAUNE (1952) Germany

Directed by Arthur Maria Rabenalt
Produced by Günther Stapenhorst
Screenplay by Kurt Heuser
Based on the novel, Alraune, by Hanns Heinz Ewers
Music by Werner Richard Heymann
Cinematography by Friedl Behn-Grund
Edited by Doris Zeltmann
Production companies: Deutsche Styria-Film GmbH and Carlton Film GmbH
Distributed by Gloria-Filmverleih GmbH; release date: October 23, 1952; running time: 92 minutes

Cast:
Hildegard Knef as Alraune
Erich von Stroheim as Jacob ten Brinken

Karlheinz Böhm as Frank Braun
Harry Meyen as Count Geroldingen
Rolf Henniger as Wolf Goutram
Harry Halm as Doctor Mohn
Hans Cossy as Mathieu, the coachman
Gardy Brombacher as Lisbeth, the maid
Trude Hesterberg as Fuerstin Wolkonska
Julia Koschka as Olga Wolkonska
Denise Vernac as Mademoiselle Duvaliere
Arno Ebert
Willem Holzboer

Plot: A scientist, Jacob ten Brinken (Erich von Strotheim), has a grown daughter named Alraune (Hildegard Knef) [pronounced Al-ra-owneh] who has come to live with him under mysterious circumstances. She is first seen by a trio of young men: Frank Braun (Karlheinz Böhm), a medical student, his friend Count Geroldingen (Harry Meyen), and an artist, Wolf Gourtram (Rolf Henniger).

As they come to the estate to call on Dr. ten Brinken, they are all three intrigued and smitten by her on first sight. Alraune is well educated and dresses like all women of her means; ten Brinken has spared no expense on her behalf. As she is free to be who she is, she strikes up flirtatious acquaintences with all three men.

Frank Baum is very curious about her. At one point he confronts her in a laboratory, where she is standing in front of a cage containing an ape woman. She is friendly and stands her ground, which impresses him somewhat. She is also fond of a mandrake root, said to be the source of magic.

Her companion and bed mate is Olga Wolkonska, a young and impressionable woman. She falls for Count Geroldingen but he has no time for her; he is smitten with Alraune. While she and Alraune are sleeping one evening, Olga takes a potion for sleep, and finds herself in trouble. What she has taken is something else and she has fallen falls unconscious. Alraune wakes and sees Dr. Mohn (Harry Halm) administering to the young woman. He asks her if she knows anything about it, and Alraune does not. Dr. Mohn takes Olga out of the room and to the hospital.

The next day, Alraune is introduced to Mademoiselle Duvaliere (Denise Vernac), who is to be her tutor and companion. Dr. ten Brinken is anxious that Alraune is becoming "wild and untamable". Alraune accepts the woman's blandishments but is perturbed by the limitations being placed on her.

Later, Alraune dresses for riding on horseback, and tells the coachman, Mathieu (Hans Cossy) she will be going out by herself. Mathieu is concerned that she has never done this before, he should go with her, but Alraune protests that she needs to be alone and goes out anyway.

When she reaches the gate, Frank Braun is there waiting for her on horseback. Just as they go down the road together, the rain starts and they are caught in a thunderstorm. Together, they head toward the boat house, where they spend time under its roof until the storm stops.

Still later, she meets Wolf Goutram at his apartment and poses for a rather provocative portrait of her dressed in fencing clothes and brandishing an epee'. They share a kiss or two. Then she goes back to her house.

Sometime later, she sees Mathieu bathing himself at the horse trough, and asks him to take her riding in the caleche. Reluctantly he agrees. His wife is desperate to see him not associate with the mistress but he says he must obey orders.

He takes her out in the caleche and two horses. As they reach a crest of the hill, he loses control of the horses. They accelerate to a hard gallop and head for what looks like a cliff overlooking the river. Alraune manages to jump off the caleche and lands among some bushes, while Mathieu still struggles to control the horses. Before he can jump too the horse break free of their yokes and the caleche goes over the cliff. The coach rolls over Matthieu and kills him.

That evening, a group of men and Alraune return to the house with Matthieu's body, intending to bury him. Alraune has never witnessed a death before. Matthieu's wife is distraught, goes to Alraune and slaps her in the face. Struck by the wonder of it all, Alraune goes home and asks ten Brinken to explain it all to her, but he puts it off.

Fade to: Dr. Mohn speaks to the artist while he is painting a mural featuring a group of women against a backdrop of very Art Neuveau motifs. After that, Wolf is honored at a féte which displays his finished work. Alraune is dressed in a gown which is a bit off the shoulder, but she says she cannot find her jewelry.

The maid, Lisbeth (Gardy Brombacher) is questioned by Dr. ten Brinken and Dr. Mohn. Incensed by their accusations, she leads them to her room and turns out her own drawers. But Dr. Mohn finds a necklace among the underwear.

That evening, Alraune takes turns dancing with her father, Dr. Mohn, and finally Frank Baum. Baum is critical of her about her dalliances with his companions, but she is not going to take it from him. Indignant with jealousy, he leaves her standing on the floor alone.

That winter, Alraune visits Wolf, who is now critically ill. Frank Baum and the Count are also there. Wolf is tender as he thanks her for all her attention and friendship. Then he dies. Alraune is in shock. Frank Baum becomes tender again, and they share a brief and intimate meeting in his apartment. He loves her, and she loves him. He mentions taking her to Paris. She says that she will go wherever he does.

Back home, Alraune confronts her father with her intentions regarding Frank Baum. Dr. ten Brinken is forceful when he tries to explain why she cannot go with her young man. She is not an ordinary woman. Alraune is confused. The doctor opens the portrait painted by Wolf and a safe, where he withdraws a book with the title "ALRAUNE" and practically throws it at her.

Alraune opens the book and reads the truth: she is a humunculous, a product of artificial insemination. She is not really human, but a byproduct of experimentation. She is a freak.

Alraune throws down the book and runs out into the garden, where Frank Baum is waiting for her. She can barely explain what has happened. Frank picks her up and takes her back to the house, but ten Brinken shoots her. Frank lowers her carefully to the ground, but it is too late. She dies.

Frank is distraught and attacks the doctor for his callous disregard for his own daughter, but it is too late. Alraune has transformed back into a mandrake root. END

Analysis and additional notes: I had my reservations about this film. I had seen the plot for the original silent film but it was lost. This particular film was rife with insinuation but the only science in it was a few scenes near the beginning and the last few scenes at the end. In between we see the operatic trials and tribulations of a singular young women who apparently had no mother, and her father dotes on her but is very standoffish at the same time.

In this case, three young men get caught up in Alraune's sphere of influence. They are all smitten by her. Only two men die: Wolf the artist, and Matthieu the coachman. Her life appears to be marred by tragedy, as we see when people around her die. This is not her fault, and yet those who serve are eager to blame her for the results. She is independent and headstrong, with a strong will to live and an equal desire to do as she pleases. This does not mean that she is amoral, as some have come to believe. It simply means that she treated others with the same respect as herself.

She is also very vulnerable, as is shown when she does not understand the truth about herself. What do you say to someone who has been living a lie not her own? Dr. ten Brinken wanted something from her, but what it was is not made clear. And in the end, the experiment failed. He had to shoot her? I don't think so. But that is up to the writers.

I have seen commentary on other sites saying that she is amoral and "soul-less". I did not see that. She was forthright, she was stalwart, she was self-contained. That is not amorality, and that is not lack of soul. In the film we see her emote about as freely as anyone else. You could see it in her face, you could see it in her eyes. Wooden? I don't think so. I think the critics should stop using hystrionics as a measure for convincing emotion. I've seen men act emotionless and wooden and yet no one says anything about them. Nuff said.

The plotting and cutting was a bit sharp. Time has no meaning in this film. We go from one scene to another without any true sense of the passage of time. What may have been hours seemed more like minutes; what may have been months seemed more like hours.

As for the costuming, I don't think I saw Ms. Knef wear the same outfit twice. It was like watching a model on the runway march out, trot her stuff and then walk off again. If this was meant to help project the idea of "the perfect woman", it did not convince me. If she was the perfect woman, then why did everyone see her as a pariah? It makes no sense. I suppose that she is meant to be seen as monster with a beautiful face, not a perfect human being.

As a matter of fact, no one is perfect. The human body is constructed two halves at a time. And sometimes facial symmetry will give that away. That is why some people's eyes are not in a straight line. One will be lower or higher than the other. The eyebrows will be higher or lower. One side of the mouth will be lower than the other. If you don't believe me, look really hard in the mirror.

As for the scientific method apparent in Dr. ten Brinken's experiment, I am wondering when it got away from him. He treated Alraune like a lab rabbit. For him, she had no emotions or soul. She was a thing. I don't know about you but I think that he started in the wrong place at the wrong time. You don't treat anyone like a thing.

If the whole story was of an experiment, I am reminded of the *Star Trek* episode "Requiem For Methuselah", in which an immortal being named Flint has created an android and tests her emotional quotient on Captain Kirk. He has named her "Rayna Kapec". He encourages her to dance and socialize with Kirk, who then falls in love with her, having found what he thinks is the perfect woman. He proposes to her and says they will be together on the ship.

This goes against Flint's plans for her.

Kirk and Flint soon come to blows over this and do battle for her. It turns out that Rayna Kapec is also fully formed in her personality, and when she rebels and says that she will make her own decisions about who to love, the conflict of emotions rage inside her until she dies. Flint reveals that he had designed her to be a lifelong companion and equal intellect, but now he will be alone.

It turns out that she is the last of a long line of androids, each of which has malfunctioned in some way or another. Flint is left to die in his own time.

Kirk, meanwhile, is mournful for his lost love, emotionally and logically. As he falls asleep, Spock melds with him and says softly, "forget."

For its strange and complex scripting I give *Alraune* 2 stars out of 4. For the acting I will give it 3. IMdb gives it only 6/10, while Rotten Tomatoes gives it no rating at all.

Production: There are no further notes on this film.

Reception: In a contemporary review, <u>Variety</u> noted that "in the early 1900s, when the H. H. Ewers novel *Alraune* cut a swatch in the German-language world [...] the very thought of artificial insemination of humans was mentionable only in whispers." and that "times and sensations change." The review opined that Knef's acting had "limited range" and that von Stroheim produces "only a laboured setting for a range of costumes changes and phony thunderstorms for the lethal Alraune."

Lethal. Phehh.

RADAR MEN FROM THE MOON (1952) A serial of 12 chapters

Directed by Fred C. Brannon
Written by Ronald Davidson
Music by Stanley Wilson
Distributed by Republic Pictures; release date January 9, 1952; September 30, 1957 reissue
Running time: 12 chapters (167 minutes, serial); 100 minutes (TV)
Budget: $172,840 (negative cost: $185,702)

Cast:
George Wallace as Commando Cody.
Aline Towne as Joan Gilbert
Roy Barcroft as Retik, Ruler of the Moon.
William Bakewell as Ted Richards
Gayle Kellogg as Dick
Peter Brocco as Krog
Clayton Moore as Graber
Bob Stevenson as Daly
Don Walters as Govt. Agent Henderson

Plot: Commando Cody (George Wallace) is a civilian researcher and inventor with a number of employees at his beck and call. He uses a streamlined helmet and an atomic powered rocket backpack attached to a leather flying jacket. Cody also uses a rocket ship which is able to reach the Moon.

When the U.S. finds itself under attack from a mysterious force, one which can wipe out entire military bases and industrial complexes, Commando Cody concludes that the Earth is coming under attack from the Moon. He flies his rocket ship there and confronts the Moon's dictator, Retik (Roy Barcroft), who boldly announces his plans to both conquer Earth and then move the Moon's entire population there using spaceships.

During the next 11 chapters, Cody has returned to Earth, and his associates Joan Gilbert (Aline Towne), Ted Richards (William Bakewell) and Dick (Gayle Kellogg), battle an elusive lunar agent named Krog (Peter Brocco) and his gang of human henchmen led by Graber (Clayton Moore) and Daly (Bob Stevenson).

Krog and his men use ray cannons powered by Lunarium to disrupt the defense forces and weaken public morale.

After a second trip to the Moon, in which he captures a sample ray cannon for duplication in his lab, Cody tracks Retik's minions to their hideout, where Krog is killed by one of his own devices. Graber and Daly subsequently die in a car chase over a cliff.

Retik flies to Earth to take personal charge of his collapsing operations but is blasted out of the sky by one of his own ray weapons. END

Chapter titles: Moon Rocket - Molten Terror - Bridge of Death - Flight to Destruction - Murder Car - Hills of Death - Camouflaged Destruction - The Enemy Planet - Battle In The Stratosphere - Mass Execution, a recap chapter - Planned Pursuit - Death of the Moon Man

Analysis and additional notes: There has been some confusion about this serial because it borrows quite a bit from *King of The Rocket Men*. But it introduces a new character, Commando Cody, who wears Jeff King's livery throughout. This serial is not a sequel. It is a retooled adventure, with different characters altogether. There is little exposition as to who Commando Cody is, where he originated, and how he amassed his fortune.

One could compare him to Tony Stark, the rich industrialist and inventor of the Marvel universe, who inherited his fortune from his father Howard, who in turn was an allusion to the famous real life inventor and aviator Howard Hughes. But we see Cody take on the villain all by himself, while his friends take on the Earth element of the conspiracy.

The budget for this project was not enough to make it more than another adventure replete with fist fights, gunfights, bad rockets, and a complement of bad robots to complete it. Once again, the robots are so badly designed one wants to punt them into the river.

But since it was broken up into 12 pieces we only suffered for a little while each week. The serial is seriously formulaic, which meant that perhaps Republic Pictures was running out of juice. There was not enough science in it to justify the cost for the props. So I really can't call it science fiction but science fantasy.

For its long and plodding scripts I give it 2 stars out of 4. IMdb gives it only 4.6/10, and Rotten Tomatoes gives it no rating. Only 33% of their audience liked it.

Production: *Radar Men From The Moon* was the most expensive Republic serial of 1952. It was filmed between October 17 and November 6, 1951 under the working title *Planet Men From Mars*; the serial's production number was 1932.

However the numbers were interpreted, in practice the budget for this serial was so tight that a stunt double was not always used for lead actor George Wallace. His nose was broken by accident while filming an energetic fight scene with actor Clayton Moore. Wallace was also suspended in midair, lying on a board with the rocket suit's jacket closed around it, in front of a rear projection screen for the flying sequences. Wallace performed his own stunts, including taking off into the air by jumping onto a springboard that would send him up and over the camera rig.

A repainted Juggernaut vehicle from the *Undersea Kingdom* serial is also reused as Retik's lunar tank. All spaceship footage was filmed new for the serial. *Radar Men From The Moon* shows outer space as brightly lit and the characters walking on the Moon in normal Earth gravity and daylight without pressure suits. His laboratory building is actually a Republic Pictures office building with a prop "Cody Laboratories" sign.

Two different aerodynamic helmets were used with the Commando Cody rocket backpack. The lighter weighted version was used only in the stunt sequences. The visors of both helmets were always getting stuck open or closed.

Release: *Theatrical:* *Radar Men From The Moon's* official release date is January 9, 1952, although this is actually the date the 6th chapter was made available to U. S. film exchanges.

Republic's next new serial, *Zombies of The Stratosphere*, which also used some of the Cody flying suit and spaceship footage, followed in the summer and began as a sequel to *Radar Men*. For unspecified reasons, Republic changed the character names of Cody and Joan at the last minute.

In between these two serials, Republic had begun filming on its first attempt at a TV series, *Commando Cody: Sky Marshal of The Universe*, but stopped production after the first three episodes were filmed to begin work on *Zombies of The Stratosphere*. After that serial was finished, Republic resumed filming of 9 more episodes of the Cody TV series. After it was completed, Republic released it also as a theatrical serial instead of a TV series.

This serial was reissued on September 30, 1957 between Republic's *Zorro's Black Whip* and *Son of Zorro*. The final original Republic serial was *King of The Carnival*, released two years earlier in 1955.

Television: *Radar Men From The Moon* was one of 26 Republic serials syndicated for television in 1966 as 100 minute TV feature films under their Century 66 package marketing name. The title given the TV movie was *Retik The Moon Menace*. In 1979, The Firesign Theatre used segments of this and other serials in their made for TV comedy movie, *J-Men Forever*.

Trivia: In 1989 the serial regained notoriety as the first shorts shown by the cult series *Mystery Science Theater 3000*. The first 8 ½ chapters of this Commando Cody serial were lampooned before their main feature of the week. Only half of the 9th installment was shown, with the excuse being "the film broke".

Critical reception: In his 1984 book *In The Nick of Time*, author William C. Cline dismissed the serial as a "quickie".

Copyright: Because of a failure to renew the copyright, *Radar Men From The Moon* lapsed into public domain in 1979.

RED PLANET MARS (1952)

Directed by Harry Horner
Produced by Donald Hyde and Anthony Veiller
Screenplay by Anthony Veiller and John L. Balderston; based on the play Red Planet
by John Hoare and John L. Balderston
Music by Mahlon Merrick
Cinematography by Joseph Biroc
Edited by Francis D. Lyon
Production company: Melaby Pictures

Distributed by United Artists; release date May 15, 1952
Running time: 87 minutes

Cast:
Peter Graves as Chris Cronyn
Andrea King as Linda Cronyn
Herbert Berghof as Franz Calder
Walter Sande as Admiral Bill Carey
Marvin Miller as Arjenian
Willis Bouchey as President
Morris Ankrum as Secretary of Defense Sparks
Robert House Peters, Jr. as Dr. Boulting, Mitchell's assistant
Orley Lindgren as Stewart Cronyn
Philip Bayard Veiller (Bayard Veiller II) as Roger Cronyn

Plot: A scientist named Chris Cronyn (Peter Graves) and his wife Linda (Andrea King), are conducting the search for extraterrestrial life on Mars, which is shown in several photographs of Mars in which canals which are dark during certain seasons are filled with water from ice mountains at the polar ice caps. It is claimed that the canals are artificial constructs, suggesting that there is a civilization on Mars.

Dr. Cronyn has built a special radio transmitter next to his house with which to send coded signals to Mars. Meanwhile, another scientist in the Andes who works for the Russians, a man named Calder (Herber Berghof), has built a similar transmitter, only to pick up the signals from San Diego and relay them to his superiors in the Kremlin.

Cronyn's friend and colleague Admiral Bill Carey (Walter Sande) is a frequent visitor and close friend to his two boys, who are both precocious and interested in the project. He provides a third world view which tempers Cronyn's enthusiasm with reason.

Cronyn's wife is especially spooked about her husband's project. She presumes that it will lead to another World War. Cronyn is having trouble finding the proper message to send to Mars, to test his theory, when his older son suggests he use Pi (3.1415629...) to contact the Martians, if there are any.

Cronyn tests this by sending one digit at a time in intervals of 3. The messages are bounced back. Then, miraculously, the rest of the number follows. Finally, he thinks he are onto something.

Meanwhile, the Russians are getting nervous about their transmitter. Ticked off by his isolation and constant harassment by the agents, Calder demands that they leave him alone to do his work. He says that he is tricking Cronyn into giving him the results of his transmissions, and that they don't have to be constantly breathing down his neck. The agents must tread carefully in his presence as he is presenting something of a dilemma.

While the scientists are running this interplanetary race, the messages back speak of their methods for producing food, their energy sources and their uses, and their manipulation of water. When this news reaches the public, industries all over the Earth begin to collapse. Coal miners are put out of work, steel workers also, as the sudden realization that Mars is ahead of Earth renders our usual way of life useless.

This is an erroneous path to take, and the use of resources on Earth have nothing to do with what is happening on Mars. Yet this knowledge becomes a presage to apocalypse. People go to their banks to withdraw cash, while others hide in their churches to pray for salvation. There is looting and riots as the world goes wild.

The latest transmissions soon turn inexplicable. Biblical passages speaking of turning swords into plowshares, being kind to one another, (based on the Sermon on the mount), and other visions of world peace, cause whole governments to collapse as the people begin to rebel against tyrants and return to a simpler life and democracy.

A group of rural Russians crowd around an ancient radio which they must hide from the soldiers of the new premier, who delights in torturing his own people. It turns out later that the elder among them is a Russian orthodox bishop, and his people allow frequent invasions by soldiers who are looking for religious articles of faith.

While this is going on, Calder is sinking deeper into chaos, thanks to his alcoholism, and he is rebelling against his handlers and the premier. At one point he is speaking defiantly to them over the radio when an avalanche buries his radio shack under deep snow and tears his transmission tower down. The Russians presume he has died in the disaster and abandon their project.

Meanwhile, Dr. Cronyn must suffer the gauntlet of reporters and the curious lining the road near his house, and must go through a gate which is now guarded by the military. At one point a protester throws a brick at his wagon's window and smashes it. When he gets to the house he cannot stand the sounds of the news and orders his older son to turn it off (it is a flat screen TV he is watching, with the remote control a mouse with several controls on it). The Cronyn family are under siege for having contacted Mars in the first place. The detractors fail to point out that it was their own stupidity which had caused the economic chaos they are suffering, as if Mars was a part of the Earth.

In Russia, the rural group of farmers set up their roadside shrines and begin to pray openly. While they are doing this, a troop of soldiers arrives in jeeps and open fire on them, slaughtering them to the last man. Yet others take up the slogans and chant on.

The President (Willis Bouchey) is concerned about the results the transmissions are having, as is the military minds at the Pentagon. Cronyn convinces them that the messages are benign and that he is still trying to properly interpret what he has been receiving.

Only his wife Linda appears to know the answer: Mars must be one society and they have conquered their own violent instincts, turning from war to a unified peace. The answer must be through scripture, from the passages being sent. Her husband is skeptical about this, but the information is undeniable. Somehow, Mars has achieved world peace through faith.

Meanwhile, in Russia, the premier is faced with an onslaught of religious protesters, who destroy his buildings one by one, singing hymns and overcoming his vaunted armies with peace. The armies cannot resist joining in, so a quiet coup takes place.

As the situation on Earth slowly returns to normal through disarmament and prayer, Cronyn and his wife are discussing what to do next, when Calder enters their radio shack and confronts them with the truth. The last 3 transmissions were from him. "Look at the chaos I have caused," he says. He wants the Earth to return to war, and destroying the world is his aim. The whole project is a fraud. He claims to want all credit for the transmissions because he manufactured them. Then he threatens Cronyn and his wife with a gun.

Subtly, Cronyn disconnects a valve to the hydrogen line and lets the gas go free; apparently there has always been a leak, and since then Cronyn had discouraged smoking in the lab. Linda volunteers to light the fatal cigarette, but Cronyn tells her to go into their house and mind their two boys. They will need her most. But she refuses. The boys will go on, she says.

Suddenly, the transmitter's receiver goes haywire and the screen is active with banded static. Another transmission is coming through, but not from Calder. Calder panics and shoots the trnsmitter, igniting the gas. All three are consumed in the explosion.

Later, the President gives thanks to the two heroes and posthumous medals, for sacrificing their lives to prevent another war. Admiral Carey has adopted the orphaned boys, and embraces them as their new father. END

Analysis and additional notes: This was a weird one. Apparently in the cold war there was room for scientific fantasy, in which the two superpowers were at odds with each other but were sidelined by a third party. In this case, Mars. Or was it Mars? We don't know because events do not show even one Martian in the mix.

We see the canals changing color with the Martian seasons, but that is no evidence of habitation by an advanced civilization. We see also evidence of "artificial formations" on the surface, but no obvious movement of features beyond what is natural. We do not see structures. We do not see roads or aircraft of any kind. Perhaps, as other films have suggested, the Martians live underground.

Whatever is the truth, the film suggests that somehow Mars is ruled by God. I prefer an elevated figurehead like a Pope or Archbishop, rather than a divine being which probably has better things to do. It makes Mars far too important to the well being of humanity, and minimizes our own efforts at achieving world peace.

We do not know which transmissions are genuinely from Mars because of Calder's constant interference with getting a clear signal. The last transmission, however, is telling. At the end, Calder is not where he can transmit anything, and that part will ever be a mystery. When did the real transmissions begin to occur? The explosion destroyed everything.

The title is a little ambiguous. *Red Planet Mars*. What does that mean? Does it say Mars is communist, or is it a comment on the state of affairs in the world at that time? Or it could be literal. It's up to you to decide.

For its rather forward thinking if ultrareligious theme and the interesting interchange between Mars (?) and Earth, I give it 3 stars out of 4. IMdb gives it 4.9/10, while Rotten Tomatoes gives it no rating but only 27% of viewers liked it.

Production: There appear to be no notes about this. Since this was a rather low budget film I don't think anyone was terribly proud of it.

Critical response: When the film was released, the staff at <u>Variety</u> liked the film, writing, "Despite its title, Red Planet Mars takes place on terra firma, sans space ships, cosmic rays or space cadets. It is a fantastic concoction [from a play by John L. Balderston and John Hoare] delving into the realms of science, politics, religion, world affairs and Communism...Despite the hokum dished out, the actors concerned turn in creditable performances."

<u>The New York Times</u>, while giving the film a mixed review, wrote well of some of the performances: "Peter Graves and Andrea King are serious and competent, if slightly callow in appearance, as the indomitable scientists. Marvin Miller is standard as a top Soviet agent, as are Walter Sande, Richard Powers and Morris Ankrum, as Government military men, and Willis Bouchey, as the President."

Allmovie critic Bruce Eder praised the film, writing, "Red Planet Mars is an eerily fascinating artifact of the era of the Red Scare, and also the first postwar science fiction boom, combining those elements into an eerie story that is all the more surreal because it is played with such earnestness."

The film critic Dennis Schwartz panned the film in 2001, writing, "One of the most obnoxious sci-fi films ever. It offers Hollywood's silly response to the 1950s 'Red Scare' sweeping the country and promoted by the McCarthy senate hearings looking for commies under every bed cover. To realize how dumb this Cold War film is, try this question of the plot's summary on for size: Can it be that the Martians are signaling Earth and that their leader is actually uttering the very word of God? This is one of those really bad propaganda films that has no entertainment value, as it shows how paranoic this country can be and how it can use religion at the drop of a radio signal to promote materialism and Christianity as a superior way of life than communism. This one might be the strangest and most twisted Red Menace films of all time. It ends with a hydrogen explosion in the lab killing two good American scientists and one lousy ex-Nazi scientist now working for the Russian Communists. The last message heard from Mars is an abbreviated one (thank God!): 'Ye have done well my good ...' then there is just silence. The film leaves one with the impression that Mars is ruled by God."

ZOMBIES OF THE STRATOSPHERE (1952) A serial of 12 chapters
Directed by Fred C. Brannon
Produced by Franklin Adreon
Written by Ronald Davidson
Music by Stanley Wilson
Cinematography by John MacBurnie
Distributed by Republic Pictures; release date: July 16, 1952
Running time: 12 chapters (167 minutes- serial)
70 minutes (feature); budget: $176,357

Cast:
Judd Holdren as Larry Martin
Aline Towne as Sue Davis
Wilson Wood as Bob Wilson
Lane Bradford as Marex
Stanley Waxman as Dr Harding
John Crawford as Roth
Ray Boyle as Shane
Craig Kelly as Mr Steele
Leonard Nimoy as Narab
Robert Garabedian as Elah

Plot: Larry Martin (Judd Holdren), a leader in the Interplanetary Patrol, detects a rocket coming to Earth. He takes to the air in his rocket suit and helmet to investigate. He discovers that Martian invaders, led by Marex (Lane Bradford), have landed on Earth. Since Mars is now orbiting too far from the Sun and its ecology has been dying, the Martian invaders want to shift Earth's orbit so Mars will orbit closer to the Sun. They plan on achieving this by using hydrogen bomb plans stolen from Earth scientists to cause the two planets' orbits to swap, using specifically placed atomic explosions on both worlds.

Martin also learns that the Martians have Earth accomplices in the forms of the traitorous Dr. Harding (Stanley Waxman), and two gangsters, Roth (John Crawford) and Shane (Ray Boyle), who bedevil him and his associates Sue Davis (Aline Towne) and Bob Wilson (Wilson Wood).

The Martians set up a base in a cave that can only be reached from underwater, where they begin constructing their bombs. They have brought a robot with them to supplement their human associates in acquiring supplies and funds to complete the project.

Eventually, Larry and his comrades gain the upper hand: Marex kills Harding when he attempts to surrender, Roth and Shane are killed when Larry turns the robot against them, and the Martians are brought down in flames in their rocket ship after a furious stratosphere raygun battle with Larry in his own spacecraft.

Marex's Martian aide, Narab (Leonard Nimoy) survives the crash and, while badly injured, tells Larry where to find the underwater cave with the activated bomb in it. Then he dies.

Larry arrives in time to defuse the bomb just seconds before it explodes. The day has been saved. Later, Bob Wilson tells Larry that it is a good thing the "zombies" from Mars did not succeed. The question remains: will the Martians invade again, or have they learned their lesson? END

Analysis and additional notes: Ok. I did not sit through 12 chapters individually, I opted to watch a colorized version with the beginning and ending credits taken out. Nevertheless, aside from the cheaky title and the continual fist fights, gun battles, car cliffhangers, as well as the badly made robots, the storyline was dreadfully unscientific and there is no explanation for this new rocket man. He is introduced without any prior exposition. Commander Cody suddenly disappeared to be replaced with this trio of heroes, two of whom do little to help out. The onus of battle against the Martians and their erstwhile minions lies with Larry Martin.

It was dull and incapable of any real science. The only elevated moment comes at the end, when Narab tells Larry how to defuse the bomb. After that it is mere denouement.

The title alone was misleading; alluding to actual zombies instead of an incidental line in the film. The Martians were not zombies nor were they zombie-like. So aside from the terrbile plot and the gratuitous violence, it was not a zombie serial.

Also, though the Martian leader Marex claimed he would create an army of robots using the one present as a model, he never did. The single robot was also remote controlled, so it failed as an actual thing of violence. It was as clunky and rough and uncontrollable as previous robots, so despite all claims that it was "high tech", it functioned as a mere distraction, not an advantage to the Martians. It was more of a source of intimidation if nothing else.

If this had been an actual invasion, there would have been more than one Martian ship and more sophisticated weapons for Marex to use. I read one viewer commenting that this serial was akin to one or more Edward Wood, Jr. films, which were low on the radar in terms of ratings.

For its lackluster plot and incomprehensible script, I give *Zombies of The Statosphere* less than 1 star out of 4. IMdb gives it a 5.7/10, while Rotten Tomatoes has no score for it yet. There is a mention, with a poster, but nothing else.

Chapter titles: The Zombie Vanguard - Battle of the Rockets - Undersea Agents - Contraband Cargo - The Iron Executioner - Murder Mine - Death on the Waterfront - Hostage for Murder - The Human Torpedo - Flying Gas Chamber a re-cap chapter - Man vs. Monster - Tomb of the Traitors.

Production: The serial is best remembered as one of the first screen appearances of a young Leonard Nimoy, who plays Narab. In 1958 a feature film version of this serial, retitled *Satan's Satellites*, was made by editing down the serial's footage to feature film length.

Zombies of The Stratosphere was scripted as a sequel to the successful *Radar Men From The Moon*, which introduced Commando Cody, played by George Wallace; and interrupted production on a planned TV program also built around that character, titled *Commando Cody: Sky Marshal of The Universe*, with Judd Holdren now starring as Cody. Then, just as filming began on this serial, the name of the hero was changed from Commando Cody to Larry Martin; but he retains all the same sidekicks (also renamed), high tech props and laboratory facilities that Commando Cody had in the previous serial, *Radar Men From The Moon*.

An addition to the Rocket Man backpack and helmet, used for the first time in this serial, is a two-way radio about the size of a lunchbox. Larry Martin wears it hanging heavily from his belt when dressed for flying. This radio is also seen in some stills of Cody in *Commando Cody: Sky Marshal of The Universe*. The radio usually disappears when Commando Cody is in flight. Martin also uses an ordinary police revolver instead of the ray gun favored by Cody in earlier and later serials.

Zombies of The Stratosphere was budgeted at $172,838, but the final negative cost was $176,357 (a $3,519, or 2%, overspend). It was the cheapest Republic serial of 1952 and was filmed between April 14, and May 1, 1952. At 17 days of principal photography, it is tied with *King of The Carnival* for the shortest filming period of all Republic serials. The serial's production number was 1933.

Zombies of The Stratosphere reused the "Republic Robot", along with stock footage of it in action and black and white footage from a Republic full color Roy Rogers film. The serial is also heavily padded with footage from *King of The Rocket Men* (1949). Although the Zombies serial has Martians as the villains, they are not the same Martians as shown in the earlier Republic serial *The Purple Monster Strikes*. The robot was first seen in *Undersea Kingdom* (1936) and prominently featured in *Mysterious Doctor Satan* (1940).

Stunts: Dale Van Sickel as Larry Martin (doubling as Judd Holdren) and Tom Steele.

Special effects: All the special effects in *Zombies of The Stratosphere* were produced by the Lydecker brothers, Republic's in house physical and model effects team. Their flying effects, using a dummy running along a wire, were first used in Republic's *Darkest Africa* (1936) and with greater impact in their *Adventures of Captain Marvel* serial (1941).

Release: *Theatrical: Zombies of The Stratosphere*'s official release date is July 16, 1952, although this is actually the date the 6th chapter was made available to film exchanges..

A 70 minute feature film version, created by heavily editing down the serial footage, was released on March 28, 1958, under the new title *Satan's Satellites*.

Television: Zombies of The Stratosphere was one of two Republic serials later colorized for 1990s television broadcast.

Home video releases: during 1991, the serial was released in original full length and black and white on two videodiscs from The Roan Group; in 1995 by Republic Pictures Home Video in the U.S. on VHS edited to 93 minutes and colorized, and a 2-DVD set from Cheezy Flicks Entertainment in 2009 at full length and original black and white.

Reception: critics and viewers found the serial to be relatively dull and unimaginative, not as interesting as *Radar Men From The Moon*. The use of stock footage from earlier serials is not quite as overwhelming as seen in the earlier or later Cody outings, as greater emphasis is placed on fistfights rather than scenes using the rocket backpack. Holdren's performance is seen as stiff and amateurish, especially when compared to the professionalism of the old Republic pros who surround him on screen.

ABBOT AND COSTELLO GO TO MARS (1953)

Directed by Charles Lamont
Produced by Howard Christie
Written by D.D. Beauchamp, Howard Christie, and
Music by Joseph Gershenson and Henry Mancini
Cinematography by Clifford Stine
Edited by Russell Schoengarth
Production company: Universal-International
Distributed by Universal Pictures; release date: April 6, 1953
Running time: 77 minutes
Budget: $762,446; box office: $1.25 million

Cast:
Bud Abbott as Lester
Lou Costello as Orville
Mari Blanchard as Allura
Robert Paige as Dr Wilson
Horace McMahon as Mugsy
Martha Hyer as Janie
Jack Kruschen as Harry
Joe Kirk as Dr. Orvilla
Jean Willes as Capt. Olivia
Anita Ekberg as Venusian Guard

Renate Hoy (Miss Germany) as Handmaiden
Harry Shearer as Boy

Plot: Orville (Lou Costello) is the oldest orphan at the Hideaway Orphans Home. He accidentally winds up inside a truck heading to a top secret laboratory, where he is placed under the guidance of lab worker Lester (Bud Abbott) to help load supplies onto a rocket ship.

While on board with Lester, Orville hits the ignition button and the rocketship blasts off, flying across the country to New Orleans, where Mardi Gras is in progress. They exit and witness "hideous creatures" and "alien beings", which are actually costumed celebrants, and conclude that they have successfully landed on Mars.

Meanwhile, two escaped convicts, Harry the Horse (Jack Kruschen) and Mugsy (Horace McMahon), enter the rocketship, put on the available spacesuits, and head to New Orleans to rob a bank. Lester and Orville, also clad in spacesuits, are wrongly accused of the crime and rush back to the rocketship, where Mugsy and Harry force them to launch into outer space.

After landing on Venus, the four men are quickly captured by female guards and brought to Queen Allura (Mari Blanchard), who informs him that Venus is inhabited only by women, as men were banished a long time ago. She takes more than a liking to Orville, however, and decides that he can stay if he promises to be true to her. He agrees and, as a show of his new power as the queen's consort, has Harry and Mugsy imprisoned for their crimes.

Mugsy then convinces one of the female guards to flirt with Orville to prove to Queen Allura that Orville cannot be trusted. Orville "takes the bait" and the Queen orders all the men to leave Venus.

Upon returning to the Earth, they are lauded as heroes. Queen Allura, who is watching the celebration from Venus, sends a spaceship to Earth which drops a cake on Orville's head. END

Analysis and additional notes: Of course, there were serious moments in this film, but they were overshadowed by the hilarious antics of our reluctant heroes. We don't know why Orville is so attractive to women, and Lester is driven mad with jealousy, a common theme in most of these comedians' films.

Harry and Mugsy seem unfazed by the fact that they ended up on a different planet, with beings who are human and behave like humans. I dare say that, had the Venusians been something else entirely they would have lost the advantage.

This film can therefore be dubbed as "comedy" and not science fiction, because the rocket ship is the only item associated with science, and the Venusians do not contribute anything to the designation.

While the New Orleans sequence presented a bit of diversion, it was also distracting.

Finally, they do not go to Mars. At all. Instead, they end up on Venus. As was the theme with the planet, named after the goddess of love, there were women living there like amazons. That was not unusual, and also did not contribute anything scientific to the plot. So the title was terribly misleading. I would have preferred it to be "Abbott and Costello Go To Venus".

I have never found Abbott and Costello to be funny. Costello adopted the unfortunate habit of calling for his partner's help far too often, and their kitch was never really humorous given the situations they were placed in. I never laughed.

For the quirky plotline and the rocket ship I'll give it 2 stars out of 4. IMdb gives it 6.5/10, and Rotten Tomatoes gives it 33% fresh while 45% of their auidence liked it.

Production: Principal photography took place between August 1 and August 28, 1952. Shortly after the film's release, Abbott and Costello appeared on *The Colgate Comedy Hour* and did a comedy sketch in which they attended the film's premiere.

The Venusian cars featured in the film were later used in the science fiction feature *This Island Earth* (1955). The Venusian women were played by contestants in the Miss Universe competition. Anita Ekberg, the winner of the Miss Sweden competition, was among the ensemble.

Science fiction author Robert A. Heinlein wrote a film treatment in 1950 called "Abbott and Costello Move To The Moon" that may have inspired the film's screenplay.

Abbott and Costello Go To Mars features a 9 year old Harry Shearer, who later went on to star in *This Is Spinal Tap* and on the animated Fox comedy series *The Simpsons*.

Home media: The film has had two DVD releases, the first as part of The Best of Abbott and Costello Volume Three, released on August

107

3, 2004, and the second as part of Abbott and Costello: The Complete Universal Pictures Collection, released on October 28, 2008.

In popular culture: In April of 2018, the film was shown on MeTV's *Svengoolie* program in Chicago. Series host Rich Koz as Svengoolie took humorous swipes at the film as well as giving some background info on the supporting cast.

There appear to be no awards granted for this film. I think it was a bit too strange for any kind of recognition, and it was not that good to begin with. Besides, at the time it was made science fiction was so far out of the mainstream as a genre it was not recognized by many academies or award institutes for film. It did not fit comfortably inside any criteria to justify an award.

ABBOTT AND COSTELLO MEET DR JEKYLL AND MR HYDE (1953)

Directed by Charles Lamont
Produced by Howard Christie
Screenplay by Lee Loeb and John Grant; Story by Sid Fields and Grant Garett; inspired by *The Strange Case of Dr Jekyll and Mr Hyde* (1886 novella) by Robert Louis Stevenson
Music by Joseph Gershenson
Cinematography by George Robinson
Edited by Russell Schoengarth
Production company: Universal-International
Distributed by Universal Pictures; release date: August 12, 1953
Running time: 76 minutes
Budget: $724,805; box office: $1.2 million

Cast:
Bud Abbott as Slim
Lou Costello as Tubby
Boris Karloff as Dr. Henry Jekyll / Mr. Hyde
Craig Stevens as Bruce Adams
Helen Westcott as Vicky Edwards
Reginald Denny as Inspector
John Dierkes as Batley

Plot: A rash of murders is plaguing London, and the police are baffled. A newspaper reporter, Bruce Adams (Craig Stevens), finds one of the victims while coming home from a pub one night and calls the police.

The next day, two American policemen, Slim (Bud Abbott) and Tubby (Lou Costello), who are working for the London Police Force, respond to a mob fight at a Women's Suffrage Rally in Hyde Park. Reporter Adams, young suffragette Vicky Edwards (Helen Westcott), Slim, and Tubby, all get caught up in the fray and wind up in jail.

Later, Vicky's guardian Dr. Henry Jekyll (Boris Karloff), bails Vicky and Adams out. Tubby and Slim are thereafter kicked off the police force. Unknown to anyone, Dr. Jekyll has developed an injectable serum which transforms him into Mr. Hyde. When Jekyll notices a mutual attraction developing between Vicky and Bruce, he has more thoughts of murder, injects himself, and transforms once again into Hyde in order to terrorize Bruce.

Meanwhile, Tubby and Slim decide that, in order to get back on the police force, they must capture this "monster" (Hyde). That evening, Tubby spots Hyde, who Slim mistakes for a burglar. They decide to follow Hyde into a music hall where Vicky is performing and Adams is visiting her.

Tubby annoys an actor in a tengu mask by mistaking him for the monster, and gets called "balmy". A chase ensues, and Tubby traps Hyde in a wax museum. However, by the time he brings the Inspector (Reginald Denny), Adams, and Slim to the scene, Hyde has already reverted to Dr. Jekyll. Tubby is scolded by the Police Chief Inspector once again. The "good" doctor asks Slim and Tubby to escort him to his home.

Once at Jekyll's home, Tubby goes off exploring and winds up drinking a potion which transforms him into a large mouse. After he recovers, Tubby and Slim try to bring news of Jekyll's activities to the Inspector, but the Inspector refuses to believe them.

Later, when Vicky announces to Jekyll her intent to marry Bruce Adams, Jekyll does not share her enthusiasm and transforms into Hyde right in front of her. Bent on murdering Vicky, Hyde attacks her.

Just in the nick of time, Bruce, Slim, and Tubby save her and Hyde escapes. During the struggle, Jekyll's serum needle is dropped into a couch cushion, which Tubby accidentally falls onto and injects himself, transforming him into a Hyde-like monster.

Another madcap chase ensues, this time with Bruce chasing Jekyll's monster and Slim pursuing Tubby's monster, both believing they are after Jekyll himself. The police are frustrated and confused by the monster's seemingly impossible ability to run all over London unfettered and invisible. But Bruce spots Hyde lurking near the wharf and gives chase.

Bruce's pursuit of Hyde ends up back at Jekyll's home, where he and Hyde struggle. Then Hyde falls from an upstairs window to his death, revealing his true identity as Dr. Jekyll when he reverts to normal form.

Slim then brings Tubby's monster to the Inspector. In their struggles to control him, Tubby bites the Inspector and four other officers before reverting to himself. Before Slim and Tubby can be derided by the Inspector once again, he and his men have transformed into monsters themselves, and chase Slim and Tubby out of the office. END

Analysis and additional notes: This film was more scientific than the previous one, which means I think the producers learned their lesson. As with a lot of films of the time which celebrated London and her denizens, the situations were more humorous than grim.

There was a genuine effort to portray the fogbound darkness of the city at night, but the ribbon of comedy throughout the film destroyed the darkness with absurd sight gags and lines. Abbott and Costello were better than they were before. The comedy was a little tighter and better organized.

Certainly, adding Boris Karloff to the mix was a bonus, as he was a versatile and skillful veteran actor already. Comedy was actually no stranger to him, but he played the "villain" (as Dr. Jekyll) admirably with a straight face throughout. I would say that this particular film is worth watching just for his performance alone, since the two leads were not really as effective as the subscript called for.

For its engaging intemix of comedy and science fiction I give *Abbott and Costello Meet Dr. Jekyll and Mr. Hyde* 2 stars out of 4. IMdb gives it 6.7/10, while Rotten Tomatoes gives it 63% fresh rating, and 64% of its audience liked it (to date).

Production: The movie was filmed between January 26 and February 20, 1953 and received an "X" rating in Britain because of the scenes with Mr. Hyde. Furthermore, Boris Karloff only played Dr. Jekyll and did not play Hyde. Once the transformation sequences were over, Hyde was played by stuntman Eddie Parker, who remained uncredited. We don't know if this is what the script called for, but Karloff was aged enough to deem him unable to perform some of the acrobatic stunts Hyde called for. Since Hyde was an almost opposite model from Dr. Jekyll, Eddie Parker gave the monster all he had. Still, since Jekyll's jealousy made him do bad things for the wrong reasons, he can also be called the villain.

Reception: Many reviewers complained that, in this version, there was no struggling of body in the transformation between Dr. Jekyll and Mr. Hyde, giving the impression that Dr. Jekyll himself was evil and enjoyed Mr. Hyde's predations.

Other reviews complained of the lack of a strong script; calling the production cheap and hastily organized. One critic, Steve Crum of the Kansas City Kansan, gave the film 3 stars out of 5, saying, "Bud and Lou meet another monster for infrequent laughs."

On December 31, 1952, Variety said, "A rousing good time for Abbott and Costello fans is contained in this spoof on fiction's classic bogeyman [from stories by Sidney Fields and Grant Garrett]. The fat & thin comics combat Boris Karloff as the fictional dual personality in the very broad doings, and Karloff's takeoff on the character adds to the chuckles dished out by A & C."

Awards: So far, none have been given to this film.

Home media: The film has been released twice on DVD, on "The Best of Abbott and Costello Volume Four", on October 4, 2005, and again on October 28, 2008 as part of "Abbott and Costello: The Complete Universal Pictures Collection".

THE BEAST FROM 20,000 FATHOMS (1953)

Directed by Eugène Lourié
Produced by Jack Dietz and Hal E. Chester
Screenplay by Fred Freiberger, Eugène Lourié, Louis Morheim, and Robert Smith; based on The Fog Horn (short story) by Ray Bradbury
Music by David Buttolph
Cinematography by Jack Russell
Edited by Bernard W. Burton
Production company: Jack Dietz Productions

Distributed by Warner Bros.; release date: June 13, 1953
Running time: 80 minutes
Budget: $200,000; box office: $2.25 million

Cast:
Paul Christian as Professor Tom Nesbitt
Paula Raymond as Lee Hunter
Cecil Kellaway as Dr. Thurgood Elson
Kenneth Tobey as Colonel Jack Evans
Donald Woods as Captain Phil Jackson
Ross Elliott as George Ritchie
Steve Brodie as Sgt. Loomis
Jack Pennick as Jacob Bowman
Michael Fox as ER doctor
Lee Van Cleef as Corporal Jason Stone
Frank Ferguson as Dr. Morton
King Donovan as Dr. Ingersoll
James Best as Charlie, radar operator

Plot: Far north of the Arctic Circle, a nuclear bomb test, dubbed "Operation Experiment", is conducted. Right after the blast, physicist Thomas Nesbitt (Paul Christian) muses, "What the cumulative effects of all these atomic explosions and tests will be, only time will tell."

The explosion awakens a 200 foot long carnivorous animal known as Rhedosaurus, thawing it out of the ice where it had been held in suspended animation [for how long?]. Nesbitt is the only surviving witness to the beast's awakening when his observation camp was destroyed by it, but has been dismissed out of hand as being "delirious". Despite the skepticism, he persists, knowing that what he saw was the truth.

The Beast begins making its way down the east coast of North America, sinking a fishing ketch off the Grand Banks, destroying another near Marquette, Canada, wrecking a lighthouse in Maine, and destroying buildings in Massachusetts. By now, the scientific community is not so skeptical.

Nesbitt eventually gains allies in palaeontologist Thurgood Elson (Cecil Kellaway) and his young assistant Lee Hunter (Paula Raymond) after one of the surviving fishermen identifies the dinosaur from a collection of drawings. On plotting sightings of the Beast's movements on a map for skeptical military officers, Elson proposes that the Beast is returning to the Hudson River area, where fossils of Rhedosaurus were first found. The Beast appears to have a homing instinct akin to pigeons or other migratory birds. Only this is no bird.

In search of the undersea Hudson River Canyon, Professor Elson is killed after his diving bell is swallowed by the Beast, which eventually comes ashore in Manhattan. A later newspaper report of its rampage lists "180 known dead, 1500 injured, damage estimates $300 million". A minor blip in the damage caused by other events. Still, it is concerning.

Meanwhile, military troops led by Colonel Jack Evans (Kenneth Tobey) try to stop the Rhedosaurus with an electrified barricade, then blast a hole with a bazooka in the Beast's throat, which drives it back into the sea. Unfortunately, it bleeds all over the streets of New York on its way, unleashing a prehistoric contagion which begins to infect the populace, causing even more fatalities. The infection precludes blowing up the Rhedosaurus or even setting it ablaze, lest the contagion spread further.

It is then decided to shoot a radioactive isotope into the Beast's neck wound with hopes of burning it from the inside, killing it without releasing the contagion. Easier said than done.

When the Rhedosaurus comes ashore and reaches Coney Island's amusement park, military sharpshooter Corporal Stone (Lee van Cleef) takes a rifle grenade loaded with a potent radioactive isotope, and climbs on board a roller coaster. Riding the coaster to the top of the tracks, so he can get to eye-level with the Beast, he fires the isotope into its open neck wound.

The creature thrashes about in reaction, causing the roller coaster to spark and setting the amusement park ablaze when it collapses to the ground. Stone dies in the conflagration. The park becomes completely engulfed in flames. The Rhedosaurus eventually dies from isotope poisoning and heat stroke. END

Analysis and additional notes: Thanks to the amazing stop motion effects by Ray Harryhousen, we are treated to some real scientific problems, whether they are caused by atomic experiments or not. However, there are several inconsistencies which the script either deliberately or accidentally ignored. A dinosaur which has lain in the ice for millions of years will not revive. Even if thawed it would go into immediate necropsis and decay. Also, we know that the dinosaurs went extinct over 65 million years ago, ice or not.

While we are told that the Rhedonosaur has a homing instinct, this was argued for several decades. One side of paleontology claims that all land dinosaurs were the progenitor of modern bird species, while the other argues for a reptilian branch. No matter what the scientists say, modern birds may have descended from a smaller branch of dinosaurs akin to *Archaeopterix*, because we have seen that reptile species have not changed much in 65 million years. Crocodiles and alligators, snakes, and other similar reptiles have mostly remained exactly as they were long ago without much adaptation.

The release of a contagion of ancient virus or bacteria was also a bit of the scientific thrill. We don't know what kind of diseases may have existed millions of years ago. Since DNA research is beginning to uncover mysteries of the Paleogene era [a period ranging from 66M years ago to 2.5M years ago], we may learn what is really there and if they are the progenitors of modern diseases such as flu and bubonic plague.

Most species of dinosaurs were not as indestructible as one would assume. If they were reptilian, their skins were as supple and colorful as those of modern reptiles, but apart from the pangolin and the tortoise, their skins were not impervious to fire. So the idea that the only way to destroy the Rhedosaur was by shooting a radioactive isotope into the wound was a bit of a stretch. It would most likely die from the wound alone, without such overkill.

On the other hand, if the dinosaurs gave rise to many bird species, they would have a homing instinct which led them to return to the same birthplace year after year to breed. Note that I am talking about bipeds or quadrupeds, not fish or arthropods. But again this is mere speculation because more DNA research is needed to identify the origins of fossils already recovered. Science requires slow and methodical steps, not a rush to conclusions.

In this film, the producers took it for granted that most people knew about the world of the dinosaurs, but at least they tried to present a scientific approach to the story rather than ramble on without any basis in fact. Once they posited the premise, that a dinosaur could be revived after an era long sleep encased in ice, one had to buy the bit. Not a horror film but a "what if" scenario, which neatly fits in to the science fiction genre.

I have a problem with the title. What 20,000 fathoms? The depth of the Rhedosaurs ice prison was rather close to the surface. I would have preferred it to be called "The Beast" and leave it at that.

For its fast and engaging pacing, special effects, and animations, I give *The Beast From 20,000 Fathoms* 3 stars out of 4. IMdb gave it 6.7/10, and Rotten Tomatoes gave it rating of 94% fresh; 67% of their audience liked it.

About the author: Ray Douglas Bradbury (August 22, 1920 – June 5, 2012) was an American author and screenwriter. He worked in a variety of genres, including fantasy, science fiction, horror, and mystery fiction.

Widely known for his dystopian novel *Fahrenheit 451* (1953), and his science fiction and horror story collections, *The Martian Chronicles* (1950), *The Illustrated Man* (1951), and *I Sing the Body Electric* (1969), Bradbury was one of the most celebrated 20th and 21st century American writers. While most of his best known work is in speculative fiction, he also wrote in other genres, such as his early novel *Dandelion Wine* (1957) and the fictionalized memoir *Green Shadows, White Whale* (1992).

Recipient of numerous awards, including a 2007 Pulitzer Citation, Bradbury also wrote and consulted on screenplays and television scripts, including *Moby Dick* and *It Came from Outer Space*. Many of his works were adapted to comic book, television, and film formats.

Upon his death in June of 2012, <u>The New York Times</u> called Bradbury "the writer most responsible for bringing modern science fiction into the literary mainstream".

Production: *The Beast from 20,000 Fathoms* had a production budget of $200,000. It earned $2.25 million at the North American box office during its first year of release and ended up grossing more than $5 million. Original prints of *Beast* were sepia toned.

The film was announced in the trades as *The Monster From Beneath The Sea*. During preproduction in 1951, Ray Harryhausen brought to Dietz and Chester's attention that Ray Bradbury had just published a short story in the <u>The Saturday Evening Post</u> called *The Beast From 20,000 Fathoms* (it was later anthologized under the title "The Fog Horn"). This story was about a marine based prehistoric dinosaur that destroys a lighthouse. A similar sequence appeared in the draft script of *The Monster From Beneath The Sea*.

The producers, wishing to share in Bradbury's reputation and popularity, promptly bought the rights to his story and changed the film's title to match the story's title. Bradbury's name was used extensively in the promotional campaign. They also had an on screen credit that read "Suggested by the Saturday Evening Post Story by Ray Bradbury".

An original music score was composed by Michel Michelet, but when Warner Bros. purchased the film they had a new score written by David Buttolph. Ray Harryhausen had been hoping that his film music hero Max Steiner, under contract at the time with Warner Bros., would write the film score. Steiner had written the landmark score for RKO's *King Kong* in 1933. Unfortunately for Harryhausen, Steiner had too many commitments to allow him to do so, but as it turned out Buttolph composed one of his most memorable and powerful scores, setting much of the tone for giant monster film music of the 1950s.

Some early conceptual sketches of the Beast showed that at one point it was to have a shelled head and at another it was to have a beak. Creature effects were assigned to Ray Harryhausen, who had been working for years with Willis O'Brien, the man who created *King Kong*. It was he who decided that the shell and the beak were superfluous.

The monster of the film looks nothing like the Brontosaurus of the short story. The film creature is instead a kind of prehistoric sauropod which was somewhat quadrupedal in stature. It was unlike any real carnivorous dinosaur and more closely resembled a rauisuchian. A drawing of the creature was published along with the story in The Saturday Evening Post.

At one point, there were plans to have the Beast snort flames like a dragon, but this idea was dropped before production began due to budget restrictions. The concept, however, was still used for the film poster artwork. Later, the Beast's nuclear flame breath would be the inspiration for the original Japanese film *Gojira* (1954, Godzilla).

In a scene of the film, while attempting to identify the Rhedosaurus, Professor Tom Nesbitt rifles through dinosaur drawings by Charles R. Knight, a man whom Harryhausen claimed as an inspiration for the Beast's design.

The dinosaur skeleton in the museum sequence is artificial; it was obtained from storage at RKO Pictures where it had been constructed for their classic comedy *Bringing Up Baby* (1938).

The climactic roller coaster live action scenes were filmed on location at The Pike in Long Beach, California, and featured the Cyclone Racer entrance ramp, ticket booth, loading platform, and views of the structure from the beach. Split matte, incamera special effects by Harryhausen effectively combined the live action of the actors and the roller coaster background footage from The Pike parking lot with the stop motion animation of the Beast destroying a shooting miniature of the coaster.

Reception: In his review of *The Beast From 20,000 Fathoms* for The New York Times, Armond White was not impressed with the story: "And though the sight of the gigantic monster rampaging through such areas as Wall Street and Coney Island sends the comparatively ant-like humans on the screen scurrying away in an understandable tizzy, none of the customers in the theatre seemed to be making for the hills. On sober second thought, however, this might have been sensible".

The Variety review focused more on the impressive special effects: "Producers have created a prehistoric monster that makes Kong seem like a chimpanzee. It's a gigantic amphibious beast that towers above some of New York's highest buildings. The sight of the beast stalking through Gotham's downtown streets is awesome. Special credit should go to Ray Harryhausen for the socko technical effects".

Culture Mag critic Christopher Stewardson rated the film 3.5 stars out of 5.

Legacy: The film's financial success helped spawn the genre of giant monster films of the 1950s. Producers Jack Dietz and Hal E. Chester got the idea to combine the growing paranoia about nuclear weapons with the concept of a giant monster after a successful theatrical rerelease of *King Kong*.

In turn, this craze included *Them!* the following year about giant ants, the *Godzilla* series from Japan that has spawned films from 1954 into the present day, and two British features helmed by *Beast* director Eugène Lourié, *Behemoth, The Sea Monster* (UK 1959, US release retitled *The Giant Behemoth*), and *Gorgo* (UK 1961).

The film *Cloverfield* (2008), which also involves a giant monster terrorizing New York City, inserts a frame from *The Beast From 20,000 Fathoms* (along with frames from *King Kong* and *Them!*) into the hand held camera footage used throughout the film.

The Beast From 20,000 Fathoms was nominated for AFI's Top 10 Science Fiction Films list.

A brief cut on televison also appears in *Gremlins 2: The New Batch* (1990).

CAT WOMEN OF THE MOON (1953)
Directed by Arthur Hilton
Produced by Jack Rabin and Al Zimbalist
Written by Roy Hamilton
Music by Elmer Bernstein
Cinematography by William P. Whitley
Edited by John A. Bushelman
Distributed by Astor Pictures
Release date: September 3, 1953; running time: 64 minutes

Cast:
Sonny Tufts as Laird Grainger
Victor Jory as Kip Reissner
Marie Windsor as Helen Salinger
William Phipps as Doug Smith
Douglas Fowley as Walt Walters
Carol Brewster as Alpha
Suzanne Alexander as Beta
Susan Morrow as Lambda
Bette Arlen as Cat-Woman
Roxann Delman as Cat-Woman
Ellye Marshall as Cat-Woman
Judy Walsh as Cat-Woman

Plot: Using a spaceship furnished with wooden tables and rolling chairs, a scientific expedition to the Moon consisting of four men and a woman land on the moon in their rocket ship and begin to explore the landscape. It is desolate and arid, and they soon discover that their air tanks are depleting rapidly.

Acting on a supposition by their junior member, they enter a series of caves. Before long, they learn that there is air in the cavern they have just entered. They doff their space suits and begin to explore the interior, only to encounter a giant spider, which they shoot to death.

Deeper into the interior they encounter a race of women who are the last survivors of a 2 million year old civilization. The women live under a monarchical hierarchy. Their leader is called Alpha (Carol Brewster), and she alone gives the orders and makes the decisions. She is always guarded by her lieutenants, Beta (Suzanne Alexander) and Lambda (Susan Morrow). They appear to be blessed with the power of telepathy, but they do not reveal this to the astronauts.

They wear black unitards and their hair is swept up into beehives. They also wear heavy makeup which gives them a cat-like appearance.

At first they are welcoming and they give food and drink to the astronauts, while Alpha gains control of the female astronaut named Helen Salinger (Marie Windsor), manipulating her to convince the men that they should stay. Alpha explains that there are no men, so that their society has been matriarchal out of necessity.

At first, the men are pleased with the idea but unwilling to stay, eager to return to the space ship, which had been damaged in the landing, and repair it before they take off.

During a short interlude, while the astronauts are resting, Alpha and Beta argue over their situation. It is revealed that the cavern can only support their ancient society for so long, but their air supply is also running out. Alpha wants to hijack the rocket after the repairs are done and leave the men behind to suffocate in the deep cold of the moon. Beta is reluctant, having fallen for one of the men. But Alpha's mental prowess is higher than hers. Eventually Beta relents.

Meanwhile, Lambda rebels and tells the "guests" the truth behind the secrecy. They realize that they are in serious danger, and escape the confines of the underground city to retrieve their suits. But when they arrive at their hiding place the suits are gone. While they are deciding what to do next they are attacked by another giant spider, sent by Alpha to kill them. Kip Reissner (Victor Jory) takes out a revolver and shoots the arachnid.

Upon being forced to return to the cavern city, they discover that the cat women can teleport themselves from location to location easily. Kip confronts them about the missing suits. Using Helen to bargain for them, they gradually break down the barrier between races and learn more about the rocket, space travel, and how close the moon is to Earth. They volunteer to assist with the repairs.

Soon afterward, Beta manages to get the upper hand with Alpha and stabs her to death. Seizing the crown, she puts it on her head and declares that she is queen. She orders the men to be seized and killed, and convinces Helen that she should join their order as their sister. But Helen also rebels, and warns the men that they all should leave now. The leader of the expedition, Laird Grainger (Sonny Tufts) says that they will leave when it is opportune. Then Helen is again overcome by Beta's influence.

Meanwhile, Beta manages to get Walt Walters (Douglas Fowley) alone and stabs him to death. Lambda sees this and runs to Doug Smith (William Smith) to tell him what she has seen. They share a brief but intimate moment, and Doug promises to protect her.

That evening the cat women perform a ritual dance to celebrate the coronation of the new queen. But Beta is not there. She and Helen, along with another cat woman, make a break for the rocket clad in the stolen suits. Lambda teleports to the mouth of the cavern in order to delay them, but she is killed by Beta.

Kip arrives and fires several shots, killing the cat women but sparing Helen. Once Beta dies, Helen is freed from her mind control. She and the men don their suits and run for the rocket, which has been fully repaired. They take off and leave the remaining cat women behind, along with the crumbling civilization which had died long ago. END.

Analysis and additional notes: This could have been a better film had it not been for the total lack of exposition which would have made sense of it. We are shown that air is precious, but why not keep the suits on? And there are two of those big hairy spiders, not just one. When I watched this film it seemed as if they were running on a $50 budget. And with it, the usual male accoutrements: cigarettes, matches, a gun. And only one gun, not six or seven. No actual preparation. No budget for costumes which would have better fitted an advanced, ancient civilization. No actual grasp of physics.

Instead, it came off as a sort of war between the sexes, with the men being on top as usual. The cat women were shown as intelligent and clever, to a certain point. But their leaders were both power hungry and foolish, a deadly combination. It is not dwelt upon that there are only a few of them in total, and the evidence that their civilization is dead reside in a few murals placed outside the galleries of the cavern, showing nothing but ruin.

One would think that if their civilization was so advanced in the first place, they would have left the moon for sunnier climes already in their own space ships. Never mind hijacking a rocket ship from Earthlings just taking a stroll into the unknown.

For the terrible roman a'clef and ill conceived scripting, I give it 1 star out of 4. IMdb gives it 3.7/10 (ouch!) and Rotten Tomatoes gives it no rating, but only 33% of their audience liked it.

Production: Apart from a few notes on the type of film and sound there are no notes. A few comments of trivia noted that the suits were obvious leftovers from previous films, and that Sonny Tufts was apparently in his cups when this film was made. But such things are not based on actual fact and there are no historical notes.

Critical reception: Upon the film's release, Variety magazine wrote: "This imaginatively conceived and produced science-fiction yarn [an original story by producers Zimbalist and Rabin] takes the earth-to-moon premise and embellishes it with a civilization of cat-women on the moon ... Cast ably portray their respective roles ... Arthur Hilton makes his direction count in catching the spirit of the theme, and art direction is far above average for a film of this calibre. William Whitley's 3-D photography provides the proper eerie quality".

The New York Times wrote: "They (The Cat-women) try to get their hands on the visitors' rocket ship, hoping to come down here and hypnotize us all. Considering the delegation that went up, it's hard to imagine why".

The Encyclopedia of Science Fiction calls the film absurd, but notes that it "qualifies as one of the most influential science fiction films ever made" as it influenced later films "in which astronauts discover decadent, all-female (or almost all-female) civilizations on other planets, including *Fire Maidens From Outer Space* (1956), *Queen of Outer Space* (1958), *Nude On The Moon* (1961), [and] *Voyage To The Planet of Prehistoric Women* (1968)."

Legacy: An original two-projector, polarized 3D-format showing of *Cat-Women of The Moon* was featured at the first 3D Film Expo at Hollywood's Grauman's Egyptian Theatre in September 2003, and also at the 3-D At The Castro film festival, at the historic Castro Theatre in San Francisco, on October 17, 2006.

The 1995 Englewood Entertainment VHS video release was in a red and blue anaglyph 3D format.

The first "flat" version of *Cat-Women of The Moon* was released on DVD by Image Entertainment.

Since 2007 The L. A. Connection improvisational comedy troupe regularly screens the film in its live "Dub-a-vision" performances.

Cat-Women of The Moon was used as the title of two programs about sex in science fiction, broadcast on BBC Radio 4 in August and September of 2011. They were presented by the writer Sarah Hall, and produced in Manchester by Nicola Swords. They featured a number of British writers, including Iain M. Banks, China Miéville, and Nicola Griffith.

Cat-Women of The Moon was remade five years later as *Missile To The Moon* (1958), which was also released by Astor Pictures.

The film was the inspiration for performer Pat Benatar to change her appearance for one Halloween, which assisted in her acquiring a record deal.

Cat-Women of The Moon inspired several songs on Shakespeare's Sister's second album *Hormonally Yours*, among them their UK number one hit "Stay".

The opening track of *Is It Man Or Astroman* uses the opening narration from the film prior to the start of the song "Taxidermist Surf".

COMMANDO CODY:
SKY MARSHALL OF THE UNIVERSE (1953)
(Also known as 'Commando Cody')
Directed by Harry Keller, Franklin Adreon, and Fred C. Brannon
Written by Ronald Davidson and Barry Shipman
Music by Stanley Wilson
Cinematography by Bud Thackery
Editor: Cliff Bell Sr.
Release - Original network: NBC

Original release: July 16 – October 8, 1955
1 season; 12 episodes; running time/episode: 25-30 minutes

Cast:
Judd Holdren as Commando Cody
Aline Towne as Joan Gilbert
William Schallert as Ted Richards (Chs. 1-3)
Richard Crane as Dick Preston (Chs. 4-12)
Gregory Gaye as The Ruler
Craig Kelly as Commissioner Henderson
Peter Brocco as Dr. Varney (Chs. 1-2)
Lyle Talbot as Henchman Baylor (Chs. 4,5,6,7,9,10)
Mauritz Hugo as Henchman Mason (Chs. 4,5,6,9,10)
Joanne Jordan as The Queen of Mercury (Ch. 12)
Gloria Pall as The Moon Girl
and a cast of extras

Plot: Dangerous weather and climate changes are ravaging the Earth. Masked scientist Commando Cody (Judd Holdren) is approached by the U.S. government to investigate. Among the tools at his disposal are an atomic powered flying suit with an aerodynamic helmet and a newly designed and built rocketship.

With his colleagues Joan Gilbert (Aline Towne) and Ted Richards (William Schallert), later replaced by Dick Preston (Richard Crane), he ascertains the disasters are being caused by alien forces, led by a mysterious "Ruler" of unknown planetary origins, with occasional help from hired, Earth-born criminals.

Warding off various dangers, Cody and his associates are able to methodically close in on the culprits and reveal that The Ruler (Gregory Gaye) is from Venus. In the final episode The Ruler meets his end on Mercury with the help of the Mercurians, who never liked the guy anyway. END

Analysis and additional notes: As with many serials of the 1940s and 50s, this one involved a long and involved as well as complex plotline, rife with fist and gun fights, criminal minions, and the usual clunky looking robot. There is always only one robot, with three being the maximum. As usual, the robot(s) is always under remote control, meaning that it is far from effective to its purpose.

As for Commando Cody, the subtitle "Sky Marshal of The Universe" is overstating the case. First of all, Cody does not leave the Earth until almost the very end. Second, he only goes as far as Venus and does not even leave the Solar system. To say that his jurisdiction covers the entire univere means he would most likely die of exhaustion, if we were to take it at all seriously.

Since there was at least two fist fights per episode it seemed as if the producers were trying to string the plot out as far as possible. It also made for impatient and bored watching. If you have a chance, you are better off watching one of the feature films constructed from the remains. It would make better sense.

Science fiction? Yes, to a certain extent, but one must suspend one's disbelief to accept it as such.

For its vague attempt at a storyline I give it 1 star out of 4. IMdb gives it 6.2/10, but Rotten Tomatoes has no page for it.

Chapters titles: Enemies of the Universe - Atomic Peril - Cosmic Vengeance - Nightmare Typhoon - War of The Space Giants - Destroyers of The Sun - Robot Monster From Mars - The Hydrogen Hurricane - Solar Sky Raiders - S.O.S. Ice Age - Lost In Outer Space - Captives of The Zero Hour.

Production: *Commando Cody* was originally filmed as a 12 part television series, but union contract issues forced Republic Pictures to first exhibit it through regular movie theaters as a weekly serial. While the TV episodes build on each other in chronological order, the serial episodes lacked the traditional cliffhanger endings that characterized all previous serials.

The *Sky Marshal* serial is a prequel to Republic's *Radar Men From The Moon* theatrical serial. The first episode has characters Joan and Ted, Commando Cody's established sidekicks in *Radar Men*, applying for their jobs and meeting Cody for the first time.

There was a substantial break between filming the first 3 and last 9 episodes of the TV series, during which time Republic set about filming a Cody serial sequel called *Zombies of The Stratosphere*, also starring Judd Holdren as Cody, Aline Towne as Joan, and Wilson Wood as Ted. For reasons unknown, however, Republic Pictures revised these principal characters' names; thus "Commando Cody" became "Larry Martin" instead.

The third TV episode ends with the apparent death of The Ruler, suggesting that Republic may have reconsidered filming the remaining 9 TV episodes and planned to cut the 3 it had finished into a regular science fiction feature film.

By the time work finally resumed on the *Sky Marshal* series, Republic had lost actor William Schallert as Cody's male colleague "Ted Richards". A replacement was found in Richard Crane, a year before his best remembered role as the title character on the science fiction TV series *Rocky Jones, Space Ranger*. The Ruler also gained a female sidekick, played by Gloria Pall, though she had almost no screen dialogue or action.

Flying jacket and helmet: *Commando Cody* reuses the Rocket Man flying jacket and helmet first seen in Republic's 1949 serial *King of The Rocket Men*. Stock footage was also used from their other serials, including *The Purple Monster Strikes*. The *Sky Marshal* series also recycles characters, sets, props, and concepts from the *Radar Men* serial. Two streamlined, bullet shaped prop helmets were again used with the Rocket Man costume. The first was made of lighter weight materials and worn only during the various stunt action scenes. During filming, the single hinged visors on both helmets frequently warped and would stick open or closed.

When not in his flying jacket and helmet, Cody wears a black military tunic with many insignia and a cap, instead of the regular business suit seen in the *Radar Men* serial. Cody also wears a black domino mask to hide his identity. Holdren always suspected this was due to producers not wanting to take a chance that he might walk out if any future demands for a higher salary were not met, as Clayton Moore had done on the popular *The Lone Ranger* television series. The mask presumably served to conceal any change of actor should the part ever need recasting, even though the change of lead with a domino mask had not worked well in the case of the *Lone Ranger* series.

Setting: As the story opens, it is the near future as seen from the perspective of the early 1950s. Earth is in radio contact with civilizations on planets in our solar system, as well as planets in other, distant solar systems, and Commando Cody has just built the world's first spaceship. The rest of the world appears unchanged by these galactic developments.

The exterior of Cody's headquarters building is actually a Republic Pictures office building.

For the serial, a number of new outer space scenes were filmed that had not been seen before in the other Republic serials, including "space walks" for several exterior spaceship repairs; aerial raygun duels between "hero" and "enemy" spaceships; and black star fields, rather than daylight and cloud spotted skies, for backgrounds when Cody's or the villain's spaceships were shown outside the Earth's atmosphere.

Cody and his associates use special badges that conceal radios to communicate with one another, prefiguring similar communication badges used more than 30 years later in *Star Trek: The Next Generation*. There were futuristic props and sets, as well as shots of the intricate model rocket special effects work of Republic's Howard and Theodore Lydecker; the spaceships of Cody and The Ruler are the same basic shooting miniature with different attachments and markings added to make them appear different.

Release: The serial was subsequently broadcast nationally on television in 1955 by Republic's TV arm, Hollywood Television Service, on NBC stations. The chapters were already filmed with a run-time of 25 minutes each, so they required no editing or expansion to fit a half-hour TV slot.

Television series or movie serial? The release of *Commando Cody* as a weekly theatrical serial, despite having been filmed as a TV series, has led to controversy among serial purists. Should it be included in Republic's canon of serials, or should it be considered a separate, stand alone, limited run science fiction action TV series? The filmed TV episodes were first titled and numbered as "Chapters" on all theatrical release prints and in Republic's advertising, while the later broadcast TV series, with changes made, lived on in syndication for years, long after the movie serial finished its 12 week run in theaters.

The serial episodes are complete but with the same general plot line as the one running through the TV series: the Ruler is always trying to destroy the Earth. Although there are no traditional cliffhanger endings, each serial chapter has a partial resolution at its end: the episode's primary henchman always escapes. The TV episodes continuity must be shown in their correct order, rather than being seen in the serial's interchangeable chapters.

Reference works on movie serials, however, generally exclude the serial version of *Sky Marshal*, or simply mention it in passing as a later Republic TV series.

DONOVAN'S BRAIN (1953)

Directed by Felix E. Feist
Produced by Allan Dowling and Tom Gries
Written by Curt Siodmak (novel), Hugh Brooke (adaptation), and Felix E. Feist (screenplay)
Music by Eddie Dunstedter
Cinematography by Joseph F. Biroc
Edited by Herbert L. Strock
Production company: Dowling Productions
Distributed by United Artists; release date: September 30, 1953
Running time: 83 minutes

Cast:
Lew Ayres as Dr. Patrick Cory
Nancy Davis as Janice Cory
Gene Evans as Dr. Frank Schratt
Steve Brodie as Yocum
Tom Powers as Donovan's Washington Advisor
Lisa Howard as Chloe Donovan (credited as Lisa K. Howard)
James Anderson as Chief Tuttle (credited as Kyle James)
Victor Sutherland as Nathaniel Fuller
Michael Colgan as Tom Donovan
Peter Adams as Mr. Webster
Harlan Warde as Treasury Agent Brooke
Shimen Ruskin as Tailor

Plot: Dr. Patrick Cory (Lew Ayres) and his wife Janice (Nancy Davis) live in a mountain retreat where Cory tries to keep a monkey's brain alive after having removed it from the monkey's skull. It does not last long, and Dr. Cory feels he has failed. He has been studying the electrostatic impressions of brain activity to determine how the brain functions. His wife encourages him to try again, but he doubts he will succeed anyway. Together, Janice and Cory's assistant, Dr. Frank

Schratt (Gene Evans) try to cheer him up, when a phone call interrupts their conversation.

The private plane of prominent businessman Warren Donovan has crashed near Cory's cabin, and rescuers request Cory's help since he is the closest physician. Time is of the essence. Donovan is seriously injured and not expected to live, so Cory tries to keep his brain alive in the man's body. But his vital functions fail, one by one. Then Cory has an idea. He takes the businessman's brain for experimentation, and manages to keep the brain alive in an electrified saline solution, connnected by two electrodes to a circuit.

Dr. Schratt is alarmed by this violation of a physician's ethics, and says that Cory cannot simply take the brain of a human being this way. But Cory is adamant. He must continue his studies, and this is the only way he will learn. Besides, he says, what is a human being but his brain? As long as it is alive, Donovan is alive, not dead. Schratt is sufficiently cowed enough that he will continue to assist Cory.

Schratt discusses the situation with Janice, who is herself a scientist. He and she agree that they will monitor Cory's studies to make sure he does not go over the line.

Later, Cory is dozing over his notes, and begins writing something in his journal. It appears to be a note in Donovan's own handwriting, telling him where to go and who to see. When Cory wakes, he glances down at it and is terribly shocked, then becomes excited as he realizes that Donovan's brain has not only survived, it has been communicating with him through some form of telepathy.

He shares this observation with Schratt and Janice but they are skeptical of his claim.

Gradually, Cory begins to exhibit Donovan's personality traits such as smoking cigars, using ruthless personal manipulation, and walking with a limp, even using a tailor to build suits for him based on Donovan's tastes in clothing. He takes an apartment in a luxury hotel without the resources to pay for it, claiming that he works for Donovan and that all questions should go to Donovan's lawyer.

Janice and Schratt suspect that Donovan's consciousness is using telepathic mind control to overpower Cory's free will.

In the meantime, a news photographer named Yocum (Steve Brodie) discovers that Cory has illegally stolen Donovan's brain and demands money to keep his mouth shut. This open and brazen extortion annoys Dr. Cory (and by extension Donovan), but there is little he can do about it, having just earned a hard won grant from the insititute he works for. He continues to manipulate stocks and other holdings based on Donovan's commands to enrich himself in order to execute Donovan's commands. He will not tolerate any question as to his identity, to his lawyer's consternation.

While Cory is occupied with this, Donovan takes control of Yocum's mind and forces him into a fatal car crash. During this time, Cory returns to normal and feels free to protest he is in command of his own brain.

After realizing that Donovan can control only one person at a time, Janice and Frank plot to destroy the brain. If Janice could distract Cory long enough, Frank would shoot Donovan's brain, ending his control over Cory. However, Frank's plan goes wrong when Donovan forces Frank to shoot himself. Janice and Cory stroll outside for a time, and while watching a thunderstorm gather, hear the gunshot, then another when Frank shoots himself.

Suddenly, Donovan takes over Cory's mind and tries to strangle Janice, when lightning strikes their home and sets it on fire. The fire destroys Donovan's brain, releasing Cory forever. Cory and Janice race inside to discover that Frank has been injured, and drag him outside. The three watch while the house burns down, free at last. END

Analysis and additional notes: This film was actually more rational and intelligent than most. Not only did it establish who or what the monster is in a few short scenes, it maintained an even handed scientific rationale for Cory's experiments, his methods, and the understandable reaction to the idea that Donovan's brain not only survives, it has the willpower to overcome its limitations and communicate via telepathy.

We don't know exactly how this is possible, but given the powerful personality trapped inside the five pounds of flesh which was its receptacle, it would only be a matter of time before it would regain its power over others. Through Cory's behavior in town we learn that Donovan is a powerful financial magnate demanding to have his way no matter what. He is not above forcing people to do his bidding, money or not. He also thinks he is far above the law, even resorting to murder when it suits him. It becomes clear that he has built his fortunes on deeds which we are not privy to, but which must have been shady. But now, even death cannot stop him from doing his own will.

Science has extended his life, but science is also his undoing. The clear philosophy which runs throughout the plot is that man is not God, and cannot expect to be one. Actions have consequences.

For its great plotline and flow of dialogue I give *Donovan's Brain* 3 stars out of 4. IMdb gives it 6.1/10, and Rotten Tomatoes gives it a rating of 55% fresh, while 25% of their audience liked it. Perhaps it was a bit too cerebral for some (I kid!). But it was a vast improvement over some of the clunkers which were pumped out like so much chaff during the mid 1950s.

Production: There are appear to be no other notes of any significance. As a matter of trivia, Nancy Davis was soon to become Nancy Reagan, wife of Ronald Reagan, at the time *Donovan's Brain* was filmed.

FOUR SIDED TRIANGLE (1953)

Directed by Terence Fisher
Produced by Michael Carreras and Alexander Paal
Written by Paul Tabori and Terence Fisher
Based on the novel Four Sided Triangle by William F. Temple
Music by Malcolm Arnold
Cinematography by Reg Wyer
Edited by Maurice Rootes
Production company: Hammer Film Productions
Distributed by Astor Pictures (USA) and Exclusive Films (UK)
Release date: May 25, 1953 (UK); running time 81 minutes

Cast:
Barbara Payton as Lena Maitland/Helen
James Hayter as Dr. Harvey
Stephen Murray as Bill Leggat
John Van Eyssen as Robin Grant
Percy Marmont as Sir Walter
Glyn Dearman as Bill (as a child)
Sean Barrett as Robin (as a child)
Jennifer Dearman as Lena (as a child)

Kynaston Reeves as Lord Grant
John Stuart as a Solicitor
Edith Saville as Lady Grant

Plot: Dr. Harvey is a rural physician who relates an unusual occurrence that happened in his village. The bulk of the story is told in flashback.

Bill and Robin are boyhood friends who compete for the affections of Lena, a beautiful girl about their own age. But Lena's family moves away, and in adulthood the two men become scientists together. They collaborate to design the Reproducer, a machine that can exactly duplicate physical objects.

Soon afterward, Lena returns to the village, and Bill and Robin's forgotten childhood feelings return. In time, they abandon their work on the Reproducer, and Robin leaves the village to learn his family's business. Bill is disappointed to discover that Lena loves Robin and intends to marry him.

Hopeless that he can ever win Lena's affections, Bill convinces her to allow him to use the Reproducer to create a duplicate of her. The experiment succeeds, and Bill names the duplicate "Helen". Because Helen is an exact copy, when she is introduced to Robin she also falls in love with him. Confronted with a dilemma, the duplicate Helen becomes despondent and morose over the idea that she should marry Bill, now that she had been introduced to Robin.

Bill believes that electroshock therapy can be used to erase his Helen's knowledge of Robin. Not wishing to compete with Lena for Robin's affections, Helen agrees to the therapy.

Bill convinces Lena to help him with the procedure. The process proceeds as planned, but the apparatus overheats, explodes and causes a terrific fire, which spreads rapidly throughout the house.

Robin and Dr. Harvey arrive in time to rescue a woman from the fire. Bill and the other woman perish in the flames. Harvey, having been briefed on the situation by Robin, discovers that the woman has amnesia. The two men wonder which woman they have saved. Dr. Harvey recalls that Bill had to start Helen's heart with a device that he attached to the back of her neck, leaving two scars.

Robin convinces the woman to bend forward on the examining table and is relieved to find that there are no marks on the back of her

131

neck. It is the true Lena. Later, they marry, having put the terrible events of the past few weeks behind them. END

Analysis and additional notes: This was a rather unique film which blended science fiction with a romance. We are shown the childhood which our three characters share, their play and their lifelong affection for each other which lasts into adulthood.

But at some point, their scientific experiments make it possible for the two men, Bill and Robin, to share Lena in a bizarre 4 sided triangle (hence the title), in which the duplicate begins to feel rather out of luck. Being the outsider, the duplicate Lena has the same personality and physical attributes as the original, but she must reconcile herself with the idea that Bill created her to become his lifelong mate. She cannot.

This brings up the ethical conflict about cloning, only this is a reproduction and not a clone. Helen is an exact copy, with memories which belong to the original. A clone is a genetic copy but the clone's personality is a blank slate which must be filled with new and different memories and experiences. Because Helen is an exact copy she is tortured by the situation she is in. It was not fair for Bill to demand that she behave like Lena, because apart from her name she *is* Lena. This bizarre situation would not have stood for long, because Helen was already cracking up over it.

The writers cleverly resolved the issue by killing one of the Lenas. Tragically, the doomed woman must be Helen. I really don't know what would have happened to the plot if Helen had survived instead of Lena. Would Robin have married her? Somehow I doubt it. After some dithering and possibly separating to sort out the mess, either Helen or Robin would have left town to start over, leaving the other to mourn the loss. The happy ending was a deliberate ploy to leave the audience guessing until the very end. Kind of ghoulish, really.

For its clever but awkward staging and soft science, I give *Four Sided Triangle* 2 stars out of 4. IMdb gives it 5.9/10, and Rotten Tomatoes gives it no rating, but only 27% of their audience liked it.

Production: *Four-Sided Triangle* was an early effort by Hammer Films. The laboratory set includes an elaborate grouping of retorts, alembics, rheostats, and neon tubing. This chaotic, improvised laboratory setting has been contrasted with the sophisticated labs portrayed by Universal Horror pictures of the 1930s.

The picture relies on a minimum of trick photography and special effects, which may have been compromised by its limited budget.

Differences from the novel: Four-Sided Triangle features some differences from the original novel by William F. Temple. In the novel, the duplicate (named Dorothy and nicknamed Dot) falls into depression for being married with Bill while she's in love with Robin. She has a breakdown and has to go on vacation with Bill to recover.

When they return, Bill starts working on a power generator which explodes, killing him. Lena tries to convince Robin to accept both her and Dot, but he refuses. A couple weeks later, Lena and Dot have an accident while diving on a river. One of them dies and the other is seriously injured.

Dr. Harvey and Robin are startled when they discover that the surviving woman can't recall anything after the duplication, and suppose she's repressing all the painful memories, so she must be Dot. Dr. Harvey finds in Bill's notes about the marks on Dot's neck and tells Robin, convincing him that the survivor is Lena.

In an epilogue, he reveals that he also discovered a note in which Bill recalls that, during the vacation, Dot had undergone plastic surgery to erase the marks, but destroyed it so Robin and Dot can be happy.

INVADERS FROM MARS (1953)

Directed by William Cameron Menzies
Produced by Edward L. Alperson and Jr.
Written by John Tucker Battle (story) and Richard Blake
Music by Raoul Kraushaar
Cinematography by John F. Seitz
Edited by Arthur Roberts
Production company: National Pictures Corp.
Distributed by Twentieth Century Fox Film Corp.
Release date: April 9, 1953; running time: 77 minutes

Cast:
Jimmy Hunt as David MacLean
Arthur Franz as Dr. Stuart Kelston
Helena Carter as Dr. Patricia Blake
Leif Erickson as George MacLean

Hillary Brooke as Mary MacLean
Morris Ankrum as Col. Fielding
Walter Sande as Police Sgt. Mack Finlay
Max Wagner as Army Sgt. Rinaldi
Milburn Stone as Army Capt. Roth
Douglas Kennedy as Police Officer Jackson
Charles Cane as Police Officer Blaine
Bert Freed as Police Chief A.C. Barrows
Fay Baker as Mrs. Wilson
Janine Perreau as Kathy Wilson
John Eldredge as Mr. Turner
Charles Gibb as Lt. Blair
Gil Herman as Maj. Clary
Bill Phipps as Sgt. Baker
Luce Potter as the Martian in Glass Globe
Lock Martin as Mutant Martian Guard
Max Palmer as Mutant Martian Guard
Barbara Billingsley as Kelston's Secretary
Todd Karns as Jim, Gas Station Attendant
Robert Shayne as Dr. William Wilson
Frank Wilcox as Pentagon Chief of Staff
William Forrest as Gen. Mayberry
Richard Deacon as M.P. Confirming Gen. Mayberry's Identity

Plot: Late one night, youngster David MacLean (Jimmy Hunt) is awakened by a loud thunderstorm. From his bedroom window he sees a large flying saucer descend and disappear into the sandpit area behind his home. After rushing to tell his parents, his scientist father (Leif Erickson) goes to investigate David's claim.

When his father returns much later in the morning, David asks him what he saw, but the man is now cold and hostile, telling the boy that it is none of his business. Then, David notices an unusual red puncture along the hairline on the back of his father's neck. David realizes something is very wrong; he has noticed that certain townsfolk are acting in exactly the same way.

Later in the day his father disappears altogether.

Through his telescope, David sees neighbor Kathy Wilson suddenly disappear underground while walking in the sandpit. David flees to the police station for help and is eventually placed under the protection of a health department physician, Dr. Pat Blake (Helena Carter), who slowly begins to believe his story. He is not being hysterical, but rationally intelligent for a young boy. But he is clearly disturbed by his experience.

When Mrs. MacLean (Hillary Brooke) arrives at the police station, she is cold and unemotional when she tries to collect David. But David will not go. Dr. Blake notices this and insists that the boy stay with her, as she has not determined his emotional state and will require more tests. Reluctantly, David's mother accepts the argument and says she will return to claim her son once the tests are complete.

With the help of local astronomer Dr. Stuart Kelston (Arthur Franz) and Dr. Blake, David concludes that the flying saucer is likely the vanguard of an invasion from the planet Mars, now in close orbital proximity to Earth. It is a plausible argument, so Dr. Kelston contacts the U.S. Army and convinces them to investigate, as an important government rocket research plant is located nearby, and George MacLean was an employee.

Closer observation shows that there is something strange going on around the sandpit, and also several people are seen trying to sabotage the plant. When they are caught in flagrante delicto, they promptly die of a brain hemorrage. It's the sabotage which is the problem.

In short order, the Pentagon assembles troops and tanks under the command of Colonel Fielding (Morris Ankrum) to investigate these incidents. The trail of clues lead back to the sandpit, and the army surrounds the saucer landing site, posting it off limits to civilians.

Standing well away from the army search, Dr. Blake and young David are suddenly sucked underground. They are captured by two tall, slit-eyed green humanoids and taken via tunnels to the flying saucer. Inside, they face the Martian mastermind: It has a giant green head with a humanoid face atop a small, green partial torso with several green arm-tentacles, and is encased in a transparent sphere. The Martian is served by the tall mutants.

The Martian declares (via telepathy) that Mars has decided to colonize the Earth. Dr. Blake is frightened, but protests that they have no right to do this. With the usual argument that Mars is dying, the being gives other orders to the mutants.

Dr. Blake is seized by the mutants and forced onto a table, where David sees a device emerging from somewhere over her head. It contains a needle which is used to implant the mind control circuit directly to the base of the skull. She is unconscious and no sound will alert her.

Once their disappearance has been noticed, army troops locate and blow open an entrance to the tunnels. Colonel Fielding and a small detachment make their way to the saucer entrance. The noise interrupts the mutants at their work, so they go toward it, leaving David and Dr. Black alone in their lab. David manages to deflect the device and drags Dr. Blake away as the implantation fails. She awakens slowly, and David coaxes her out of the lab. Somehow they find their way to the army in the tunnel, where they tell Fielding what happened.

The troops and Colonel Fielding, with Dr. Blake and David in tow, open fire on the pursuing mutants as their group escapes the saucer. After a short running battle in the tunnel, the men are trapped by a landslide, cutting off their means of escape.

David thinks quickly and proposes that they use sound to clear the rubble, based on the source of the blasters the mutants employ. The army men assemble a projector using mutant equipment and, emitting a signal, help to clear the slide.

The sound kills the mutants and threatens the mastermind, who orders the saucer powered up to depart.

In the meantime, Colonel Fielding, David, Dr. Blake and the men return to the surface. Orders are given for everyone to quickly leave the area: Fielding's troops have planted timed explosive charges aboard the saucer, which are ready to detonate.

Fielding tells David and Dr. Blake to run downhill away from the sandpit, and artillery opens fire on the field, as the charges ticking timer slowly approaches zero. It seems like the run is taking forever, as memories of the last few days crowd in on the boy.

As the flying saucer emerges from the sand and begins its escape, the sandpit expodes, destroying it. Then the boy blacks out.

When he awakens, David is suddenly back in his bed during a thunderstorm. He runs into his parents' bedroom, confused and frightened. Once he relates his story, they reassure him that he was just having a bad dream, telling him to go back to sleep.

When he returns to his bed, more wind and loud thunder is heard. David climbs out of bed again, goes to his window, and sees the very same flying saucer in his nightmare slowly descending into the sandpit, to which he declares, "Gee whiz"! END

Analysis and additional notes: The first time I saw this film it was badly mangled by the editing process for commercials. I was too young then to notice the details. Parts of it seemed inexplicable. Others got lost in translation. It was a bit of a popcorn thriller. But when I saw it again just recently, there was a whole raft of interesting aspects to this movie that could not be ignored.

1) Mind control. Here we see actual instrumentality at work. The devices are deadly. A person brought under control loses his natural desire for free will, and becomes unemotional. The added feature that the devices are designed to destroy the subect's brain if failure occurs is chilling.

2) The backgrounds are almost Daliesque in presentation. There are no ceilings. The walls are plain and solid colored, even in spaces where there should be some decoration. Certain furniture is exaggerated. A clock on one wall is simple and rather overlarge, suggesting that time is of the essence. A door in the police station is entirely too tall for an average person. These are the first clues to me that this is a dream and not reality.

3) The fact that the entire plot is a dream, and a premonitory one at that. The boy dreams everything which occurs except at the very end, when everything which has happened is happening again. Is it real or memorex? I have seen other films which employ this gimmick, but few which are spot on.

4) David, being an ordinary boy by all accounts, was more rational and intelligent than most others. It helps that his father was a scientist, even if we don't know what kind of work he did. We can safely assume that the town is populated with people who work at the rocket plant, so the scientific bent is prevalent. Environment shapes a child's temperament, and David is mentioned to have a scientist's attitude toward life. But, and there is a but, he is far more concerned with rescuing his parents than anything else. This drives his whole behavior throughout the film.

The cut of film I saw a week ago was far longer and better than the previous one. I saw scenes of the army assembling their equipment, loading tanks on trains and other equipment, and transporting them to the sandpit area. I saw the extended scenes of the army making preparations and dealing with the occasional bouts of sabotage. Even better and more rational scenes in the police station, which is manned by two and only two officers, and a disinterested detective who was already under control.

It is a pity that most productions are cut heavily for television consumption. People miss a lot of things which would make their enjoyment much better if the stations did not have to pay their pound of flesh to the ad man. This is why many of these films have been preserved by commercial free stations or websites in their entirety. Film industry museums like AFI (The American Film Institute) and commercial-free channels like TCM (Turner Classic Movies) are working hard to recover lost films and also to restore the integrity of many of them. I have mentioned this before in my previous books.

For its engaging and sometimes chilling scenarios, I give *Invaders From Mars* 3 star out of 4. IMdb gives it 6.5/10, and Rotten Tomatoes gives it a rating of 82% fresh. 55% of their audience liked it.

Production: The story makes use of a unique outre music score that consists of an ethereal, rhythmically wavering tonal composition sung in unison by a choir. It is used as both a sound effect and as the scenic score associated with the Martians. As the film's "The End" title card and end credits are displayed, the music underscores an unspoken question that only each viewer can answer: is young David still asleep, trapped in a recurring nightmare, or was his bad dream a premonition of this supposed real event?

The score is credited to Raoul Kraushaar, but Thomas Hischak's Encyclopedia of Film Composers notes that most of the score is now believed to be the work of frequent Republic composer Mort Glickman.

Visual design: An Eastman color camera negative was used for principal photography, with vivid SuperCinecolor prints struck for the film's initial theatrical release. To provide an oddly striking and vivid look to the film's images, standard Eastman color prints were used thereafter on later releases. While some film sources have claimed that *Invaders* was designed for the early 3D process, it was not filmed or released in 3D.

Invaders used occasional camera angles set lower or higher than usual to enhance the dramatic and visual impact of key scenes.

Special effects: The Martian heat ray effect showing the bubbling, melting walls of the underground tunnels was created by shooting a large tub of boiling oatmeal from above, colored red with food coloring and lit with red lights. The cooled, bubbled-up effect on some areas of the blasted tunnel walls was created by first using inflated balloons pinned to the tunnel walls. In film tests they looked like balloons stuck to the walls, so the effects crew tried smaller inflated latex condoms. Further testing showed these looked much more convincing, and the crew wound up inflating more than 3,000 and then sticking them to portions of the tunnel set's walls; in some shots, the condoms can be seen moving slightly as the Martian mutants rush down the tunnels.

Compositing of special effect scenes of the sandpit and other shots was made with a full aperture in camera, flipping negatives, and so on, allowing for more fluid and credible cinematography.

British release: (This is the better one.) A new ending and additional scenes were added in response to various objections raised by the film's British distributor. Other portions of *Invaders* were re-edited, and the original U.S. ending was dropped in favor of a more straightforward conclusion. New scenes were filmed several months after the U.S. release, including the one showing the destruction of the Martian flying saucer in the sky when the army's charges finally explode.

The British release also included a greatly expanded planetarium scene: framed pictures can be seen hanging on the planetarium walls that were not in the U.S. release; they appear to vanish and then reappear at times as the expanded and restructured scene plays out.

While the adult actors had not changed significantly, child actor Jimmy Hunt is taller, looks older, and has shorter hair in these new scenes. Hunt also wears a sweater vest in them (the vest materializes about three minutes into the scene, at which time Dr. Kelston's necktie also appears to be retied), while he and Dr. Kelston discuss various flying saucer accounts: the Lubbock Lights and the Mantell UFO incident. Dr. Kelston also identifies the various saucer models as "Type

1", "Type 2", etc.. All are rational arguments showing David's power of recall from his father's discussions; probably overheard at dinner.

After a large overhead explosion, David joins Kelston and Dr. Blake behind an Army tank for cover. The scene dissolves to the MacLean house, in David's bedroom, where he has been put to bed by Kelston and Dr. Blake. Standing at his door, they assure him his parents were surgically saved from the Martian devices implanted in the back of their necks before they imploded, and they wish him a good night. This scene dissolves to the film's "The End" title card, as the film's ethereal music reaches its crescendo in coda with the final fadeout.

Critical reception: Oscar Godbout of <u>The New York Times</u> reviewed the film strictly as entertainment for youngsters, calling it "a pictorial 'funnybook'" that would "probably frighten witless a lot of small children."

A generally positive review in <u>Variety</u> wrote: "Imaginative yarn makes full use of astronomical and lab equipment as well as Government atomic research installations as backgrounds to heighten the realism. Highlight, however, is a Martian ray gun which can cause the earth to part into subterranean passages. All this has been effectively filmed by John Seitz in Cinecolor."

<u>Harrison's Reports</u> declared it "A pretty good science-fiction melodrama, photographed in Cinecolor. The story, as in most pictures of this type, is highly imaginative, but it is packed with suspense from start to finish and should thrill the action fans, especially the youngsters."

Film historian Paul Meehan considered *Invaders From Mars* as "one of the best of the 50s invasion cycle", and "in hindsight", one of the most influential of the period, setting the scene for other "abduction films".

Critic Patrick Legare wrote of the film, "Originating during the science-fiction/Red-Scare boom of the '50s, Invaders From Mars is an entertaining little picture that holds up reasonably well".

Author and film critic Leonard Maltin awarded the film three out of a possible four stars. In his review on the film, Maltin called the film "starkly stylish".

Influence: *Invaders From Mars* impressed some kids who grew up and became filmmakers. Don Coscarelli's original 1979 *Phantasm* has some plot similarities, while Brad Bird's *The Iron Giant* makes references to the film, as well as to other iconic science fiction features, particularly those from the 1950s.

Remake: In 1986, *Invaders From Mars* was remade using the same title; it was directed by Tobe Hooper and stars Karen Black, Hunter Carson, and Timothy Bottoms. The original film's child star Jimmy Hunt played the police chief.

IT CAME FROM OUTER SPACE (1953)

Directed by Jack Arnold
Produced by William Alland
Screenplay by Harry Essex; story by Ray Bradbury
Music by Herman Stein
Cinematography by Clifford Stine
Edited by Paul Weatherwax
Production company: Universal Pictures
Distributed by: Universal-International; release date: May 27, 1953
Running time: 80 minutes

Cast:
Richard Carlson as John Putnam
Barbara Rush as Ellen Fields
Charles Drake as Sheriff Matt Warren
Joe Sawyer as Frank Daylon
Russell Johnson as George
Dave Willock as Pete Davis
Robert Carson as Dugan, reporter
Virginia Mullen as Mrs. Daylon
Kathleen Hughes as Jane, George's girl
Paul Fix as Councilman (uncredited)
Robert "Buzz" Henry as Posseman (uncredited)

Plot: Author and amateur astronomer John Putnam (Richard Carlson) and schoolteacher Ellen Fields (Barbara Rush) watch a large meteorite crash near the small town of Sand Rock, Arizona. They awaken a neighbor, Frank Daylon (Joe Sawyer), who has a helicopter, and all three fly to the crash site.

Putnam climbs down into the crater and notices a partially buried round object in the crater's pit. He comes to the realization, after he sees a 6 sided hatchway close, that this is not a meteorite but a large alien spaceship. The hatchway's noise starts a landslide that completely buries the craft.

Putnam's story is later scoffed at by Sand Rock's sheriff (Charles Drake) and the local news media. Even Ellen Fields is unsure about what to believe but still agrees to assist Putnam in his investigation.

Over the next several days, local people disappear; a few return, but they act distant or appear somewhat dazed and not their usual selves. Convinced by these and other odd events, Sheriff Warren comes to believe Putnam's story that the meteorite is actually a crashed spaceship with alien inhabitants. But, being the overly aggressive sort, he then organizes a posse to hunt down the invaders at their crash site.

Putnam hopes to reach a peaceful solution to the looming crisis. Alone, he enters a nearby abandoned mine, which he thinks will connect to the now buried spaceship and its alien occupants. At first it is too dark to see, but he directs his flashlight inward.

What confronts him is a large single eye, on a being which is part octopus, part jellyfish. It communicates with him by telepathy. In this encounter, the alien will not permit him beyond that point, and explains that they had crashed to earth by accident. They intend to stay on Earth only long enough to repair their damaged craft and leave.

When he learns this, Putnam vows to try and facilitate their departure but explains that several people have disappeared. The alien replies that he requires their human forms to perform the labor they cannot do. The persons themselves will not be harmed in any way and are being kept safe.

Putnam concludes that the aliens must be able to shape shift into human form in order to appear human and move around Sand Rock unobserved, in order to collect their much needed repair materials. In doing so, however, they fail to reproduce the townspeople's exact personalities, leading to suspicion and eventually to the deaths of two of the aliens so far.

To protect the aliens from the sheriff and his posse, Putnam manages to seal off the mine entrance with explosives in order to give them the time they still need to finish their spaceship's repairs.

However, the aliens have decided to destroy themselves and their spaceship, now that they have been discovered. Putnam reasons with their leader at length and convinces them to instead finish the repairs while he, as a sign of the aliens' good faith, takes the captives outside to the sheriff and his posse.

The alien allows that Putnam is the first human who has shown uncommon restraint to his people, and there is room for further discourse in the future. They come to the agreement and the people are allowed to leave, while the spacecraft emerges from its tunnel hideaway a short time later and departs into space.

Putnam's fiancee' Ellen asks him if they are gone for good. He responds, "No, just for now. It wasn't the right time for us to meet. But there will be other nights, other stars for us to watch. They'll be back." END

Analysis and additional notes: No doubt *It Came From Outer Space* was intended to be a popcorn thriller or horror film. But it was the first story where the aliens are completely different from humanoid forms, while a reasoning human being and amateur scientist interacts with respect to them for being what they are.

We see a careful diplomacy taking place between beings, rather that the usual confrontation with guns and artillery. True, a couple of alien duplicates are shot, but the aliens are benign enough not to respond in like kind. There is even a suggestion that the aliens may come back to engage in further diplomacy. They have given no hint that they were going to conquer the Earth. They are simply down for repairs. This was a refreshing change from the usual gunplay from previous films and serials.

For its intelligent and absorbing screenplay I give *It Came From Outer Space* 3 stars out of 4, and for the acting the same. IMdb gives it 6.6/10, and Rotten Tomatoes certifies it 81% fresh. 53% of their audience liked it.

Production: The screenplay by Harry Essex, with input by Jack Arnold, was derived from an original and lengthy screen treatment by Ray Bradbury. Screen legend says that Bradbury wrote the screenplay but Harry Essex merely changed the dialogue and took the credit.

Unusual among science fiction films of the era, the alien "invaders" were portrayed by Bradbury as creatures stranded on Earth and without malicious intent toward humanity. The film can be interpreted as a metaphorical refutation of the xenophobic attitudes and ideology of the Cold War. Bradbury said "I wanted to treat the invaders as beings who were not dangerous, and that was very unusual". He offered two story outlines to the studio, one with malicious aliens, the other with benign aliens. "The studio picked the right concept, and I stayed on". In 2004, Bradbury published in one volume all four versions of his screen treatment for *It Came From Outer Space*.

Filming took place on location in and around the California towns of Palmdale, Victorville, and the Mojave Desert, as well as on Universal's sound stages.

The film's uncredited music score was composed by Irving Gertz, Henry Mancini, and Herman Stein.

Universal's makeup department submitted two alien designs for consideration by studio executives; the rejected design was saved and then later used as the "Metaluna Mutant" in Universal's 1955 science fiction film *This Island Earth*.

The special effects created for the alien spacecraft consisted of a wire-mounted iron ball, with hollowed out "windows" and with burning magnesium inside.

The Arizona setting and the alien abduction of telephone lineman and two other characters are fictionalized story elements taken from Bradbury's younger life when his father moved the family to Tucson, Arizona, where he worked as a telephone lineman.

Urban legend has it that an extra in an Army corporal's uniform seen at the "meteor" crash site is comedy writer-performer Morey Amsterdam. While the briefly glimpsed extra does indeed resemble Amsterdam, no hard evidence (e.g., cast call bureau records, interviews with Amsterdam) has ever confirmed this is actually him.

The most recent DVD re-release of *It Came From Outer Space* comes with a documentary titled "The Universe According to Universal". It was written and directed by David J. Skal and has audio commentary by Tom Weaver, in which Weaver notes the extra's similarity to Morey Amsterdam.

Reception: *It Came From Outer Space* was released in June 1953. By the end of the year it had accrued $1.6 million in US and Canadian distribution rentals, making it the year's 75th biggest earner.

Barbara Rush won the Golden Globe award in 1954 as most promising female newcomer for her role in the film. The film was nominated for AFI's Top 10 Science Fiction Films list.

In 1992, Patricia Bosworth counted *It Came From Outer Space* as one of a number of 1950s Hollywood anti-Communist propaganda films in which "aliens from outer space serve as metaphors for the Soviet menace." Bosworth's inclusion of the film as anti-Communist propaganda is at odds with both The American Film Institute and story author Ray Bradbury, who stated, "I wanted to treat the invaders as beings who were not dangerous, and that was very unusual."

No Earthlings are killed or injured in the film by the aliens. If they were intended to be stand-ins for the Soviet Union/Communists, as Bosworth professes, their presence in an Arizona town is antithetical to how Communist surrogates were portrayed in Hollywood science fiction films during the Cold War.

It should be noted that Bosworth blames her father's death in 1959, which she labels a suicide, on his being targeted by the Hollywood Blacklist. Her father, defense lawyer Bartley Crum, died later of an alcohol and barbiturate overdose.

Reviews: The New York Times review by A. H. Weiler noted "the adventure ... is merely mildly diverting, not stupendous. The space ship and its improbable crew, which keep the citizens of Sand Rock, Ariz., befuddled and terrified, should have the same effect on customers who are passionately devoted to king-sized flying saucers and gremlins."

"Brog" in Variety opined that "Direction by Jack Arnold whips up an air of suspense in putting the Harry Essex screenplay on film, and there is considerable atmosphere of reality created, which stands up well enough if the logic of it all is not examined too closely ... story proves to be good science-fiction for the legion of film fans who like scare entertainment, well done."

Since its original release, the critical response to the film has become mostly positive.

Bill Warren has written that "Arnold's vigorous direction and Bradbury's intriguing ideas meld to produce a genuine classic in its limited field."

Jonathan Rosenbaum described the film as "[A] scary black-and-white SF effort from 1953."

Phil Hardy's The Aurum Film Encyclopedia: Science Fiction observed: "Dark desert roads and sudden moments of fear underline Arnold's ability as a director of Science Fiction films, and

145

Essex's/Bradbury's lines match his images superbly." FilmCritic.com opines that the film "moves terribly slowly (despite an 80 minute running time) because the plot is overly simplistic with absolutely no surprises."

Cultural references: It Came From Outer Space is one of the classic films mentioned in the opening theme of the musical The Rocky Horror Show and its film adaptation.

The narration in the Siouxsie and the Banshees song "92 Degrees" from the 1986 album Tinderbox contains dialog from the film.

Video releases: Universal digitally restored It Came From Outer Space and in October 2016 released it on Blu-ray. The film is presented in its original widescreen polarized 3D, with three-track stereophonic sound. Also included is a non-3D "flat" version in mono sound. Both 3D and flat trailers are also included. Rounding out the Blu-ray package is a documentary on Universal's 3D films and a "making of" voice-over commentary track.

Sequel: A made-for-TV sequel entitled It Came From Outer Space II was released in 1996, starring Brian Kerwin, Elizabeth Peña, Jonathan Carrasco, Adrian Sparks, Bill McKinney, Dean Norris, Lauren Tewes, Mickey Jones and Howard Morris. Written by Jim and Ken Wheat, it was directed by Roger Duchowny, and was his final work before retiring.

The story is essentially a remake of the first film, with former small town resident Jack Putnam (Kerwin) returning and witnessing an alien craft landing. Strange things then begin to happen, with his neighbours behaving oddly and the power going off and on.

Writing for The Radio Times, Alan Jones gave the film 1 star out of 5 and called it a "lacklustre update" which was "proof positive that 40 years of technical advances can't compensate for poor production values, boring characters and a complete lack of thrills." He summarised: "file this under "don't bother"."

Leonard Maltin called the original "intriguing" and "remarkably sober for its era, with crisp performances and real restraint, even in its use of 3-D" and the 1996 effort "a much inferior remake, rather than the sequel the title suggests."

In the New York Daily News, David Bianculli wrote that "the fact that this is a remake not a sequel, yet carries the suffix II anyway, is a clue about how clearly the makers of this new version were thinking when they made it. In other words, not very."

THE LOST PLANET (1953)
Directed by Spencer Gordon Bennet
Produced by Sam Katzman
Written by Arthur Hoerl and George H. Plympton
Music by Ross DiMaggio
Cinematography by William P. Whitley
Edited by Earl Turner
Distributed by Columbia Pictures; release date: June 4, 1953
Running time: 15 chapters

Cast:
Judd Holdren as Rex Barrow
Vivian Mason as Ella Dorn
Michael Fox as Dr. Ernst Grood
Forrest Taylor as Prof. Edmund Dorn
Gene Roth as Reckov
Ted Thorpe as Tim Johnson
Karl 'Killer' Davis as Karlo, aka Robot R-4
Jack George as Jarva
Frederic Berest as Alden
John L. Cason as Hopper
Lee Roberts* as Wesley Brenn, aka Robot R-9
Nick Stuart as Darl
Leonard Penn as Ken Wopler
Joseph Mell as Lah

Cast Notes: Though the screen cast lists I. Stanford Jolley in the role of Wesley Brenn, he is obviously not playing the part. Lee Roberts plays Brenn and Jolley does not appear at all in this serial.

Unlike the *Captain Video* serial, *The Lost Planet* has a female character, Professor Dorn's daughter Ella (Vivian Mason), who strides about the Lost Planet (Bronson Canyon) in a fetching female version of the Video Ranger uniform.

Plot: Dr. Ernst Grood has succeeded in winning control over the planet Ergro as the first step in his desired conquest of the Universe.

Reporter Rex Barrow, his photographer Tim Johnson, Professor Edmund Dorn and his daughter Ella are all captured by Grood, who plans to make use of the professor's knowledge. With the help of the professor's inventions, Rex is able to free Ergro of Grood's domination, while Grood is sent on an endless voyage into space. END

Analysis and additional notes: I did try to watch this one, from beginning to end, but I could not. The staging was cheesy, the acting worse, and the props and set design really needed work. As with other films and serials, I conclude that they were trying to build a blockbuster on a $50 budget.

Books on the sound serials generally conclude that this is one of the worst serials ever made, but it still has points of interest. The bizarre performance of Michael Fox (1921–1996) as the villainous Dr. Grood is particularly memorable. This is one of Fox's first screen roles. He went on to a long and distinguished career as a character actor in dozens of feature films and hundreds of TV series right up to his final illness and death.

The Lost Planet really should stay lost, and I have nothing further to say about it. For its flaws rather than its good parts, I give *The Lost Planet* 1 out of 4 stars. IMdb gives it 5.1/10, while Rotten Tomatoes does not even have a page for it.

Chapter titles: Mystery of the Guided Missile - Trapped by the Axial Propeller - Blasted by The Thermic Disintegrator - The Mind Control Machine - The Atomic Plane - Disaster in The Stratosphere - Snared by The Prysmic Catapult - Astray in Space - The Hypnotic Ray Machine - To Free The Planet People - Dr. Grood Defies Gravity - Trapped in a Cosmo Jet - The Invisible Enemy - In the Grip of The De-Thermo Ray - Sentenced To Space

Production: *The Lost Planet* was the last of only three science fiction serials released by Columbia. This serial was, despite the characters' names, essentially a sequel to *Captain Video*, from which stock footage was taken for this serial. It was originally known as *The Planet Men*.

Michael Fox recalled that writer George Plympton would deliberately write lines that he thought the actors couldn't say such as "The atom propulse set up a radiation wall which cut off the neutron detonator impulse!"

Critical reception: In the opinions of Harmon and Glut, *The Lost Planet* is a "rather shoddy, low budget space cliffhanger."

THE MAGNETIC MONSTER (1953)

Directed by Curt Siodmak and Herbert L. Strock (uncredited)
Produced by Ivan Tors and George Van Marter
Written by Curt Siodmak and Ivan Tors
Narrated by Richard Carlson
Music by Blaine Sanford
Cinematography by Charles Van Enger
Edited by Herbert L. Strock
Production company: Ivan Tors Films
Distributed by: United Artists; release date: February 18, 1953
Running time: 76 minutes

Cast:
Richard Carlson as Dr. Jeffrey Stewart
King Donovan as Dr. Dan Forbes
Jean Byron as Connie Stewart
Harry Ellerbe as Dr. Allard
Leo Britt as Dr. Benton
Leonard Mudie as Howard Denker
Byron Foulger as Mr. Simon
Michael Fox as Dr. Serny
John Zaremba as Chief Watson (as John Zarimba)
Lee Phelps as City Engineer
Watson Downs as Mayor
Roy Engel as Gen. Behan (as Roy Engle)
Frank Gerstle as Col. Willis
John Vosper as Capt. Dyer
John Dodsworth as Dr. Carthwright
Billy Benedict as Albert
Charles Williams as Cabbie
Kathleen Freeman as Nellie (the operator)
Robert Carson as the Pilot (uncredited)
Donald Kerr as Nova Scotia Lab Worker (uncredited)

Plot: A pair of agents from the Office of Scientific Investigation (OSI), Dr. Jeffrey Stewart (Richard Carlson) and Dr. Dan Forbes (King Donovan), are sent to investigate a local appliance store. All of the store's clocks have stopped at the same time, while metal items in the store have become magnetized.

A source for this event is traced to an office located directly above the store, where various scientific equipment are found along with a dead body. There are also signs of radioactivity, but the exact cause of the store's anomalies is clearly no longer in the room or even in the immediate area.

Investigation and a request for citizen input eventually leads to a passenger airline flight carrying a scientist, Dr. Howard Denker (Leonard Mudie), who has developed signs of radiation sickness related to something he is carrying in a heavy briefcase and which he guards somewhat irrationally.

Before dying, he confesses to experimenting with an artificial radioactive isotope, called Seranium, which he had bombarded with alpha particles for 200 hours (8 days and 8 hours). Unfortunately, his microscopic creation has taken on a life of its own. The new isotope must absorb energy from its environment every 11 hours. In the process of absorption it doubles its size and mass each time, releasing deadly radiation and incredibly intense magnetic energy.

The OSI officials compute that, with its current rate of growth, it will only be a matter of weeks before the isotope becomes heavy enough to affect the Earth's rotation on its axis, eventually causing it to break out of orbit. They also discover that the isotope is impervious to any known means of destruction or to rendering it inert.

The only answer appears to be using a Canadian experimental power generator, dubbed the Deltatron, under construction in a cavern deep under the ocean somewhere in Nova Scotia. The hope is that they can bombard the isotope with so much energy in one surge that it will neutralize itself with its own "gluttony".

The two governments agree on this proposal, and the isotope is transferred to the Deltatron project, but there is a last minute objection from the engineer in charge. He will not endanger the invention with this experiment. With no time left, the lead OSI agent, Dr. Jeffrey Stewart, commandeers the huge device, which fills the whole cavern.

Stewart risks his life by activating it and revving it up to maximum output, barely escaping just before sealing off the cavern.

The machine powers up and the isotope is successfully pushed beyond its limits, completely destroying it, though the Deltatron has also been destroyed in the process. All trace of magnetism has now disappeared from the area.

The Earth has been saved. Life returns to normal, as shown by lead OSI agent, Dr. Jeffrey Stewart and his pregnant wife Connie (Jean Byron) completing the purchase of their first house and moving in shortly thereafter. END

Analysis and additional notes: Aside from the obvious mistakes in physics shown in this film, it is actually a fairly clever and suspenseful story. It was cute to imagine such a "monster" which would endanger the entire Earth with its magnetism, but the problem is that no such isotope exists or can exist.

The film does not take into account the decay rate of the isotope, and it lacks the actual sentience to "double" its size and potency like a microbe. An isotope can be altered by bombarding it with particles but it cannot "grow". So this was the first thing wrong with the film.

The second is the amount of radioactivity Dr. Denker absorbed and his isolation from the other passengers on the airliner. He was not isolated, and there is no actual explanation why the other passengers were not affected. And yet, only Dr. Denker was affected, and he was handled with bare hands by the crew. So exposure to the radiation was not treated with any reasonable care.

If it was at all possible to have a "magnetic monster" it would have affected the plane's electronics, especially its gyrocompass and other navigational controls. The plane would be in danger as long as it was in the air. Passengers' watches would have stopped, and other evidence of magnetism would have alerted the passengers that something was wrong.

Still another is the premise that such an isotope would acquire sufficient mass to shift the Earth's orbit. This has nothing to do with magnetism but with matter. The isotope, not being able to "grow", would do nothing, just as the Earth would do nothing. And since the Earth has thousands of times the mass of the isotope, it would not be affected in any way. So yeah, fun, but nonsense.

It is impossible to "neutralize" any radiation source apart from its decay rate. Instead of overpowering the isotope safely, the entire cavern and its contents should have been marked off with tape and abandoned, to continue on as a new natural reactor. There are many such similar deposits in Africa and elsewhere. The best thing to do is just stay away.

Yet, this film had its share of good stuff. The interactions between the OSI agents and the "authorities" (wherever they were) were calm and reasonable. There is a general agreement that the threat is world wide. There is no violence or gratuitous gore.

For its quirky plotline and the story overall I give The Magnetic Monster 2 stars out of 4. IMdb gives it 5.9/10, while Rotten Tomatoes gives it no rating, but only 21% of their audience liked it.

Production: *The Magnetic Monster* is the first feature film in Ivan Tors' "Office of Scientific Investigation" (OSI) trilogy, which was followed by *Riders To The Stars* (1954) and *GOG* (1954).

The Magnetic Monster marked Richard Carlson's initial foray into science fiction and horror films. He would follow it with better known titles that would forever associate him with those genres: *It Came from Outer Space* (1953), *The Maze* (1953), *Riders To The Stars* (1954), *Creature From The Black Lagoon* (1954), and such TV series as *Thriller* and *Voyage To The Bottom of The Sea.*

For the Deltatron, the film used ten minutes of footage of the atom smasher from the German science fiction thriller *Gold* (1934), directed by Karl Hartl and produced by UFA.

Though the music was composed by Blaine Sanford, it was actually conducted by Korla Pandit (uncredited).

The Los Alamos MANIAC computer was featured in an effort to lend a scientific air to the film. The UCLA Differential Analyzer from the same era is also shown briefly for the same reason.

THE NEANDERTHAL MAN (1953)

Directed by Ewald André Dupont
Produced by Ilse Lahn, Jack Pollexfen, Aubrey Wisberg and Edward Small (uncredited)
Written by Aubrey Wisberg and Jack Pollexfen
Music by Albert Glasser
Cinematography by Stanley Cortez
Edited by Fred R. Feitshans Jr.
Production company: Global Productions Inc.
Distributed by United Artists; release date June 19, 1953
Running time: 78 minutes

Cast:
Robert Shayne (listed as "Shane" in the credits) as Prof. Clifford Groves
Joyce Terry (listed as "Joy" in the credits) as Jan Groves
Richard Crane as Dr. Ross Harkness
Doris Merrick as Ruth Marshall
Robert Long as George Oakes
Jeanette Quinn as Celia
Lee Morgan as Charlie Webb
Beverly Garland as Nola Mason
Dick Rich as Sheriff Andy Andrews
Robert Easton as Danny
Anthony Jochim as naturalist at conference
Marshall Bradford as naturalist conference chair
Uncredited:
Eric Colmar as Buck Hastings
Frank Gerstle as Mr. Wheeler
William Fawcett as Dr. Fairchild
Robert Bray as Jim Newcomb
Hank Mann as naturalist
Crane Whitney as State Police Chief
Tom Monroe as unnamed man
Wally Rose as the Neanderthal Man

Plot: At home in California's High Sierras, Professor Clifford Groves (Robert Shayne) hears glass breaking and looks up in fear from his book, *Neanderthal Man and The Stone Age*. He finds his lab window smashed and the room wrecked. His adult daughter Jan (Joyce Terry) is awakened by the noise. Groves sends her back to bed, telling her that he has to go attend to business.

Meanwhile, Mr. Wheeler (Frank Gerstle) spots a huge saber toothed tiger while hunting. That night at Webb's Cafe, the locals tease him. "Three times the size of a mountain lion and got the tusks the size of an elephant - t'ain't natural," says Danny (Robert Easton). Game Warden George Oakes (Robert Long) comes in. Wheeler leaves and Charlie Webb (Lee Morgan) tells him Wheeler's story.

While driving home, a saber toothed tiger jumps onto Oakes's car. He scares it off by honking the car's horn.

Later, Oakes and Sheriff Andy Andrews (Dick Rich) make plaster casts of the giant tiger's footprints. Oakes takes one to Dr. Ross Harkness (Richard Crane) in Los Angeles. Oakes eventually convinces the incredulous Harkness that the cast is real. Harkness says he will drive up that weekend to investigate.

When Harkness stops at Webb's Cafe, waitress Nola Mason (Beverly Garland) introduces him to Ruth Marshall (Doris Merrick), who is on her way to see her fiance', Groves. She has been stranded because her car has broken down on the road. Harkness drives her to Groves's house, where Jan tells them that Groves is in Los Angeles speaking before the Naturalist's Club.

There, Groves lectures the club on his theory that Neanderthal man was more intelligent than "modern man" because Neanderthals had bigger brains. The club members scoff at him and demand proof. Groves responds with insults instead of diagrams. The chairman (Marshall Bradford) adjourns the meeting, telling Groves not to come back. Groves angrily says to the empty room that he'll show them proof if that's what they want.

Jan invites Harkness to stay at their house. At breakfast, a grouchy Groves complains about Harkness being there, but Ruth insists that he remain, since his line of inquiry is similar. Reluctantly, Groves shows Harkness the lab, where several different colors of domestic cats are housed in wire cages. They all react with hostility and hissing to Groves's entrance. But they are all calmed by the presence of the housekeeper, a deaf mute called Celia (Jeanette Quinn), who feeds and cares for them. Groves explains her to Harkness, who is friendly and encouraging to her. Then, when Groves sends her out, the cats react again. Harkness takes note but says nothing.

Then Oakes arrives, and he and Harkness head out to look for the saber toothed tiger. They locate and kill it, but Harkness says he fears there are others up in the hills. He begins to suspect that there is a connection between the cats in the lab and the tigers, but keeps it to himself for now.

Back at the lab, Ruth and Groves quarrel about their deteriorating relationship. He has been so disagreeable about his ouster from the Naturalist Club and Ruth has become his target. He throws her out, then injects himself with the serum that he has been using to turn the cats into saber toothed tigers. It is a retroserum which he thinks will make him regress to the more primitive form of Man.

He reverts to a Neanderthal Man [or, what everyone once assumed they look like]. Out in the woods, he kills hunter Jim Newcomb (Robert Bray) and his dog, then returns home and becomes Groves again. When he has rested, he writes in his diary that this most recent regression was the fastest yet and the recovery was the slowest.

"I gloried in my strength and ferocity," he writes, noting also that he was overcome by the "hungry urge to kill." Then he spontaneously turns into the Neanderthal Man without the benefit of the serum and runs off into the night.

Harkness sneaks into Groves's lab and finds photos that Groves took as he regressed Celia, his control subject for his experiments. She appears to take on more hair, and her teeth go wonky, but she is not aggressive in her demeanor.

Buck Hastings (Eric Colmar) and Nola go on a picnic, where he snaps some glamour shots of her. But the Neanderthal Man kills him while Nola is behind a bush changing clothes. As she looks in horror at Buck's dead body on the ground, the Neanderthal Man carries her off kicking and screaming. There is no one else around to help her.

Sometime later, Oakes phones Jan and says that Buck has been found murdered. During the call, Celia sees Nola standing outside and alerts Harkness, who carries Nola in. She is hysterical and her clothes are torn. Buck, she says, was killed by something "not human." Then she cries, "He tried to pull me by my hair and then he ... then he ..." and collapses into tears, wailing. Jan calls Webb's Cafe, tells Webb what happened and asks him to send for the local doctor, Dr. Fairchild (William Fawcett).

Harkness shows Jan and Celia the photos of Celia being regressed to a Neanderthal Woman. Celia signs back that she has no memory of any of it. Harkness has noticed that one of the lab cats started to yowl whenever it saw a syringe. When he injects it with the serum, it turns into a saber toothed tiger and escapes through an open window.

Jan and Harkness read Groves's diary together. Groves has written that the serum works on cats, but not dogs, and not fully on women but completely on men. (Something to do with the Y chromosome?) Suspecting that Groves is the Neanderthal Man, they set out to find him before the State Police and Sheriff's posse does.

They stop at Webb's Cafe and see that Webb has been injured by the Neanderthal Man. Jan says that Ruth's door has been smashed in and that she's gone. "I reckon he got her, too," says a dazed Webb.

Dr. Fairchild tells Harkness and Jan that the posse has cornered the Neanderthal Man in a cave and that Ruth is trapped with the monster. Harkness walks to the cave, alone and unarmed, and tells Ruth to let the Neanderthal Man run away. The monster does, but then a saber toothed tiger jumps him. The posse holds off shooting for awhile as the Neanderthal Man is being mauled. Then they deal with both.

Now at home on his deathbed, the Neanderthal Man changes back to Groves one final time and utters his last words: "Better ... this ...way." END

Analysis and additional notes: Again an instance of a mad scientist who is ahoist on his own petard. We hardly know why Groves was so insistant that his experiments should create the better man. According to science, the Neanderthals were a more primitive form of Man, but lacked all the aggression of more modern man. This is the precise opposite of the kind of Neanderthal man Groves transformed himself into. One of the reasons they died out as a distinct species is that apparently they were assimilated into more modern societies until their blood line was completely integrated with ours.

Climate change and other natural factors were also responsible for their dissolution, as they were driven to warmer climes where they met with more developed societies. Even then, they predated modern man by only a few thousand years, and were apparently genetically compatible. Some scientific theories aver that Neanderthal genes are an integral part of the modern human genome.

We also see that Groves found that only cats were compatible with the serum, and the male of the species. His assertion that the Neanderthal Man's skull is larger than a Homo sapien's does not guarantee that the larger brain is any better at translating stimuli into data. For example, a whale's brain is way larger than man's but a whale lacks the faculty of speech, mathematic analysis, and so on. So the physical size of a given brain means nothing in terms of rational thought, interacting in a "civilized" manner, or any other indication of modern behavior and socialization.

We also have no examples of Neanderthal Man which are extant. We have no idea of their organizational skills or their rituals, apart from some evidence that Neanderthals interred their dead and left memento mori in the graves. There are in fact very few graves, which means that Neanderthal Man was constantly nomadic as they pursued migrating animals in the wild. One cannot assume anything else about the Neanderthals without more evidence.

I think that Groves was already mad to begin with, when he embarked on his disastrous and failed project. He was enflamed when the Naturalist Club rejected him. He did not realize the the word "naturalist" means "an expert in or student of natural history." This means studying a subject in situ and without tampering with the natural course of evolution. Groves did neither one. Instead, he hastened to force the result without thinking things through.

For its somewhat incomprehensible plotline and erroneous scientific method, I give *The Neanderthal Man* 1.5 stars out of 4, and I am being generous. IMdb gives it 4.4/10 (ouch!) and Rotten Tomatoes gives it a resounding 0! (ouch, ouch!). Only 10% of their audience liked it.

Production: The film's working title was "Madagascar". Production began in early December 1952 at Eagle-Lion Studios in Los Angeles. The film was released in the USA on June 19, 1953 and in Spain and Brazil at unknown dates. 3 minutes was trimmed from its running time when it opened in the UK, reducing its time from 78 minutes to 75 minutes. Stuntman Wally Rose was the man in the Neanderthal Man mask, not Robert Shayne.

Reception: The pressbook for the movie suggested ways theater owners could bring in the audience. One idea was to "make an oversize footprint stencil and paint them on sidewalks of streets leading to the box-office," while another was to "dress up a man in costume to simulate the 'half man-half beast' in the picture ... Use as a ballyhoo stunt in front of your theatre or in your lobby. Can also be mounted on flat top truck and sent around town."

To my knowledge, no such stunts were employed, since early reviews before its release drew yawns.

Besides, given the social atmosphere of the time, I could see a fistfight or two between theater patrons and the stuntmen. This is mostly due to a natural animosity between theater goers and people already dressed in costume who parade up and down in front of, for example, Graumann's Chinese Theater in Hollywood. There we have seen several cases of assault and battery in the last few years. Theater goers do not care to be deterred by these people, who are panhandling for their daily wages, from buying their tickets and going in peacefully.

The Neanderthal Man was not well-received by critics in 1953, when it was mentioned at all. According to the "Review Digest" in the 1 August 1953 issue of <u>BoxOffice</u> magazine, the movie was rated "fair" by <u>Film Daily</u>, <u>Harrison's Reports</u> and <u>BoxOffice</u> itself. <u>The Hollywood Reporter</u> rated it as "very poor," and calls the film "an overlong, dull conversation piece."

The movie had not been reviewed by <u>Variety</u>, <u>Parents' Magazine</u> or <u>The New York Daily News</u> some 6 weeks after its release. In <u>BoxOffice</u>'s "Feature Review," an anonymous reviewer wrote that "...the film lends itself particularly on midnight 'spook show' programs." The reviewer went on to say that it "should qualify for duty as a supporting attraction in most bookings" and that the "picture can be played with an assurance of adequate acceptance."

Many later reviewers called the movie "a variation of the Jekyll and Hyde theme," often adding the words "uninteresting" and "clichéd" to the description.

Bill Warren said the film has "almost nothing to recommend it."

Academic Michael Klossner refers to it as a "clichéd, Jekyll/Hyde rip-off," but notes favorably "the beautiful mountain settings, the colorful rustics and [Stanley] Cortez's sharp b&w photography."

The Neanderthal Man mask was frequently commented upon. Ken Hanke said it was "an appalling over-the-head mask (with stylishly wavy hair) that looks exactly like what it is."

Phil Hardy noted that the mask "didn't flex with [Wally Rose's] facial movements."

Bill Warren, as well, pointed out that "the elaborate ... mask doesn't move or flex with the performer's face, and the eyes seem to be painted on." He added that "the makeup/mask also varies throughout the film, as if different artists worked each day."

Author and film critic Leonard Maltin awarded the film 1.5 star out of 4, calling it "colorless and cheap".

General comments about *The Neanderthal Man* covered everything from direction to its overall quality as a film. Michael Hanke called it "a film that might be described as being scraped off the bottom of the barrel. That, of course, means the movie is like catnip to lovers of Bad Cinema," although adding that it is a "very low-rent production that is indefensible on every level." Nonetheless, Hanke rated the movie as 3 stars out of 5 and included it in "The Thursday Night Horror Picture Show" series, which he hosted. It ran on September 4, 2014 in the Carolina Asheville movie theater in Asheville, North Carolina.

"It was unquestionably a cheap and rapidly made film," wrote Bill Warren, "and Dupont brought none of the inventiveness to it that other directors who worked on equally shaky conditions applied to their films. The picture is unimaginative, dull and ponderous ...."

Similary, Hardy said that "DuPont, a minor talent in the best of circumstance, could bring no innovation" to the "clichéd" script.

The reviewing division of the Catholic News Service for the United States Council of Catholic Bishops called *The Neanderthal Man* a "horror clunker" with "stylized violence and hokey menace." USCCB rated it "A-II," acceptable for "adults and adolescents," but not children.

Klossner pointed to the many scientific inaccuracies in the film. He writes that "perhaps no film has expressed the horror and contempt too many people feel about primitive man as much as Neanderthal Man" and says "when Groves becomes a Neanderthal, he is a savage killer with a (completely inaccurate) apelike face and long claws."

Bill Warren agreed, noting that the Neanderthal Man "doesn't look like any reconstruction of a Neanderthal man that I've ever seen; furthermore, the creature we see behaves more like a vicious ape-man monster than the Neanderthals, who were probably not much different from Homo sapiens in general behavior."

The film also includes a sequence that Warren calls "very unusual for the period." As Nola describes her ordeal after being carried off by the Neanderthal Man, who has just murdered Buck at their picnic, her torn clothing and hysterical demeanor suggests that "the movie is clearly implying rape." No actual suggestions of rape had ever occurred in a motion picture before, though I suppose her reaction to being manhandled by the monster would easily lead to that conclusion.

PHANTOM FROM SPACE (1953)

Produced and directed by W. Lee Wilder
Screenplay by William Raynor and Myles Wilder; story by Myles Wilder
Music by William Lava
Cinematography by William H. Clothier
Edited by George Gale
Production company: Planet Filmplays
Distributed by United Artists
Release date: May 15, 1953; running time: 73 minutes

Cast:
Ted Cooper as Lt. Hazen
Tom Daly as Charlie
Steve Acton as Mobile Center Dispatcher
Burt Wenland as Agent Joe
Lela Nelson as Betty Evans
Harry Landers as Lt. Bowers
Burt Arnold as Darrow
Sandy Sanders as First Policeman
Harry Strang as Neighbor
Jim Bannon as Desk Sgt. Jim
Jack Daly as Joe Wakeman
Michael Mark as Refinery Watchman
Rudolph Anders as Dr. Wyatt
James Seay as Major Andrews
Noreen Nash as Barbara Randall

Plot: Federal Communications Commission (FCC) investigators arrive in the San Fernando Valley after what appears to be a flying saucer crash, causing massive interference with teleradio transmissions. During their investigation, they receive eyewitness reports of what appears to be a man dressed in a bizarre outfit, which appears to be radioactive and thus a public threat. Everything he touches is contaminated.

Their investigation reveals that the man is actually a humanoid creature from outer space, who is invisible without his spacesuit. They start a massive manhunt for the alien. They track him to the Griffith Observatory, where he is trapped inside and cannot escape.

A female lab assistant discovers that he can be seen using ultraviolet light. The alien tries to communicate by tapping out a code, but no one can understand it. All attempts to learn what it means meet with failure, but it is clear that the alien has not harmed anyone so far.

Now breathing heavily because his breathing gas reserves are running low, the alien is trapped on the Griffith telescope's upper platform. Because he cannot survive without his breathing gas, he finally falters and then falls to his death. His body briefly becomes visible before evaporating completely. END

Analysis and additional notes: Here we see a vague attempt to be sympathetic toward the alien, even though he is deadly to others by virtue of his radioactivity. While two schools of thought battle for supremacy, we are attracted by the uniqueness and novelty of a plot in which most of us find ourselves rooting for the alien. Picture if you will an expedition to another planet, where the natives little understand us and our mission, and attempts to communicate on a common frame of reference are doomed to fail.

For once, no one goes in with guns blazing. While the investigators must keep a respectful distance, they do try to extend a hand of some friendship. Perhaps the alien's spacecraft met with a mechanical or software failure. Perhaps some miscommunication caused him to fear the society he is trapped in. Whatever the reason, we are not allowed enough time to learn who he is or even where he comes from. For this story, it is enough that he is here. What would you do?

I must point out that this is the first film since *The Thing From Another World* (1951) in which we see a rational argument about the science behind the event carried on between the scientists. It also presaged the end of the fistfight/gunfight ridden serials in which little dialogue occurs to fill out the plot.

But also, the film had such bad production values that it was put on the "B" list of films. For this and other problems, I give *Phantom From Space* 2 stars out of 4. IMdb gives it 4.1/10, and Rotten Tomatoes does not have a rating for it. However, only 7% of their audience liked it.

Production: W. Lee Wilder formed a film production company in the early 1950s called Planet Filmplays for the purpose of producing and directing "quickie" low budget science fiction films, with screenplays co-written with his son Miles.

Phantom From Space uses stock footage of radar rigs. Some of this stock footage would later reappear in *Killers From Space* (1954).

Phantom From Space opened on May 15, 1953. Legend Films released a colorized version of the film.

Reception: Film historian and critic Glenn Erickson was humorous in his review of the film's DVD release. He wrote, "after a couple of uninspired potboilers in the late 1940s (The Pretender is actually a good movie), Wilder hit his groove of incompetence with this no-budget wonder concerning the saddest space invader on record ... Endless talky scenes alternate with the entire cast of 6 running back and forth in the old interior of the Griffith Planetarium. The poor invader is a bald Muscle Beach type in a radioactive space suit and a helmet that appears to be the same prop from Robot Monster, somewhat altered."

There are no further notes to be had on this film.

PROJECT MOONBASE (aka "Project Moon Base" in UK) (1953)
Directed by Richard Talmadge
Produced by Jack Seaman
Screenplay and story by Robert A. Heinlein and Jack Seaman
Music by Herschel Burke Gilbert
Cinematography by William C. Thompson
Edited by Roland Gross
Production company: Galaxy Pictures Inc.

Distributed by Lippert Pictures
Release date: September 4, 1953; running time: 63 minutes

Cast:
Donna Martell as Colonel Briteis
Hayden Rorke as Gen. 'Pappy' Greene
Ross Ford as Maj. Bill Moore
Larry Johns as Doctor Wernher
Herb Jacobs as Mr. Roundtree
Barbara Morrison as Polly Prattles
Ernestine Barrier as Madame President
James Craven as Commodore Carlson
John Hedloe as Adjutant
Peter Adams as Captain Carmody

Plot: Set in the future of 1970, the United States is considering building bases on the Moon. Colonel Briteis [pronounced "bright eyes"](Donna Martell), Major Bill Moore (Ross Ford), and Doctor Wernher (Larry Johns) are sent to orbit the Moon in order to survey landing sites for future lunar missions.

However, Dr. Wernher turns out to be an impostor whose mission is to destroy the U.S.'s orbital space station, which he plans to do by colliding the rocket with the station on the way back from the Moon.

While on the way out, however, Wernher inadvertently gives his identity away, but does not reveal which government he works for. In the ensuing struggle for control of the rocket, Col. Briteis has to make an emergency landing on the Moon.

Now that they have all been marooned, Dr. Wernher redeems himself by helping to establish communications with Earth, but an accident results in his untimely death.

In response to this unexpected turn of events, the U.S. authorities decide to make the immobilized spaceship the core of a new moon base. As long as it there, they consider it U.S. territory.

To avoid a scandal, the Earth based commander, General Greene (Hayden Rorke), cajoles Major Moore into proposing to Colonel Briteis. Social convention demands that they must marry so as not to have an unmarried male and female astronaut alone in close quarters for weeks. Briteis accepts, but requests that Major Moore be promoted to Brigadier General after they are married so that he will outrank her.

163

And so a rather dry and unromantic wedding ensues. END

Analysis and additional notes: I must admit that I have not read anything by Heinlein but so many films have been made from his stories that I feel I know his bibliography fairly well. I notice that he is willing to make women equal with men as far as job equality is concerned, but his women always end up dependent on the men in the end. So it is with Col. Briteis, who holds her own right up until the wedding.

We don't know why she would want to elevate Major Moore to Brigadier General so that he will outrank her. In fact, she deserves the promotion herself. But most of the producers in that time appeared to practice a mild chauvinism where women are concerned. In 1953 women occupied minor positions in the background during the Korean War rather than face actual combat situations. I suppose it's par for the course, but by the actual 1970 women were emerging as pilots and other soldierly roles during the war in Viet Nam. Please keep this in mind when watching this film.

After many films I have seen in which stock footage (chiefly that of the German V-2 rocket) was employed to depict the rockets and other craft in use, often interchagably so that we don't know the actual design of any craft, we are instead treated to animations of new rocket designs and even the orbital satellite. The animated lander on the Moon appeared to prophecy the shape of the actual lander in 1969.

However, I was disappointed with what was considered the "wardrobe of the future" in the interior scenes. We see both men and women wearing nothing but t-shirts and shorts, with a small regimental cap and some medaling, and short boots. Nothing like the heavily designed space suits in the 1970s.

There are actually no gravitational or inertial movements in the cramped "cabin", which was actually a few cots and a single wall against which the actors played. And, while it was intriguing to see communications back and forth via a flat screen television, it looked to me like the speaker was sitting on a chair on the other side of a hole in the wall framed to appear like a screen.

There was again no actual decoration which indicated to me that there was any artwork or creative touch to any of the décor; rendering the future as a flat and uninteresting time, bereft of social creativity. It made me think that after a couple of weeks of bland and uninteresting cohabitation, Briteis and Moore would be at each other's throats from the boredom alone.

For its feeble attempt at outdoing the other films, I give *Project Moonbase* (or Moon Base) 1.5 stars out of 4. IMdb gives it a harsh 2.9/10, while Rotten Tomatoes gives it no rating, but only 8% of their audience liked it.

Production: This movie and *Cat-Women of The Moon* (1953) were made using some of the same sets and costumes. The two films were then released within one day of each other. This film was shot in 10 days, rehearsal time regardless. There are no further notes.

ROBOT MONSTER (1953)

Produced and directed by Phil Tucker and Al Zimbalist
Written by Wyott Ordung
Narrated by Slick Slavin (uncredited)
Music by Elmer Bernstein
Cinematography by Jack Greenhalgh
Edited by Bruce Schoengarth and Merrill White
Production company: Three Dimensional Pictures, Inc.
Distributed by Astor Pictures; release date June 24, 1953
Running time: 62 minutes; budget: $50,000; box office: $1 million

Cast:
George Nader as Roy
Claudia Barrett as Alice
Selena Royle (credited as Selena Royale) as Mother
John Mylong as The Professor
Gregory Moffett as Johnny
Pamela Paulson as Carla
George Barrows as Ro-Man/Great Guidance
John Brown as Voice of Ro-Man/Great Guidance

Plot: Evil Moon robot Ro-Man Extension XJ-2 (George Barrows), referred to as just Ro-Man, has seemingly destroyed all human life on Earth with a Calcinator death ray; all except for eight humans that remain alive.

The survivors are an older scientist, The Professor (John Mylong), his wife (Selena Royle), his two daughters Alice (Claudia Barrett) and Carla (Pamela Paulson), his young son Johnny (Gregory Moffett), his assistant Roy (George Nader), and two space pilots (uncredited) that shortly take off in a spaceship for an orbiting space platform.

All eight have now developed an immunity to Ro-Man's death ray, having received an experimental antibiotic serum developed by the Professor. He has also developed a "wall of invisibility" (a primitive cloaking field) which enables them to hide out from Ro-Man for the time being. But it is only a matter of time before the robot will discover him and his family and friends.

Ro-Man's mission is to destroy all humans, even if it means his physically killing them one by one, before the grand plan to subjugate the Earth is complete. After fruitless negotiations with the fleeing rocket, Ro-Man, with a laser in hand, destroys the spaceship headed for the orbiting platform, killing the two pilots aboard.

He later captures and strangles the youngest daughter, Carla, then tosses Roy to his death over a cliff. After some searching he manages to capture Alice and drags her to a cave nearby, where he has set up his base of operations.

Ro-Man's mission is waylaid when he develops an illogical attraction to Alice. Upon consulting with his leader the Great Guidance, he refuses to eliminate her, saying that he knows he must kill her but he cannot. He does not understand the illogical reaction, which is possibly some form of robotic compassion. The Great Guidance judges Ro-Man to be defective, and threatens to destroy him if he does not comply. Ro-Man, in a daze of conflicting impulses, refuses and signs off.

The alien leader, the Great Guidance, teleports to Earth. The Great Guidance then attempts to finish the genocide by releasing prehistoric dinosaurs and a massive earthquake on the remaining survivors. Fade to a great white...

Johnny awakes from a concussion induced coma. Up to now, all that has happened in the story has just been a nightmare. His parents, who had been looking for him, rejoice and take him home.

Suddenly, Ro-Man, his arms raised in a threatening manner, rushes out of a cave. It seems that Johnny's nightmare was prophetic.
END

Analysis and additional notes: I was being serious about what is a terribly comic film in my description of the plot. I allowed for a certain amount of logic in the flow of the plot. But logical it was not. If, as we are supposed to presume, the robot aliens had wanted to invade and take over, doing it with one agent would never work. I could not believe in the premise.

If the story was meant to be a boy's nightmare, then he needed a good session with a psychiatrist, because he dreamed that his sister Carla was murdered by the robot monster; and his other sister Alice was abducted and held prisoner while the monster lost its objectivity. It actually says more about Johnny than whatever else is happening. But even this reveal does not justify the strange pacing and staging of the whole story.

What I could not and will never abide was the costuming, which included the costume for the evil Ro-Man. It consisted of an astronaut helmet for a head and an ape costume for the body. Hardly to be taken seriously, and hardly terrifying. I could launch into a long winded discussion of costume design, but I will spare your eyeballs.

The staging of the Professor's home base was a blank wall of a ruin against a tumble of boulders, basically out in the open and exposed to every danger; and Ro-Man makes his base a cave in the mountainside instead of his own space ship. There is very little else in the way of props (we see nothing of the instrumentality for the Professor's cloaking field), and Ro-Man's equipment operates on some other energy, because there is no wiring or connection to any external electrical source. And, what was with the bubbles emerging from it ad infinitum? Nothing is explained rationally.

For the actors' vague attempts at treating their roles with some seriousness, I give *Robot Monster* 1.5 stars out of 4. IMdb gives it 2.9/10, and Rotten Tomatoes gives it a surprising 36% fresh. 37% of their audience liked it. Apparently it holds a cult following despite its ridiculous and irrational presentation.

Production: 25 year old writer/director Phil Tucker made *Robot Monster* in 4 days for an estimated $16,000. Except for a few scenes at a house in Los Angeles and a building site near Dodger Stadium, most of the base footage was filmed outdoors in Bronson Canyon, the site of innumerable motion pictures and TV settings. Principal photography on *Robot Monster* wrapped on March 23, 1953.

Robot Monster's very low budget did not allow for a robot costume as first intended, so Tucker hired his friend Barrows, who had made his own gorilla suit, to play Ro-Man; Tucker then added the space helmet. Nightclub comic Slick Slavin reportedly filmed an opening prologue for the movie which has since been lost.

Robot Monster is similar in its plot to *Invaders From Mars* (1953), released a month earlier by 20th Century Fox. Both films contain a young boy stumbling upon an alien invasion and who is captured as he struggles to save his family and himself. As the alien commences the final destruction of Earth, the boy awakens to find it was all a dream. Claudia Barrett recalled in an interview that the film's original screenplay was designed as reality, but director Tucker changed his mind and then shot a new twist ending that showed the film's story has been a boy's dream, which was (naturally) premonitory.

In *Robot Monster*'s opening credits, "N. A. Fischer Chemical Products" is given prominent credit for the "Billion Bubble Machine", used as part of Ro-Man's communication device for reporting to his superior, the Great Guidance.

3D: *Robot Monster* was shot and projected in dual-strip, polarized 3D. The stereoscopic photography in the film is considered by many critics to be of a high quality, especially for a film whose crew had little experience with the newly developed camera rig. Producer Al Zimbalist later told The New York Times that shooting the film in 3D added an extra $4,510.54 to the budget.

Special effects: *Robot Monster*'s special effects include stock footage from *One Million B.C.* (1940), *Lost Continent* , and *Flight To Mars* (1951); a brief appearance of the *Rocketship X-M* (1950) spaceship boarding; and a matte painting of the ruins of New York City from *Captive Women* (1952).

Film score: *Robot Monster*'s music was composed by Elmer Bernstein, who also composed *Cat-Women of The Moon* the same year; and later, the more prestigious *The Great Escape*, *The Magnificent Seven*, *The Ten Commandments*, and Michael Jackson's *Thriller* music video.

Bernstein recalled he was stuck in a period where he was "greylisted" because of his left wing politics and only offered minor films, but said he enjoyed the challenge of trying to help a film. Wyatt

Ordung stated that Bernstein scored the film with an 8 piece orchestra, and Capitol Records expressed interest in producing an album from it.

Release: *Robot Monster* was released by Astor Pictures on June 24, 1953, at a runtime of 62 minutes.

Reception: *Robot Monster* was originally released with the Three Dimension Pictures short *Stardust In Your Eyes*, starring nightclub comedian Trustin Howard as Slick Slaven. In December of 1953, the Los Angeles Times reported that "theater men" considered the film "one of the top turkeys of the year."

The film is frequently considered one of the worst movies ever made, with film historian Leonard Maltin calling it "one of the genuine legends of Hollywood - embarrassingly, hilariously awful...just dig that bubble machine with the TV antenna."

Robot Monster was included as a selection in the 1978 book *The Fifty Worst Films of All Time (And How They Got That Way)*.

Despite rumors to the contrary, *Robot Monster* received some decent reviews, and it grossed $1 million during its initial theatrical release, more than 62 times its original investment. It was quickly sold to television, where its infamy slowly spread to new generations of cult movie fans. They liked it because it was egregiously bad. Who knew?

The Los Angeles Times called it "a crazy mixed up movie ... even children may be a little bored by it all".

A review in Variety noted, "judged on the basis of novelty, as a showcase for the Tru-Stereo Process, Robot Monster comes off surprisingly well, considering the extremely limited budget ($50,000) and schedule on which the film was shot."

Harrison's Reports called it "the poorest 3-D picture that [has] been made so far", adding, "The story is completely illogical, and the supposed monsters from another planet are laughable. Even the acting, at times, is ridiculous."

Aftermath: In December of 1953, it was reported that director Phil Tucker tried to commit suicide at the Hollywood Knickerbocker Hotel. He was only saved because he had written a suicide letter and sent it to a newspaper, who sent a reporter and some detectives to the hotel. He was discovered with a pass in his pocket from the psychopathic ward of a veteran's hospital.

In the letter, Tucker said he had not been paid for *Robot Monster* and was unable to get a job. "When I was refused a job - even as an usher," Tucker wrote, "I finally realized my future in the film industry was bleak." It was revealed that Tucker and the producer had quarreled, and film exhibitors had instructions not to let Tucker in to see the film unless he paid admission.

In *Keep Watching the Skies!*, a comprehensive history of 1950s and early 1960s American science fiction films, author Bill Warren claimed that Tucker's attempted suicide was due to depression and a dispute with the film's distributor, who had allegedly refused to pay Tucker his contracted percentage of the film's profits.

This would suggest that the production company had no knowledge of tort law, and risked being legally shut down for refusing to pay a sum they could not afford. If they were that cheap, they should not have been in business to begin with.

The actors connected to *Robot Monster* included George Nader, who won the Golden Globe in 1955 as "Most Promising Male Newcomer of the Year"; although his award was not tied to his *Robot Monster* performance. He signed with Universal Studios, where he starred only in secondary features, while other new male stars, like Tony Curtis and Rock Hudson, were assigned to major film roles.

Selena Royle, an MGM stock player, had a durable film career beginning in 1941, but it ended in 1951 when she was branded a Communist sympathizer. She refused to appear before the House Committee on Unamerican Activities and eventually cleared her name. But by then the damage to her reputation had already been done; she made only two additional films, *Robot Monster* being her last. No doubt she found another line of work.

In popular culture: A brief scene from *Robot Monster* can be seen in the 1984 music video for The Cars' single "You Might Think".

The film was featured in a 1986 episode of the Canned Film Festival, and a 1989 episode of *Mystery Science Theater 3000*.

Ro-Man is seen in the 2003 film *Looney Tunes: Back in Action*.

Ro-Man was the inspiration for the fictional monster SCP-2006, from the SCP Foundation online writing community, which launched in 2008.

In the 2010 animated film *Megamind*, the character Minion (voiced by David Cross) resembles Ro-Man, with the body of a gorilla and a transparent head with a fish in it.

SPACEWAYS (1953)

Directed by Terence Fisher
Produced by Michael Carreras
Written by Paul Tabori and Richard Landau; based on a radio play
by Charles Eric Maine
Cinematography by Reginald H. Wyer
Edited by Maurice Rootes
Production company: Hammer Film Productions
Distributed by Lippert Pictures (US) and Exclusive Films (UK)
Release date: August 7, 1953; running time: 76 mins

Cast:
Howard Duff as Dr. Stephen Mitchell
Eva Bartok as Dr. Lisa Frank
Alan Wheatley as Dr. Smith
Philip Leaver as Professor Koepler
Michael Medwin as Dr. Toby Andrews
Andrew Osborn as Dr. Philip Crenshaw
Cecile Chevreau as Vanessa Mitchell
Anthony Ireland as General Hayes
Hugh Moxey as Colonel Alfred Daniels
David Horne as Minister

Plot: Engineer Dr. Stephen Mitchell (Howard Duff) is part of a British space program that plans to launch a satellite that will permanently orbit earth. At a cocktail party, it is announced to the program's staff that the satellite project has been approved by the Defense Council.

Mitchell's wife Vanessa (Cecile Chevreau) is not enthusiastic about the new project, nor with having to live at a high security military base in such utter secrecy. During the party, she sneaks away with Dr. Philip Crenshaw (Andrew Osborn), with whom she is having an affair. Dr. Mitchell leaves the party with Dr. Lisa Frank (Eva Bartok), a mathematician on the project who is in love with him.

So far they are carrying on a purely Platonic friendship, where Lisa is always encouraging and supportive. But the standard operating procedure is that no staff member may engage in a romantic affair with another. Mitchell confesses to her that his marriage is on the rocks. Lisa asks if he ever loved Vanessa. Mitchell hedges for a moment, then finally says no.

When Mitchell returns home, he has an argument with Vanessa about her affair with Crenshaw. He had been made aware of her having kissed Crenshaw after she left the party with him. Vanessa discloses her displeasure with Mitchell. He would rather fly into the stars than to give her the lavish lifestyle she prefers. Mitchell says nothing while she vents her spleen, then tells her flat out that marrying her was a mistake. Then he leaves to commiserate with his partners, leaving her alone with her intransigence.

The satellite rocket soon launches, but it does not reach its maximum altitude. During the investigation of the cause both Crenshaw and Vanessa have mysteriouly disappeared. Dr. Smith (Alan Wheatley) secretly investigates and comes to the conclusion that the two were murdered by Dr. Mitchell. He claims Mitchell hid their bodies in the spacecraft's fuel tanks, and the weight displacement of the bodies caused the lack of enough fuel to make the first launch successful.

Smith approaches Mitchell with the accusation and reveals that Crenshaw was also a spy, who had concealed having a degree from a German university in order to get on the project. Mitchell denies having any knowledge of this. He is as surprised about it as Smith.

Mitchell decides to go into space on the second rocket in order to prove his innocence. Smith confesses to Mitchell that he believes him, but he must do his job properly. Mitchell does not hold this against Smith, but argues that in order to discover the truth he must go forward. Smith leaves with the promise that he will do just that.

Lisa comes forward to tell Mitchell that she believes him, and will do all she can to help. But the crew complement has already been selected and she is not on the list. They touch hands; it is the only physical contact they have had since their last meeting.

Smith discovers that there was a new team member added just prior to the disappearance, and that a security guard had died in an "accident" a week earlier. Crenshaw had appeared on the scene rather suddenly after the guard's death.

Soon afterward, Smith and the police discover that Crenshaw and Vanessa are actually hiding out in a seaside cottage. Crenshaw has been planning to head to the east instead of going to America, as he had promised Vanessa. He is confronted by Smith about it.

During a violent scuffle between Crenshaw and Smith, Vanessa is accidentally shot. She dies without a word. Crenshaw is arrested and charged with espionage and the murder of the security guard.

After the second rocket launches into space, Mitchell is surprised to see that Lisa is on board. She had convinced Toby Andrews (Michael Medwin) to let her go on the flight instead of him. Toby was always supportive of her and saw the logic in her argument. Together they check the fuel tanks on board, but find no bodies in them.

Mitchell and Lisa jettison the spaceship's second stage but the operation fails, resulting in an explosion that causes their spacecraft to go out of control. They are tossed and jostled as the rocket begins to tumble off course. They are faced with the possibility that the rocket will never return to Earth.

Their pilot releases the fail-safe, saving them from destruction and allowing the spaceship to return safely to Earth. Lisa and Mitchell pledge their love to each other and plan to marry. END

Analysis and additional notes: As with most British films, this one approached the idea of space travel as a means to an end, rather than as an exciting adventure in space. In fact, the film was really a romance and murder mystery than actual science fiction.

Against the backdrop of a space mission we are presented a story of love and marriage, challenges to both and also the fact that Vanessa's lover turns out to be a foreign spy. I don't know what he told Vanessa to convince her to run away with him, but whatever it was she was a chump for believing him. I chalk it up to pure hormonal foolishness than any actual love being exchanged.

There was no actual science in it. Aside from a short mention of the mechanics involved with space flight, the only real adventure in space is when the second stage failed to jettison. It was almost as if the whole space mission was in the background of the main plot. So while the approach was in all seriousness, I would not call it the most stellar film in the science fiction firmament.

For its seriousness throughout and pacing of direction (Fisher always directed his films as going from point A to point B with a minimum of fuss), I give *Spaceways* a resounding 2 stars out of 4. IMdb gives it 5.1/10, while Rotten Tomatoes gives it no rating, but only 14% of their audience liked it.

Production: Principal photography on *Spaceways* took place at Ray Studios, Windsor, England from mid-November of 1952 to early January 1953. Some of the scenes of the spaceship taking off were special effects shots taken from *Rocketship X-M* (1950).

Reception: *Spaceways* was not well received by critics, and its poor production values soon relegated the film to the bottom of theater playbills and drive-ins, mainly as fill in fodder.

Film reviewer Glenn Erickson, writing in <u>DVD Savant</u>, noted: "The disappointment of Spaceways is finding out that it is really a lukewarm murder mystery in a science fiction setting".

There are no further notes on this film.

THE TWONKY (1953)
Directed by Arch Oboler
Produced by A.D. Nast, Jr. (executive producer), Arch Oboler (producer), and
Sidney Pink (associate producer)
Written by Henry Kuttner and C.L. Moore (story; as Lewis Padgett) and Arch Oboler (screenplay); based on "The Twonky" (1942 short story) by Henry Kuttner and C.L. Moore
Music by Jack Meakin
Cinematography by Joseph F. Biroc
Edited by Betty Steinberg
Distributed by United Artists; release date: June 10, 1953
Running time: 84 minutes

Cast:
Hans Conried as Kerry West
Janet Warren as Carolyn West
Billy Lynn as Coach Trout
Edwin Max as the Television Deliveryman

Gloria Blondell as the Bill Collector
Evelyn Beresford as Old Lady Motorist
Bob Jellison as the TV Shop Owner
Norman Field as the Doctor
Stephen Roberts as Head Treasury Agent
Connie Marshall as Susie
William Phipps as Student
Lenore Kingston as Offended Phone Operator #2
Alice Bakes as Offended Phone Operator #1
Brick Sullivan as Cop

Plot: After seeing his wife (Janet Warren) off on her trip to visit her sister in another town, Kerry West (Hans Conried), a philosophy teacher at a small town college, goes inside his home to contemplate his new purchase: a television set. It is a small box with a screen in its own stand, a wooden affair painted what appears to be white. He has had it installed in his office but has not turned it on yet.

Sitting down, he places a cigarette in his mouth and is about to light it when a solid beam of light shoots from the television screen, lighting it for him. Unaware of what has taken place, it is only when the television lights his pipe that West realizes that his television is behaving abnormally.

West soon discovers that the television can walk and perform a variety of functions, including dishwashing, vacuuming, and cardplaying. When the television deliveryman (Edwin Max) returns to settle the bill, the television materializes copies of a five dollar bill in order to provide payment. Yet the television soon exhibits other, more controlling traits, permitting West only a single cup of coffee and breaking West's classical music records in favor of military marches, to which it dances.

After West demonstrates the television to his friend Coach Trout (Billy Lynn), the coach declares the television set to be a "twonky", the word he used as a child to label the inexplicable.

Trout concludes that the Twonky is actually a robot committed to serving West. When he tests this hypothesis by attempting to kick West, the Twonky paralyzes his leg. After tending to the coach, West attempts to write a lecture on the role of individualism in art, but the Twonky hits him with beams that alter his thoughts and censors his

175

reading. When West appears in his class to give his lecture the next day, he finds himself unable to do more than ramble on about trivialities.

Frustrated, West goes to the store from which his wife had ordered the television and demands that they take it back or exchange it. But the salesman refuses, saying that only Mrs. West can make such an order, since she was the one who bought it.

Meanwhile, at West's house, the coach has summoned members of the college's football team and ordered them to destroy the Twonky. West arrives with the television deliveryman and his replacement set, only to find the players passed out in front of the machine. When West wakes them up, they appear to be in a hypnotic state mumbling that they have "no complaints," a condition the Twonky soon inflicts on the deliveryman as well.

Upstairs, Trout theorizes that the Twonky is from a future "super state" that uses such machines to control the population, which the Twonky soon demonstrates by walking into the room and altering his mind so that he no longer believes there is a problem.

As the recovering Trout tries to leave the house, the police storm past him into the house in response to a call made by the device seeking female companionship for West, followed by Treasury men tracking down the bogus $5 bills manufactured by the set. It is all chaos which West is hard put to manage on his own.

When the law enforcement officers try to arrest West, the Twonky places all of them in a trance, and they leave without a complaint.

Terrified, West escapes the house and goes to the local bar, when he proceeds to get drunk, presumably to drown his troubles. But when he finally returns home, the Twonky turns its light beam on him and makes him terribly sober. He is barely able to deal with this when a bill collector arrives and demands payment for various objects the Twonky ordered. West is unable to account for the order. But then the Twonky mesmerizes the collector and sends him on his way.

Just then, West's wife has returned home. In a desperate bid to spare her the Twonky's treatment, West lures the Twonky to his car and places it in the trunk. Then, he tries to crash the car by a variety of means but is frustrated by the Twonky's ability to control the vehicle. Spotting another vehicle parked alongside the road, West pulls over and abandons his car, then hitches a ride from the other driver, an elderly Englishwoman.

His relief at having escaped is soon negated by the woman's erratic driving, and by the discovery that the Twonky was able to move itself into her car's trunk. When the Twonky tries to stop the woman's reckless driving, it precipitates a crash that destroys itself. West is free at last. END

Analysis and additional notes: Coming off like a typical *Twilight Zone* episode, The Twonky is a delightful romp through an adventure which tells of robots and mind control. It was meant to be a satire of television and its addictive properties. But instead it was a warning to many: don't rely too heavily on this technological terror you have constructed.

After all, in 1953 we began to see how addictive it was. Soon after World War II, the television was introduced into the public sector as a medium of news and entertainment, and took off as thousands, then millions, began to buy the sets and place them in their homes. At the time only a few networks had channels so the entertainment was sparse but important. So too the news, which was presented in half-hour and hourly segments. From then until now, television gradually replaced radio.

Even then, the motivation for television was a means of distraction from other events, which the viewing public has no knowledge of, and even knowing, has no control over.

Today, more than 70 million households own at least one television set, but slowly but surely streaming online is beginning to replace cable.

Nevertheless, *The Twonky* seems a relatively bland film to some, but to me it presented a situation we are ill prepared for. The machine robot was adept at judging its surroundings, and able to influence and control the minds of many. I don't understand why it did not try to control Professor West with its mind ray, but it did not. Perhaps it saw him as the only real connection it had with the world.

It used intimidation and threats a great deal. It spent West's money as if he was made of it. There was no logic in its approach to the world it was in. It could be that it could move in time but was defective.

There was also no explanation as to its arrival in the world of its past. What happened? Was there an accident? Was it sent back in time deliberately? What kind of world did it come from? So in a way it is frustrating not to have those questions answered.

For its quirky yet scary plotline and able acting on the part of Hans Conreid I give The Twonky 2 stars out of 4. IMdb give it 5.6/10, and Rotten Tomatoes gives it no rating. Only 17% of their audience liked it. True it was more comedy than science fiction but surely more people would have remembered it.

Production: The Twonky was based on a 1942 short story by the established science fiction author Henry Kuttner, writing with his wife and frequent writing partner C. L. Moore, while using their pseudonym Lewis Padgett.

Arch Oboler had completed the film in 1951, but it did not find a distributor at the time. After he finished the 3D film, *Bwana Devil* (1952), *The Twonky* was finally released by United Artists. Hans Conried, later a noted character actor in other films and finally in the cartoon series' *Fractured Flickers, Rocky and Bullwinkle,* and *Aesop and Son,* had his first leading role in the film.

Reception: The Twonky did poorly at the box office and critics saw the poor production values as a major problem. When interviewed in 1970, Hans Conried recalled that he told the producer that *The Twonky* would probably bomb at the box-office (which it did), whereupon the producer genially replied "That's all right. I need a tax write-off this year anyway."

THE MAZE (1953)

Directed by William Cameron Menzies
Produced by Richard Heermance
Executive producer: Walter Mirisch
Screenplay by Daniel Ullman
Based on The Maze by Maurice Sandoz
Music by Marlin Skiles
Cinematography by Harry Neumann
Edited by John Fuller
Production company: Allied Artists Pictures Corporation
Distributed by: Allied Artists Pictures Corporation
Release date: July 26, 1953; running time: 80 minutes

Cast:
Richard Carlson as Gerald MacTeam
Veronica Hurst as Kitty Murray
Katherine Emery as Edith Murray
Michael Pate as William
John Dodsworth as Dr. Bert Dilling
Hillary Brooke as Peggy Lord
Stanley Fraser as Robert
Lilian Bond as Margaret Dilling (as Lillian Bond)
Owen McGiveney as Simon
Robin Hughes as Richard Roblar

Plot: In a castle in the wild highlands of Scotland, two butlers are in a tizzy about their master, who has just died of natural causes. Working alone, the lead butler named William (Michael Pate), tells his companion Robert (Stanley Fraser) to deal with the body while he makes sure that the next of kin are notified. There is a quiet and private funeral, and the butlers proceed to dig and fill in the grave alone. William then dispatches a letter to the laird's nephew.

Meanwhile, in Edinborough, there is an engagement party held for Gerald MacTeam (Richard Carlson) and his fiancee' Kitty Murray (Veronica Hurst). They slip off into the study of her aunt's home to exchange promises and vows and to look on the future. They appear deeply devoted to each other.

Soon afterward, a letter is delivered to Gerald from Craven Castle. In it is news of his uncle's death and an invitation to visit the castle, there to accept his role as master of the estate. Kitty is impressed; she had no idea she would be marrying into royalty.

Gerald says he should visit before the wedding to make sure the offer is legitimate and to assess if the castle is suitable to live in. He pledges that it should not take more than a week to do this. Kitty encourages him to go and return as soon as possible, as all the plans have already been made. Besides, she says, it will give her time to pick out her trusseau without his trodding underfoot.

Gerald goes. The promised week goes by, then another few days. Kitty is distraught with worry, while her aunt Edith (Katherine Emery), who is not sure of the bond to begin with, says that perhaps Kitty has made a mistake in trusting Gerald. Kitty replies that she has a bad feeling about the whole thing, but cannot imagine why he has not kept in touch with her, at least to explain the delay.

The next day, a letter arrives in the post from Gerald. But to Kitty it is depressing. The castle is real enough but Gerald writes that he must break off their engagement. He does not explain why, only that their engagement was a bad idea and that he cannot honor their troth.

Kitty is distraught again. This does not even sound like Gerald. She cannot accept his denial as they had ever been open with each other and had no secrets between them. Aunt Edith suggests that perhaps it is for the best. But Kitty insists that there is something wrong. She is determined to go to Craven Castle and find out what. Edith says she will go along as chaperone. She does not want her niece to go there all alone.

Together, they take a cab from the train station (we don't see the mode of transportation, just the cab) to Craven Castle. The cab stops just outside the gate to the estate. While Kitty and Edith are making comments about the outside of the castle, the cabbie moves their suitcases from the running board to the ground and then drives away. Thus stranded there, the women pick up their cases and walk toward the front door.

Kitty lifts the door knocker and pounds it into the wood. There is no answer. She tries again. The door opens finally and William is surprised at first. There is a flash of lightning and then thunder as a storm is threatening rain. William asks who they are, then reluctantly admits them to the castle just as the rain begins to fall.

The castle itself is entirely made of stone inside and out, consisting of three floors connected by a staircase. At night, much of it remains in the darkness lit only by candlelight. There is no modern technology of any kind: no telephones, no electricity, no appliances. Everything is as it was since the 18th century.

William is brusque and officious. He explains that master Gerald is already in bed and should not be disturbed. He then says that they must obey the rules of the house, among which is the rule that they must be locked in their rooms at night. That Robert will move their luggage up to their rooms for them. Then they must be gone by the next morning.

Kitty and Edith are led upstairs to a sumptuous suite of adjoining bedrooms with a connecting door, where William lights the fireplace and the candles, then bids them good night. When he goes out, he locks the doors. Kitty and Edith are trapped for the moment. [There is nothing about a bathroom. We presume that there is at least a small privy, but it is not pointed out.]

Sometime in the night, Kitty is in bed when she hears a shuffling noise outside. She looks at the bottom of the door and spots a massive shadow moving past it, but cannot divine what it could be.

The next morning, Kitty finds her door unlocked. She visits her aunt and finds that Edith has contracted a head cold. Edith thinks it is not that bad, but Kitty decides it is a sufficient excuse to stay one more day. She goes down into the kitchen, where William is working, and insists on preparing a breakfast tray for her aunt. While they are engaging in a mild argument Gerald enters the room and faces her with some dismay.

He has aged about 20 years, and his hair has turned gray. He looks at her with a cold expression, nothing like Kitty's Gerald. Kitty is shocked at his appearance but says nothing about it. Gerald asks her what she is doing there. She says she could not believe the engagement is broken off over a broken down castle. He is as adamant as William that she and her aunt should leave and never return. Then he leaves the kitchen.

Kitty finally delivers the tray to Edith and explains what happened. Edith is complacent as she suggests that maybe Gerald has realized their marriage would be a mistake. Kitty refuses to accept it. She says that the Gerald she just saw was nothing like the Gerald who left Edinborough. She insists that something is terribly wrong. Why should she and Edith be locked inside? Why are there bricks over the windows? Why no views of the maze, which was mentioned in the travel brochure?

For this Edith has no answers. It is all a mystery to her.

After breakfast, Kitty finds a small window in the kitchen which faces onto the maze. It is somewhat run down and unkempt. At its center is a swimming pool and deck. She can see there is a gate to the maze with a sign on it saying "Keep Out". She determines to visit the maze.

She then writes a letter to several of Gerald's friends with a view to get help for Gerald, among them is Dr. Bert Dilling (John Dodsworth), who is a prominent doctor and psychologist. A group of them are adventuring in Scotland and should be able to help him. Then she goes out to find the post box. William sees her doing this but offers no interference, but no aid either.

Kitty wanders along looking for the box but finds nothing at first. She ventures closer to the maze as she does so. She finds the gate open and enters the maze, but goes only a few steps before the estate gardener warns her not to go too far in. Stymied, Kitty asks the gardener to post the letter for her. He warns her about the atmosphere in the castle, then assents with a tip of his hat and moves off down the road with the envelope in hand.

That evening, Kitty confers with Edith about the letter. Edith insists that she is feeling much better and can leave, but Kitty asks her to wait. If the letter was truly delivered she wants to be at Craven Castle when Gerald's friends arrive. Then, they both conspire to steal one of the keys from William or Robert to escape their evening prison.

During a mild upset outside their rooms, Kitty manages to remove one of the keys from a lock and together she and Edith go to explore the upper floor, where Gerald's rooms are supposed to be. They enter a bleakly furnished set of rooms where there are nothing but bookshelves. Edith says there is nothing worth looking at here, when she spies a shuffling shape escaping through a secret door. She screams at the shock, then collapses in a dead faint.

Gerald, William and Robert discover them, and Gerald has Edith transferred back to her bedroom. Gerald and Kitty hold a brief argument about their intrusion, where Kitty reveals her dissatisfaction about their accomodations. What is going on? Why should she and her aunt be locked in every night? What is the secret of Craven Castle?

Gerald says only that they must leave the very next morning, or he can't answer for the consequences. She leaves him in a sad huff. Gerald tells William to make sure all the rooms are locked next time.

The next morning, Kitty and Edith are packing their suitcases and preparing to leave, when the door knocker is heard outside. William goes to answer the door and finds four of Gerald's friends outside: Dr. Dilling, his wife Margaret (Lillian Bond), his friend Simon (Owen McGiveney) and his girlfriend Peggy Lord (Hillary Brooke). They have arrived in a souped up roadster and are eager to visit Gerald. WIlliam is about to deny them entry when Gerald appears at the door and commands him to let them in.

All seems well, at first, but Gerald tells them the rules of the house. It seems a bit off-putting, but then Bert offers that it's the house rules so they must be obeyed. While Gerald is seeing to their rooms, Kitty approaches Bert and asks his opinion. Bert is concerned, as are the other friends. He thinks that Gerald is close to a psychotic break, but does not know the cause. Kitty tells the friends what happened to her aunt and they all decide to approach the situation with kid gloves.

After dinner, Gerald tells them that they must be in their rooms by 11 o'clock, to be locked in until the morning. They agree and are locked in together soon after. While William is busy seeing to their imprisonment, Kitty steals another key and lets Edith out. Together, they head to the window overlooking the maze and see the candlelit shadow moving toward the center.

Wasting no more time, the two women leave the castle by a side door and walk toward the maze. The gate has been left open. They hear noises among the hedges and try to find their way toward the center. Along the way, Edith and Kitty are separated. Desperately, they try to find their way back, when Edith confronts a giant half human toad or frog. Shocked yet again, she screams and faints, while the toad monster hops away frantically.

Kitty comes upon her and tries to revive her, when Gerald, William, and Robert arrive. Gerald directs the two butlers to pick Edith up and take her back to her room. He then leads Kitty toward the castle, where the toad has hopped up the stairs to Gerald's rooms.

The toad keeps going far enough that he launches himself through the window and falls to his death.

The next morning, the friends are assembled in the dining room, where Gerald explains the curse of Craven Castle. He is holding a copy of *Teratology*, the study of amphibians. He says that the toad monster was the original master of the castle; a man who was born in arrested development.

He explains that the human embryo goes through several stages of evolution, from blastocyst to human. The amphibious stage was the master's prison. He was born that way and had survived from 1750 to the present day (1953). His human descendants were the castle's servants, including Gerald. His nightly sojourns to the maze pool was his only surcease from the torture of being a monster.

Now that the original master is dead, Gerald is freed from his obligations and has become the new master. William and Robert accept him freely and ask for his next command. Kitty and Edith are delighted, and his friends accept his explanation.

The curse of Craven Castle has been broken as we focus on the gravestone erected over the poor toad's final resting place. END

Analysis and additional notes: I came upon this strange gem when my AV research assistant showed it to me. It was not on the standard list of science fiction films, relegated to the monster film list. But when I saw it, I decided that there was enough science in it to be part of the SF list. Upon watching it, the film presented as a mystery, something with dark shadows and secrets. But when I saw the book *Teratology* standing prominent among the books of choice, I realized that it was about an aberration of science.

Granted, I realize that science would never accept the idea of a human toad hybrid as a consequence of birth. At the amphibious stage there would be no human arms and legs. Those materialize in the fetal stage. But the fantasy of it suggested a long succession of castle servants bound by oath to protect a monster whose only desire was to take a swim in the maze's pool. We see that the gravestone was set at 1750-1953, making him the longest living monster in the science fiction universe. The castle itself was not cursed, only its inhabitants.

While it was filmed in "3-D", there was little to suggest it was so except for the depth of field for the shots. The focus was in the foreground, while the background was indistinct and blurry. If it was real 3-D, all the levels would have been clear and sharp. I remember seeing *The Creature From The Black Lagoon* in 3-D and there were no such impediments.

For its rather centered and logical screenplay, as well as the solid performances throughout, I give *The Maze* 2.5 stars out of 4. IMdb gives it 6.0/10, but Rotten Tomatoes does not even have a page for it.

Production: No notes could be found.

Reception: Critical reception for *The Maze* were mixed, with some critics praising the film's acting, atmosphere, and direction while criticizing the finale. Author and film critic Leonard Maltin awarded the film 2 out of 4 stars, calling the finale "ludicrous and unsatisfying".

Brett Gallman from <u>Oh, The Horror!</u> gave the film a negative review, criticizing the film's "bloated" runtime, and plot development, calling it a footnote in director Menzies' career.

Dennis Schwartz from <u>Ozus' World Movie Reviews</u> awarded the film a B grade, calling it, "A moronic but entertaining horror/sci-fi film."

<u>TV Guide</u> awarded the film 2 out of 4 stars, commending the film's acting, direction, and set design, calling it above average. However, the reviewer felt that the film was somewhat hampered by its low budget.

Dave Sindelar, on his website *Fantastic Movie Musings and Ramblings* gave the film a more positive review, writing, "I have a lot of affection for this eerie horror/SF movie, though it took me a couple of viewings. The first time I saw the movie, I did get caught up in the eerie mood and the atmospheric sense of dread and tragedy that pervaded the castle, but the revelation concerning the nature of the true lord of the castle caused me to break out in laughter rather than to rear back in horror, and it ruined the movie for me. The second time I saw it, I was prepared, and was able to see beyond this flaw and appreciate how touching and sad the ending of the movie was. Part of the credit must go to Richard Carlson's excellent performance, one of the best of his I've seen."

Trivia: The plot may have been inspired by a legend associated with Scotland's Glamis Castle, the ancestral home of the House of Bowes-Lyon. According to the legend, a rightful heir to leadership of the noble house was born horribly deformed, and the Bowes-Lyon family told the outside world he had died at birth. He was then kept sequestered in a secret part of the castle until his death from old age, while the next eligible heir took his place in the succession to family leadership.

This was to be the second 3-D film designed and directed by William Cameron Menzies. Contrary to some opinion, there is no evidence to substantiate that his previous film, *Invaders From Mars* (1953), was not designed nor planned for 3-D, and certainly was not shot in this process. Menzies, who was known as a director with a very "dimensional" style (many shots focused in layers), only directed one other 3-D film previous to this: *Fun In The Sun,* a short that was shot for the aborted Sol Lesser production, *The 3-D Follies*. This would be his final film as production designer and director.

Perhaps the first film to mention the scientific discipline of teratology, and perhaps the first to discuss the discredited concept of prenatal phylogenetic evolution.

Goofs: Kitty and Edith's rooms in the castle have their windows blocked with stone. That is shown in a shot of Kitty's room the night they arrived. The only light sources are candles and the fireplaces. Yet, in the morning, both bedrooms are bathed in light as if the sun were streaming in through these blocked windows. Ooppss...

THE WAR OF THE WORLDS (1953)
Director: Byron Haskin
Producer: George Pal
Screenplay: Barré Lyndon; based on *The War of the Worlds* by H. G. Wells
Music: Leith Stevens
Cinematography: George Barnes
Distributed by Paramount Pictures; Release date August 26, 1953; Running time 85 minutes

Cast: Gene Barry and Ann Robinson along with several others [uncredited]; narrated by Sir Cedric Hardwicke

Plot: Following the opening credits, with lush and exotic music supplied by Leith Stevens, the film begins with a preamble of illustrations by space artist Chesley Bonestell showing the planets of our solar system, over which the film's narrator (Sir Cedric Hardwicke) reads the introduction to the original novel by Wells.

The visuals of a dark and barren Mars reveals the stark landscape of a race gone stagnant. Mars is no longer the verdant world it had been millions of years ago, and the Martians are envious of the green and blue world they see through their telescopes. The narrator explains why the Martians find Earth the only world worthy of invasion: all the other worlds are either too hot or too cold. Earth is just right.

Wells's novel is updated to the early 1950s and the setting moved from the environs of London to southern California; in point of fact centering on the area around the San Gabriel valley, Altadena and Pasadena (conveniently close to CalTech and the Jet Propulsion Laboratory).

Dr. Clayton Forrester (Gene Barry), a scientist and veteran of the Manhattan Project, is fishing with colleagues in the mountains when they spot a large meteor streaking across the sky. It comes crashing to earth near the town of Linda Rosa (actually Corona).

Soon afterward, a deputy in the Forestry Dept. arrives and informs Forrester that he is needed to examine the meteor; begs a cigarette or two and helps himself to a sandwich and a cup of coffee. Intrigued, Forrester tells his colleagues that he had better go see what the excitement is all about.

At the impact site, he meets a woman reporter who seems to know everything about him. His illustrious career has been well documented in major magazines and newspapers, but she does not know what he looks like. Finally he points himself out. She blushes and says that she had no idea of his good looks; naturally, she had thought he was older.

She introduces herself as Sylvia Van Buren (Ann Robinson), a reporter for a major newspaper; and then her uncle, Pastor Matthew Collins, who runs the Presbyterian church in Linda Rosa. They discuss the area and the local charm while the meteor is seen to be emitting vapor. A man approaches it and gives it a whack with a shovel. A piece of earth falls off the surface and the hot steam drives him back. It looks too hot to approach safely. Forrester says everyone should stay clear until it cools down.

Another man suggests that the place could be turned into a park. The pastor agrees and suggests that if picnic tables were to be installed it might boost tourism. The man disagrees, saying that if that happened people would bring their own lunches; he has the idea to put up a food kiosk to generate revenue. But Forrester disagrees as well, pointing out that no one knows what kind of material the meteor is made of. It could even be radioactive.

A deputy sheriff has looked into his car and points to a gadget lying in the back seat. He thinks it is a bomb because it is ticking. Forrester says it is a geiger counter, pulls it out and points the wand around the area. The most activity seems to register in the direction of the meteor crash site, bearing out his initial guess about the rock. He suggests that the area be cleared of civilians for now and a guard posted to prevent visitations for safety's sake.

The meteor appears to have slid in at a shallow angle and seems curiously lighter than normal for its large size. Forrester ponders these anomalies and decides to wait in town overnight for it to cool down before making a more thorough examination. Pastor Collins invites him to stay at his house where he can have a shave and a good meal, and mentions that the annual square dance festival would be a good way to get to know the community. Sylvia agrees.

Later, the square dance is in full swing as everyone in the small town attends. Forrester and Sylvia share food and jokes. Meanwhile, the meteor crash site is dark and quiet as three men from the town stand guard. They discuss the idea of partnering up and building a food stand with all kinds of food: hamburgers, hot dogs, even tacos and frijoles.

While they are talking, a round hatch on top of the meteorite slowly begins to unscrew. The men hear the noise and snatch up sticks to defend themselves, not sure at first what to do. Then they see the top of the meteor moving.

Suddenly, the idea that the meteorite is some kind of alien ship comes to them. Do the aliens look like us? Could they be friendly? The latino man suggests waving a white flag, because "everyone knows a white flag means we come in peace." The other men discuss this, and when they ask what to tell the aliens, one of them says, "welcome to California." These simple minded and innocent thoughts are shared among them as they move closer to the meteor.

A mechanical cobra-like head emerges, supported by a long telescoping neck. It appears to be something like a camera and a probe at the same time. It emits a peculiar pulsing and shimmering sound as it looks around, describing a circle in the dark. It has not seen the men yet. It appears to be curious about the sky and the trees.

The men see the probe and approach carefully. The latino man waves his white flag, and the machine appears to focus on them. What follows is terrible destruction as a flash of heat emerges from its eye and envelops the men, turning them into ash instantly. The heat destroys the surrounding vegetation and sets the forest on fire. Then it lashes out again and destroys a transmission tower nearby.

The power suddenly goes out at the square dance. Candles are lit as the people mill about in the dark. Dr. Forrester consults his watch to note the time of the event and discovers that his and other people's wrist watches have stopped running at the same time. His compass also points away from magnetic north and toward the location of the fallen meteorite.

Forrester and the sheriff go with a deputy to investigate and are attacked by the machine's ray. The deputy gets into the squad car and drives away (possibly to warn the town) but does not get far before he and the car are incinerated. Both Forrester and the sheriff manage to survive and call in the military. [Nice that one can simply make a phone call to the Joint Chiefs and get almost immediate action. This would never happen in real life!]

Soon, a military outpost has been established near the crash site, where Sylvia and Forrester have been consulting with a general, called Mansley, about the invasion. Forrester has tried to keep his observations about the alien craft low-key, trying to avoid provoking the general into unwarranted action; but Mansley appears to know what he is doing. He has placed a forward observation post between the base and the crash site with instructions to call if anything moves. At first, it is a case of sit and wait. More meteors are seen to crash to earth nearby. It is no longer an incidental shower. The enemy is arriving in droves.

The first machine has laid waste to the surrounding area but has not tried to leave the gully. In the first gray mist of dawn, however, that shimmering sound fills the valley, and the first machine finally emerges from the fog and stands up. It looks like a manta ray suspended tens of feet above the ground by means of some kind of invisible legs. And it is not alone, as two more appear. The observors report that the machines are moving, and there is a hurried fluster at the ground base as lights are doused and Forrester and Mansley look at what they've got through binoculars.

At first Forrester is amazed as he discusses what propulsive force the invaders may be using, decides on electromagnetism, and that they may use it for all sorts of purposes. He tells Mansley more about the ray and its effects. Mansley, however, is keen to attack the machines now. Forrester warns him to move with caution, as his own experience with the machines is that they shoot first and ask questions later. The machines advance slowly along the valley floor sweeping it for any sign of life. No one dares to move.

Meanwhile, Sylvia and Pastor Collins talk softly about the alien beings while she is pouring coffee for him. The Pastor seems to think that if the aliens are that advanced they should be closer to God for that reason alone. Sylvia begins to think her uncle is acting strange; very much out of character. She warns him not to think like that. The aliens have already sinned by killing. But then Matthew asks her if she likes Dr. Forrester. She says yes. He does, too. Then he sends her to get some more water for coffee.

While she is doing that, someone calls out, "who is that?" She drops the pitcher in her hand and runs to the window, then screams out her panic as Pastor Collins walks toward the machines, his bible raised in the air with the cross pointed toward them. He is reciting from Psalm 23, looking as if he alone and his message of peace can stop the machines.

The lead machine spots him and fires, disintegrating him instantly with its ray. Sylvia screams again.

Mansley calls out to open fire, and his men attack with everything in their arsenal, but each war machine is protected by an impenetrable force field. The Martians then use their disintegrator rays to send the rest of the military force into full retreat. The tanks are incinerated with men inside, men catch fire and fall.

Finally, Mansley declares, "let's fall back to safer ground. The Air Force will take care of these babies now."

The task force moves to the floor of the San Gabriel Valley. The machines are so far invincible. From their shelter, Forrester and Sylvia discuss more findings with the general, and Forrester thinks that there is no weapon on Earth capable of destroying the invaders. Mansley, however, thinks that the Bomb can still do it. Forrester is still skeptical, saying that the scope of the alien science is too advanced. Mansley insists that they've got to try, or there will be nothing to stop the machines from destroying their way to the coast.

Sylvia is still rattled by the experience of seeing her uncle die. She asks, "is there nothing we can do?" Forrester reassures her; everything that can be done will be.

Soon afterward we see jet fighters engaging with the machines. None survive the battle. Then the machines attack the compound.

There are scenes of open battle again. Outgunned and outmanned, Mansley and his group desert the compound before they are caught in the open. While Forrester and Sylvia flee, Mansley exhorts everyone to be gone. He is caught by a ray and disintegrated before our very eyes.

Forrester and Sylvia manage to find a small plane and climb into it. Apparently Forrester knows how to fly, and soon they are soaring over the valley trying to escape the machines. Sylvia wants to go higher, but another squadron of planes is on their way and Forrester cannot. They narrowly avoid another pod of machines and crash land on a farm, ditch the plane and dive into a small trench to endure the terrible risk of being caught in the open. They huddle together while the plane is destroyed.

Soon afterward, it is quiet just then. There is a tender moment as Forrester looks at a sleeping Sylvia. Then she comes to and panics as she finds they are still in danger. They find their way to an abandoned farmhouse, but are not there long before another meteor crash lands and barrels its way into the house. Timbers fall.

Sometime later, Forrester comes to. Sylvia has wet a cloth and is dabbing at his forehead. He sits up slowly as she explains that she has been terrified witless. The machines are now all around them. Forrester's reading glasses have been smashed but he can still see. He gets up and looks around. The farmhouse proves to be a good place to hide for the moment, but he knows it can't last.

Sylvia has found enough food to make breakfast. While she cooks, they talk about their families. Forrester has been an orphan and raised himself to be self-reliant, while Sylvia is a member of a big family but has been living in California to be near Pastor Collins. She tells a story about when she was very small and got lost. Scared to be anywhere else, she goes into a church to find sanctuary. She claims that her uncle found her. Then she declares that she could bawl her head off. But Forrester says she's not the type. She has proved she is tougher than that several times already, and looks like it has not affected her at all.

A sound outside attracts their attention. Breakfast is abandoned as Sylvia spots something moving outside. Together, they move into another room to hide, just as another meteor lands nearby and ploughs its way through the kitchen. Forrester and Sylvia are now trapped with no way to get out.

A long machine umbilical extrudes from one of the machines and snakes its way down toward the house. A strange device like a mobile camera pokes into a hole in the wall and begins to probe around, looking for the source of light and sound in the house. It moves about slowly.

On a gamble, Forrester picks something up and pitches it into the dark. The probe turns its head looking for the source. "Maybe they don't know we're here," Sylvia suggests softly. "We're not going to let them," he says. He looks around carefully and finds an axe for chopping firewood. Armed with it, he leads Sylvia away. But something alerts the probe and it turns.

Forrester attacks by throwing something, and before it can react chops off the probe's head. The umbilical withdraws quickly and retracts into the tripod. Now robbed of their hiding place, they look for another way out but the earth has covered most of the doors and windows. They finally find an open window and begin tearing away at obstructions to get out.

While they are working, we see shadows moving about outside, then while Sylvia is busy throwing away detritus, a strange hand lands on her shoulder. Frozen with horror, she slowly turns and sees a Martian looking right at her. It is a grotesque creature with what looks like a big eye divided into three segments.

Forrester sees it, pulls her to him and throws the axe he has been working with at it. The creature recoils, makes a terrible keening sound and flees. He seizes a scarf and wraps the probe's head up in it. While he is working, Sylvia points out that there is blood on the scarf. Forrester examines it closely and says that he must get it to the lab at Pacific Tech (Caltech). He says his biologist friend Marchemont will know what to do with it.

By now Sylvia is thoroughly shocked by everything which has happened and becomes hysterical. Forrester shakes her and yells until she stops. He becomes tender as he tells her there is no time to fall apart now; they must escape. Together, they manage to get out of the house as the machines destroy it completely.

Sometime later, they manage to make it to Pacific Tech, where Forrester shows the souvenirs he has gathered to his friends Marchemont and Bildebeck. When Marchemont examines the blood on the scarf, she remarks that she has never seen such weak and anemic blood cells, and that by human physical standards the Martians must be very primitive indeed. She does not elaborate.

One of the other scientists has erected a light stand and mounted the probe's head on it. He says that by examining the optics of the camera they can learn how the Martians see. Somehow, the three lenses coalesce three images into one. The color is very weak; almost black and white. The scientist guides Sylvia to the camera saying they would see why the Martians were so interested in her. There is a long protracted moment of Sylvia's face filling the screen. She is not happy with the alien machine. (We're not sure why this is relevent but perhaps it is to give Ms. Robinson something to do.)

There is a desperate meeting in Washington, D.C. about the situation as the military grants a grim press conference to the newspeople. According to reports, the machines are landing in threes. They sweep the area, secure outposts at certain points; then sweep again. The Martians are thorough in wiping out anything that moves. Cities are going dark and silent across Europe; nothing has been heard from Asia or the Pacific Rim for days. Canada has gone dark. There is a brief note of chagrin as they see a radio picture of the Eiffel Tower going down in pieces. Radio communication is practically nonexistent; and messengers arrive to deliver notes between offices.

Then a spokeman for the Joint Chiefs makes the announcement that there is little anyone can do now but evacuate any surviving populations of the cities to the shelter of the hills. The military has decided to use the Bomb.

Forrester, Sylvia, Marchemont and Bildebeck are consulted about what to do next. They set up an observation outpost in the valley some miles away from a Martian advance group. At zero hour, everyone must put on protective clothing and wear special sunglasses. The impact point is close enough that the bright flash of detonation could blind one in an instant.

From the forward bunker comes the news that the machines are moving again. Forrester studies them and says that there is some sort of protective energy blister covering the machines. (The first use of a force field for protection, which was not used again until *Star Trek*) The general thinks that still won't stop the awesome power of a nuclear blast.

Standing near the compound is a reporter who is recording the events of the day. He makes a vocal note that he is recording everything on tape should anything happen to him for future history, if there is any. Sylvia takes that with the calm tones of one who has seen everything she wanted to and then some.

The countdown begins. The Flying Wing (an impressive monstrosity of air power) takes off at Edwards AF Base and carries its deadly payload to the blast zone. At the end of the countdown, everything is bathed in bright light. Then the thunder of the blast and the pressure wave knocks things over, blows dust and sand over everyone and everything. As the mushroom cloud rises over the desert, Forrester clambers back to the window and looks at the roiling devastation through his binoculars.

The cloud is dense, hard to see through at first. Then, as if nothing had happened, the machines emerge unscathed and stroll slowly through the radioactive cloud. The general turns to Forrester and says, "this is impossible! Planes, tanks, guns, nothing affects them! The answer must lie with whatever science can think up."

He then says that if things continue this way, the Earth could be conquered in six days.

Marchemont mutters, "six days."

Sylvia says, "the same number of days it took to create it."

A panoramic montage follows of people on the move in Los Angeles, showing us whole masses of them walking along bridges and down avenues, carrying whatever they are able to, and walking into the low foothills of the mountains. While they are abandoning the city, the Pacific Tech group loads equipment into trucks and scientists into a bus. Sylvia takes the wheel of a bus and drives them away, while Forrester drives away in one of the trucks filled with instruments.

Forrester happens to be passing through the downtown garment district when he is caught in a mob of men looting the stores and carrying away anything they can. They see the truck and seize it. In the melee, Forrester tries to stop them, yelling, "you fools! You'll cut your own throats!" but is knocked out of the way. The mob drives the truck away after dumping the instruments on the road and leaves him there, stunned and half conscious.

When he recovers, he wanders aimlessly and comes on a man trying to gather money up from the street. The man remarks that "you can't buy a ride for love or money." Then it dawns on Forrester that something must have happened to Sylvia as the bus had just gone through there. He asks the man if he had seen the bus, and the man shakes his head. Forrester runs on and comes on the vehicle lying on its side, abandoned.

Now it is his turn to panic. He calls out, "Bildebeck. Marchemont. Sylvia!!" The search for a solution is lost, and the Martian war machines are laying the city to waste a block at a time. He runs farther and sits down on a bus stop bench to rest. A jeep carrying two safety officers comes to a stop and they tell him to come with them. He asks if they have seen anyone of the group. They say no; then he waves them off and resumes his search.

What follows is a fruitless marathon on the abandoned streets. He is alone, desperate, angry. Time after time he dodges the heat rays and destruction raining down around him. At some point, a war machine destroys Los Angeles City Hall [then the only tall building in the city center at that time]. He stops to gather his wits and then remembers what Sylvia had said about going into a church for safety.

He finally finds his way to a Presbyterian church, where Rev. Billy Graham prays to God to save the congregation. There, Forrester finds Marchemont and Bildebeck, who has been badly injured. He asks the whereabouts of the other scientists. Marchemont replies that they were scattered after the mob took the bus. Then he asks about Sylvia. They have not seen her. He says he must find her and says goodbye.

He then manages to get to the cathedral of St. Juliana, where the priests are helping others to pray for salvation. A war machine blasts at the cathedral. A salvo of alien fire destroys the windows and sends the refugees into a panic. Forrester calls desperately for Sylvia, who hears him and calls back. Somehow they meet and embrace as the building stones begin to fall around them.

Outside, something strange is beginning to happen. We see a machine slow down and then fall. Others begin to fall, too. We see them collide against buildings all over the world, their probe lights going out. Something is happening to the Martians.

When quiet finally descends, the refugees slowly emerge from the cathedral. Forrester sees one of the machines laying nearby. Curious, he approaches carefully as a hatch in the machine opens. A small, bulbous arm and hand emerges, blood vessels are clearly visible and pulsing. Then it grows still. Forrester looks at it closely, then peers up inside. The creature is dead.

As bells ring a quiet victory knell, the narrator explains that the Martians had no resistance against the Earthly diseases Man had grown immune to. Thus, a powerful conquering force was stopped by "the littlest of things, which God in his wisdom had put upon the Earth." END

Analysis and Additional Notes: This is one of my special favorites. Not only was it released in the year of my birth, it was one of the landmark films which I thought could never be remade. The special effects were superior for that time despite their budget constraints. George Pal did his best to make everything perfect even if the plot of the screenplay was highly derivative of the original novel by H. G. Wells. It had all the elements of excitement, terror and pathos of a great film, to rival even Sir Lew Grade's biblical potboilers.

Though I did not become an Angeleno until my teen years, the landscape of the Los Angeles area became my back yard. I am actually thinking of writing a history of Los Angeles myself as it contains many well known and overlooked features which could stand revelation to the new generation of Angelinos.

At the time, only the Jet Propulsion Laboratory and Cal Tech (California Technical University) dominated the San Gabriel valley floor, with Pasadena and Altadena being the biggest cities. Corona hosted a small airfield which is no longer there. Given the amount of space needed to produce the film without attracting a large crowd, it was relatively easy to film the external scenes there. In this century, the San Gabriel valley is almost completely built over, from the mountains to the plain of Los Angeles.

What is of particular note is the use of action and special effects to convey the terror of an alien invasion without overloading the senses. Each scenario is a story in itself, dominated by the human side of the equation. We don't actually see any Martians until the middle third of the picture, and certainly not clearly enough to frighten the audience overmuch. We see their terrible war machines throughout; as if the machines *are* the Martians. Their pilots, like the *Dr. WHO* Daleks, seem to be superfluous to the plot. How the war machines operate and move about is beyond anything anyone had ever seen before.

The story is also a bit preachy but that was the way things were back then in the 1950s. One could not make a science fiction film without bringing God into it. That is because the people responsible for making the film were religious to begin with, so they could only work through their particular idiom. I don't think an aetheist could have made it better or worse, and I like the overall plot even if the catch ending was a religious one. It still displayed the human condition in the face of certain doom at the hands of the *other*. There is no chance to propose an alternative. The Martians were bad; so they must die. End of story.

I'm not sure it would go over so well now. Given the reaction to stories with similar religious or anti-religious overtones nowadays it would probably have been a flop at the box office. Later, a credible and more terrifying version of *The War of The Worlds* (2005) was produced and directed by Steven Spielberg, starring Tom Cruise. The war machines in that film were more in line with Wells's novel, and the scenarios far more destructive and terrifying.

For its amazing special effects and credible acting I give The War of The Worlds 4 stars out of 4. IMdb gives it 7.2/10, and Rotten Tomatoes does not have any results for it.

More notes: George Pal originally planned for the final third of the film to be shot in the new 3-D process (with glasses) to visually enhance the Martians' attack on Los Angeles. The plan was dropped prior to actual production of the film, probably due to the expense of the camera work. I saw *The Creature From The Black Lagoon* in 3-D and was impressed with the underwater scenes. One could think one was really underwater, they were that good. But it was in black and white so that sort of destroyed the effect overall. Later, there was a thrust to produce more of such films in color. *House of Wax* (1953) was one of the first.

World War II stock footage was used to produce a montage of destruction to show the worldwide invasion, with armies of all nations joining together to fight off the invaders. Effects were added to demonstrate the awesome power of the Martian machines.

Wells had used the second half of his novel to make a satirical commentary on civilization and the British class system. Lyndon did not incorporate that satire into the film's screenplay, but he did add an unsubtle religious subtext (in contrast to Wells's original novel), to the point that the Martians only begin to die shortly after blasting the Los Angeles churches. I am sure it is meant to be coincidental after all, but many think it deliberate.

Special Effects: Each disintegration effect took 144 separate matte paintings to create. The sound sound effect of the snake-like probe was created by stirring a slushie, played back at a higher pitch and speed, enhanced in remix and punctuated by a piano wire plucked in the lower C octave. The resulting eerie shimmering sound was chilling indeed.

The machines also fired a green death-ray from their wingtips, generating a distinctive sound and exposing the interior of its target before disintegrating it. This weapon was substituted for the chemical black smoke weapon described in Wells' novel. The sound effect, created by striking a high tension cable with a hammer and remixed, was reused in **Star Trek** for the launch of photon torpedos in battle.

The other war machines' rays were created by mixing the backward recorded sound of three electric guitars. For many years, it was utilized as a standard "ray-gun" sound on children's television shows and the science fiction anthology series *The Outer Limits*; particularly in the episode "The Children of Spider County".

The Martian's scream in the ruined farmhouse was created by a sound mix of a microphone scraping along dry ice combined with a woman's scream recorded backwards.

St. Brendan's Catholic Church was the setting used in the final scene where the desperate people of Los Angeles gathered to pray. St. Juliana's was shown as the exterior.

A conscious effort was made to avoid the stereotypical "flying saucer" look of typical UFOs. The Martian war machines, as designed by Al Nozaki, were shaped like manta rays floating over the ground. Three Martian war machine props were made out of copper for the film. The same blueprints were used a decade later to construct the alien spacecraft in the film *Robinson Crusoe on Mars* (1964), also directed by Byron Haskin; and was supposedly melted down later for a copper drive. Fan collector Forrest J Ackerman owned a replica model made from the *Robinson Crusoe on Mars* blueprints, and was constructed by Ackerman's friends Paul and Larry Brooks.

The walking tripods of Wells's novel proved problematic for various reasons. It was finally decided to make the Martian machines "float" along on three invisible, electromagnetic legs. It was difficult to mark out the invisible legs when smoke and other effects had to be seen with the machines. However, the three leg beams were shown to create small fires where they touch the ground. More advanced and elegant than Wells's original design, they brought more of the terror of their sophistication compared to the primitive armaments of human kind into sharp relief.

The War of the Worlds had its official premiere in Hollywood on February 20, 1953, although it did not go into general theatrical release until autumn of that year. The film was both a critical and box office success. It accrued $2,000,000 in distributors' domestic (U.S. and Canada) rentals, making it the year's biggest science fiction film hit.

The *New York Times* noted the film was "an imaginatively conceived, professionally turned adventure, which makes excellent use of Technicolor, special effects by a crew of experts and impressively drawn backgrounds... Director Byron Haskin, working from a tight script by Barré Lyndon, has made this excursion suspenseful, fast and, on occasion, properly chilling."

The film was nominated for three Academy Awards, winning in the category for Special Effects in 1954.

In 2011, *The War of the Worlds* was deemed "culturally, historically, or aesthetically significant" by the United States Library of Congress and selected for preservation in the National Film Registry. The Registry noted the film's release during the early years of the Cold War and how it used "the apocalyptic paranoia of the atomic age". The Registry also cited the film's special effects, which at its release were called "soul-chilling, hackle-raising and not for the faint of heart."

After viewing the 21st century version of *The War of The Worlds* (2005) as produced by Steven Spielberg, and directed by Ridley and Tony Scott, the lasting impact of this original classic still rings with me. Call me old fashioned, but in spite of the stark simplicity of the latest incarnation, which follows the novel more closely, I found myself feeling thankful that this film was not simply a remake of the old. In some ways it was even more frightening than the original, but more closely followed H. G. Wells's novel in terms of special effects.

In spite of all of that, *The War of The Worlds* of 1953 is still my favorite, sweeping aside most other films of the 1950s in terms of its approach to the alien war machines and also the no-nonsense presentation of real terror in a world which has been so far anthropocentric. The aliens could have won, but did not.

CRΛSH OF THE MOONS (1954)

Directed by Hollingsworth Morse
Produced by Roland D. Reed, Guy V. Thayer Jr., and
Arthur Pierson
Written by Warren Wilson
Music by Alexander Laszlo
Cinematography by Guy Roe
Edited by Fred Maguire
Distributed by United Television Programs Inc.
Release date: July 10, 1954; running time: 78 minutes

Cast:
Richard Crane as Rocky Jones
Sally Mansfield as Vena Ray
Scotty Beckett as Winky
John Banner as Bavarro
Nan Leslie as Trinka
Patsy Parsons as Queen Cleolanta
Harry Lauter as Atlasan
Robert Lyden as Bobby
Maurice Cass as Prof. Newton
Charles Meredith as Secretary Drake
Lane Bradford as Lasvon
Rand Brooks as Andrews

Note: Crash of The Moons is a 75 minute 1954 American science fiction film consisting of three consecutive episodes of the television series *Rocky Jones, Space Ranger* to constitute a complete story. It was released only on 16mm for home movie rental and television syndication. It was directed by Hollingsworth Morse. This film is currently in the Public Domain.

Plot: Rocky Jones (Richard Crane) goes to save the inhabitants of Ophiuchus [pronounced "officious" in the film], a planet about to collide with a moon. However, the Empress of the planet, named Cleolanta (Patsy Parsons), is suspicious of his motives. While Rocky and his crew succeed in evacuating the planet in time, Cleolanta's pride and vanity are a major hindrance. As the last of the planet's population leaves, Cleolanta arrogantly declares that she will stay behind.

Her assistant Atlasan (Harry Lauter) refuses to allow this, picks her up against her will and carries her on board Rocky's own ship. She watches in despair as the moon crashes into her planet. The two bodies destroy one another instantly. As Rocky's ship heads for the new home planet chosen for her people, Cleolanta realizes that she had been wrong, and that, as stated by one of her underlings, "it is the people that make a nation, not the land itself".

She reconciles with Rocky and his crew, and sincerely thanks them for their efforts on her behalf and that of her people. This marks the end of the character Cleolanta in the *Rocky Jones* series. Succeeding episodes contain a new villain. END

Analysis and additional notes: This one slipped by in the night and disappeared. I did not see it. But as the following notes will reveal, the whole is the sum of its parts and not much more. I cannot rate it because I did not see it, but IMdb gives it only 3.1/10, while Rotten Tomatoes gives it no rating at all and only 14% of their audience liked it. And now to the particulars:

Rocky Jones, Space Ranger is an American science fiction television serial originally broadcast in syndication from February to November 1954. The show lasted for only 2 seasons and, though syndicated, dropped into obscurity. Because it was recorded on 16mm film rather than being broadcast live as were most other TV space operas of the day, it has survived in reasonably good condition. The film format also allowed more elaborate special effects and sets, exterior scenes, and much better continuity.

The show was based on the exploits of clean-cut, square-jawed Rocky Jones, the best known of the Space Rangers. These were Earth based "space policemen" who patrolled the United Worlds of The Solar System in the "future". Rocky and his crew would routinely blast off in a chemically fueled, upright rocketship, the Orbit Jet XV-2, which was later replaced by the nearly identical Silver Moon XV-3. They went on missions to moons and planetoids where the odds of success seemed remote yet they would always prevail.

Although they might destroy a rocketship full of unseen bad guys, their pistols were never fired at people, and conflicts were always resolved with fistfights.

Though many strange worlds were visited during the series, the alien characters usually spoke American English, and always appeared as normal humans wearing bizarre costumes and living in strange environments. The script writers did not appear to know the difference between planets, moons, stars and constellations, so that the specific locations Rocky and his sidekicks visited are generally unknown to astronomers. There was also no discussion of physics, neither relatively nor generally.

Half hour episodes were usually grouped into stories that consisted of three "chapters" that were broadcast consecutively in successive weeks. A few of the stories were complete in one episode.

Production: *Rocky Jones, Space Ranger* was the creation of Roland D. Reed. Roland Reed Productions was founded in 1950 and in 1951 Warren Wilson wrote the screenplay for the *Rocky Jones* pilot. By the end of 1951, a cast had been selected headed by Richard Crane as Rocky Jones and Our Gang member Scotty Beckett as Rocky's copilot and comic relief, Winky. The pilot was shot between January and April 1952 with the titles and effects shots being prepared in March of that year. The outdoor scenes were shot at Palomar Mountain Observatory. Post production was completed in May.

The pilot was screened on September 29, 1952. Although the premise showed potential, several characters were recast, including Vena Ray and Secretary Drake. With the new cast finally in place and screenplays prepared for the first 26 episodes, filming began in October 1953 and continued until April 1954.

A merchandising blitz began during this time. Wristwatches, wallets complete with space dollars, badges, buttons, records and clothing were produced to promote the show. A *Rocky Jones, Space Ranger* comic book was issued by Charlton. Issues 15, 16, 17 and 18 of the ongoing title *Space Adventures* were devoted to Rocky's adventures. Rocky, Winky, Vena, Bobby and Cleolanta appear prominently. The largest sponsor was the Gordon Baking Company, makers of Silvercup Bread and the original sponsor of the *The Lone Ranger* radio and television series.

The series finally premiered the week of Monday, February 22, 1954 at various days and times on stations across the United States.

Offscreen issues began almost immediately. In February of 1954, Scotty Beckett was arrested for possessing a weapon after being implicated in an armed robbery at the Cavalier Hotel in Hollywood. After posting bail, he fled to Mexico where he encountered more problems for writing bad checks and more weapons charges. After a gun battle with local police, he was incarcerated for four months, and did not return to the United States until September 1954.

By then the character of Winky had been written out of the show, replaced by Biffen Cardoza (James Lydon).

After filming of the initial 26 episodes ended, Maurice Cass (Professor Newton) died of a heart attack on June 8, 1954. An additional 13 episodes were ordered, and filming took place between August and October 1954. Lydon continued to play Biffen Cardoza, and Professor Newton was replaced by Professor Mayberry (Reginald Sheffield), while regular villainess Cleolanta, Suzerain of Ophiucius (Patsy Parsons) was replaced by Juliandra, Suzerain of Herculon (Ann Robinson).

No further episodes were ordered, and the series ended after 39 episodes. Several researchers have stated that this may have been due to the high cost of the special effects, which apparently made the series unprofitable, especially since the show was syndicated rather than being broadcast on a major network.

Characters and actors:

Rocky Jones: the quintessential action hero – brave, strong, handsome, highly moral, and always ready to defend his beliefs with action. To the women of the stories he is irresistible – even to arch villainess Cleolanta.

Winky: Rocky's faithful copilot and sidekick, the womanizing Winky was the upbeat comic relief to balance the always serious Rocky.

Vena Ray: The blonde Vena serves as Rocky's navigator and translator and was a strong female role model in some episodes. She was played by character actor Sally Mansfield.

Bobby: the young ward of Professor Newton who wants to grow up to be a Space Ranger, and no mention was ever made of his parents or origins. He was portrayed by Robert Lyden.

Professor Newton: Played by Maurice Cass. Professor Newton could always be counted on to provide the scientific explanation for the fantastic events that unfolded, and although elderly, he would often accompany the spaceship crew on their adventures.

The character of Professor Newton was replaced by Professor Mayberry upon Cass' death in 1954.

Secretary Drake: As the head of the Office of Space Affairs and the Space Rangers, Secretary Drake was a father figure to Rocky and his crew, and to him Rocky was like his own son. Secretary Drake was played by Charles Meredith.

Cleolanta: Played by Patsy Parsons. Cleolanta is the Suzerain (empress) of the planet Ophiuchus. She was usually the force behind the troubles that befell the United Worlds, but secretly had a crush on Rocky. She often berated her henchmen for not measuring up to him.

Juliandra/Noviandra: Played by Ann Robinson. Juliandra is the Suzerain of the planet Herculon and friendly to the United Worlds, and she is the one who offers the services of Biffen Cardoza as replacement copilot for the Silver Moon. She has an imprisoned mad twin sister, Noviandra, who hates the United Worlds and everything it stands for.

Pinto Vortando: Pinto is a seedy, unshaven space rogue whose presence usually meant trouble for Rocky. He was portrayed by Ted Hecht.

Bovarro: Big and boisterous, he lives with his wife and young son on the stormwracked moon Posita, one of the two "gypsy moons" (the surviving moon was called Negato) due to crash into Ophiuchus in the three episode adventure: *Crash of The Moons*. Played by John Banner.

Ranger Clark: One of Rocky's fellow Rangers. Ranger Clark operates the refueling space station O.W.9. Ranger Clark was played by William Hudson.

Moving on.

THE CREATURE FROM THE BLACK LAGOON (1954)

Directed by Jack Arnold
Produced by William Alland
Screenplay by Harry Essex and Arthur A. Ross;
story by Maurice Zimm
Music by Henry Mancini, Hans J. Salter, and Herman Stein
Cinematography by William E. Snyder
Edited by Ted J. Kent
Production company: Universal Pictures
Distributed by Universal Pictures; release date: February 12, 1954 and
March 5, 1954 (regional); running time: 79 minutes
Budget: unknown; box office: $1.3 million

Cast:
Richard Carlson as Dr. David Reed
Julie Adams as Kay Lawrence
Richard Denning as Dr. Mark Williams
Antonio Moreno as Dr. Carl Maia
Nestor Paiva as Captain Lucas
Whit Bissell as Dr. Edwin Thompson
Bernie Gozier as Zee
Henry A. Escalante as Chico
Perry Lopez as Tomas
Rodd Redwing as Luis
Sydney Mason as Dr. Matos
Ben Chapman as Gill-man (land)
Ricou Browning as Gill-man (underwater)

Plot: A geology expedition in the Amazon jungle headed by Dr. Carl
Maia and his two native assistants is digging about for specimens
when the two assistants uncover a fossilized skeleton of a hand, radius
and ulna sticking out of the river clay. It appears to be a fossil of a
species unknown to him, possibly from the Devonian period, which
may provide a direct link between land and sea animals.

Dr. Maia orders his two assistants to stay in their camp while he
visits his institute in Buenos Aires. When he leaves, we see a living
form of the fossil emerge from the water and scrape at the dock to a

flourish of eerie music. Sometime later, the two men are preparing to sleep when something attacks them, killing them both.

In Buenos Aires, Dr. Maia reunites with his friend and former student, ichthyologist Dr. David Reed (Richard Carlson) to discuss his find. Reed works at an aquarium in California, but more recently he has been a guest at Maia's institute in Brazil to study lungfish. Once he sees what is there, he insists on accompanying Maia back to the camp to study his find.

Reed persuades his boss, the financially minded Dr. Mark Williams (Richard Denning), to fund a return expedition to the Amazon to look for the remainder of the skeleton. Williams is naturally mercenary; all he knows about it is the numbers and the kudos. But eventually he relents and allows Reed to mount his expedition.

The new group hires the tramp steamer Rita, captained by crusty Lucas (Nestor Paiva). The expedition consists of Reed, Maia, Dr. Mark Williams (Richard Denning), as well as Reed's girlfriend and colleague, Kay Lawrence (Julie Adams); and another scientist, Dr. Edwin Thompson (Whit Bissell). The boat is nothing more than a glorified dinghy with room to hold about 12 men, but it will do the job, according to Lucas.

When they arrive at the camp, they discover Maia's assistants have been killed while he was away. Lucas suggests it was likely done by a jaguar, but the others are unsure. The markings found among the camp grounds do not point that way. They more closely resemble the footprints of an alligator, of which we see several prime examples frightened away by the passage of the Rita among the swamps lining the river.

A further excavation of the area where Dr. Maia found the fossil turns up nothing conclusive. Dr. Williams is ready to give up the search, but Dr. Reed suggests that, perhaps thousands of years ago, the part of the embankment containing the rest of the skeleton fell into the water and was washed downriver, broken up by the current.

Maia says that, according to the map, the tributary empties into a lagoon. Lucas calls it the "Black Lagoon", a paradise from which no one has ever returned. The scientists decide to risk it, unaware that the amphibious "Gill-man" that killed Maia's assistants has been watching them.

As the Rita glides slowly toward the lagoon, Kay watches the fauna and birds roaming among the trees, and hears their raucous calls. She finds them somewhat disturbing, but Reed assures her that she will get used to them.

Taking notice of Kay, the creature follows the Rita all the way downriver to the Black Lagoon. Once the expedition arrives, Reed and Williams go diving to collect samples of fossil remains from the lagoon floor. The creature follows them but does not attack. After they return, the two men admit there is little there to discover. But surely a water sample may reveal more.

While they are studying their data, Kay becomes enamored of the calm water and goes swimming. She is stalked underwater by the Gill-man. The underwater duet is punctuated with the Gill-man's grasping of Kay's ankle and feet, and she is briefly alarmed. But the other scientists find her too far from the Rita and calls her to come back. As she starts swimming toward the boat, Lucas tells his men to move the Rita farther into the lagoon. There, they put down a net to catch fish.

The creature follows Kay until she is safely aboard, then gets caught in the net. We see the hawsers moving, the crane moving. There is a concerted drag on the boat which nearly tips it over. Then nothing. While it escapes from the net, the creature leaves a claw behind, revealing its existence. Reed finds it among the torn netting, and Maia is excited. Perhaps this is a living example of the fossil he found.

Williams is ready to go after the creature, intending to hunt it down and kill it, ostensibly to collect another trophy of the hunt. Reed is alarmed at this and reminds him that this expedition is to collect a specimen to prove to the scientific world of its existence, not as a taxidermist's mounting on his wall. William reminds him who is paying for everything. At this, Reed backs down. But it is clear to everyone else that Williams is only after more publicity, not scientific understanding.

Now that everyone knows what they are dealing with, Maia and Reed agree that they must go down again to discover if the creature is there. While they and Kay are talking with Lucas on the deck, the creature boards the boat and tries to carry Kay off. During the melee' Thompson manages to drive it off with an oar, while Williams shoots it with a harpoon.

After this situation occurs, Lucas suggests that they lay down some fish paralyzer, a powder he keeps on board to catch fish. He says it does no real harm to the fish but may render the Gill-man inert for the time it will take to capture it.

They try this, and at first all they see are parlayzed fish on the surface of the lagoon. Lucas says he may have to laid down enough to do the job. Together, he and Reed compose clumps of the powder to toss into the deeper parts of the lagoon. Once the clumps begin to sink and shed the powder, they settle down to wait.

Subsequent encounters with the Gill-man claim the lives of Lucas's crew members, before the creature is captured and locked in a makeshift bamboo cage anchored beside the Rita. Maia and Reed argue with Williams about the creature. It has certainly shown some rudimentary intelligence, but Williams wants to use it anyway to satisfy his need for notoriety.

Again, he asserts his dominence about the expedition and orders Lucas to turn the Rita around to leave the lagoon, but Lucas reminds him that sea law says the captain is the one who gives orders aboard his boat. Defeated temporarily, Williams stands down for the moment.

A few minutes later, the creature breaks out of the cage and climbs aboard the Rita, where it damages crew and equipment until Thompson drives it away using a lantern. But the creature manages to avoid the lantern and damages it, causing a fire which burns Thompson horribly. Later, Thompson lies critically injured but ably bandaged by Kay, who is distraught about his condition.

Following this incident, Reed decides they should return to civilization. When Reed suggests he should try to recapture the creature, Kay says it has caused enough damage already, and it is probably very dangerous. But he replies that without the evidence of the creature's existence the scientific world would never accept their findings. Kay relents, and Thompson manages to say through his bandage that he would never abandon the project.

But Williams is now obsessed with capturing or killing the creature, and objects to Reed's decision. Reed has had enough of Williams' intransigence by now, and tells him off. Williams realizes that his will cannot be done, but he will do as everyone else wants.

Yet all realize they have no control over the situation as long as the creature is free.

As they try to leave the lagoon aboard the Rita, they find the lagoon's entrance blocked by fallen trees and presume the jam was caused by the Gill-man. While the others work to remove the tangle of branches, Williams tries to capture the creature, single handed and underwater. and is mauled to death for his efforts.

The creature then abducts Kay and takes her to its lair in an underwater cavern. Reed is forced to go after her alone, but armed with harpoons. When he emerges into the cavern, Kay is alone but mostly unharmed. The cavern has several skeletons lying about which closely resemble the creature. But time being of the essence, Reed must only concern himself with Kay for now.

Once they escape the cavern and return to the Rita, Reed and Maia arm themselves and wait for the inevitable attack, while Lucas tries again to free the logjam. Reed is forced to go underwater again to attach the cable, which was broken. At last, the logjam is broken up and the Rita can escape the lagoon.

The creature attacks again, but cannot avoid the bullets raining down on it. It retreats mortally wounded to the depths of the Black Lagoon, where its body sinks into the watery depths. END

Analysis and additional notes: I remember seeing this film in 3D and black and white. I was impressed with the depth of field which remained consistent throughout as I was given a pair of polarized glasses to see the film. The creature appeared to swim through water which was clear enough but somehow free of fish. Then, fish appeared but not with the creature.

There were bits of seaweed and enough sediment on the bottom to make it seem like it was real, but I realized that it was a special tank filled with water. At no time was the creature actually swimming in the Amazon river.

My knowledge of the river is that in several places, Piranha fish occupy the remote lagoons and swamps. In that case, the creature would not have gotten several yards before it was beset with a cloud of the fish, which consume anything living which happens to fall into the water, down to the very bones. Therefore the creature of the Black Lagoon was extremely lucky.

But for decades I was on the fence about whether *The Creature From The Black Lagoon* was science fiction. I mean, it starts out reasonably enough as a scientific expedition into ikthyopaleontology and devolves into a simple monster movie complete with the damsel in distress scenario. We are not told why the creature should have such an interest in the lone female scientist on the expedition. There is only a pedantic pacing to the action which makes the "Gill-man" into a villain. That it is clever enough to track the crew of the Rita to the area where its ancestors were found is not explained. The evolution and identification of the species of which the creature is a member is not explained. We don't know how many millions of years have passed between the fossilized remains and the present day of 1954, and the number is not revealed. We are simply expected to accept the scenario without question. Therefore, I feel that the importance of the film to actual science fiction remains in question.

As with all previous and current expeditions into the jungles of the Amazon, there should have been a small army of security people ensuring that the scientists were kept safe. But they all went out there alone, hardly prepared for what greeted them. That is my main bugaboo. Current scientific expeditions are peopled with many volunteers, security men, and assistants, precisely because each discovery is prone to be exploited by poachers and thieves aiming not to advance human knowledge but to make a quick buck from whatever artifacts or fossils are found. The more familiar bodies surround the dig, the less likely there would be a theft or desecration, especially with regard to uncovered tombs and other such loci.

Take *Indiana Jones and The Raiders of The Lost Ark*, for example. Not only was there the possibility that a golden idol found after a series of booby traps set in a buried temple might be stolen, the one who steals it is himself an archaeologist. He is using Indy to find the stuff for him, or so he thinks. When it comes to the actual location of the Ark of The Covenant, however, he has not done enough homework to realize that he is digging in the wrong place. Again, Indy does all his homework for him. In the end, the villain is undone, but that's not the point.

The point is that every modern expedition has been peopled enough to prevent a disaster. *The Creature From The Black Lagoon* did not cover every contingency possible, so it was not credible for me. Nevertheless, I have been told that a lot of people liked this film when it first came out.

For its somewhat simplistic presentation and the credible acting, as well as the underwater sequences, I give *The Creature From The Black Lagoon* 2 stars out of 4. IMdb gives it 7/10, while Rotten Tomatoes gives it a rating of 84% fresh. 73% of their audience liked it.

Production: Producer William Alland was attending a 1941 dinner party during the filming of *Citizen Kane* (in which he played the reporter Thompson) when Mexican cinematographer Gabriel Figueroa told him about the myth of a race of half fish, half human creatures in the Amazon River. Alland wrote story notes titled "The Sea Monster" 10 years later. His inspiration was Beauty and The Beast. In December of 1952, Maurice Zimm expanded this into a treatment, which Harry Essex and Arthur Ross rewrote as *The Black Lagoon*. Following the success of the 3D film *House of Wax* in 1953, Jack Arnold was hired to direct the film in the same format.

The designer of the approved Gill-man was Disney animator Milicent Patrick, though her role was deliberately downplayed by make-up artist Bud Westmore, who for 50 years would receive sole credit for the creature's conception. Jack Kevan, who worked on *The Wizard of Oz* (1939) and made prosthetics for amputees during World War II, created the bodysuit, while Chris Mueller Jr. sculpted the head.

Ben Chapman portrayed the Gill-man for the majority of the scenes shot at Universal City, California. Many of the surface scenes were filmed at Rice Creek near Palatka, Florida. The costume made it impossible for Chapman to sit for the 14 hours each day that he wore it, and it overheated easily. So he stayed in the back lot's lake, often requesting to be hosed down. He also could not see very well while wearing the headpiece, which caused him to scrape Julie Adams' head against the wall when carrying her in the grotto scenes.

Ricou Browning played the Gill-Man in the underwater shots, which were filmed by the second unit in Wakulla Springs, Florida.

Critical reception: The Creature From The Black Lagoon received positive reviews from critics upon its release and is now considered a classic.

Leonard Maltin awarded the film 3 out of 4 stars, writing, "Archetypal '50s monster movie has been copied so often that some of the edge is gone, but ... is still entertaining, with juicy atmosphere and luminous underwater photography sequences."

The film is recognized by American Film Institute in these lists:

2001: AFI's 100 Years...100 Thrills – Nominated

2003: AFI's 100 Years...100 Heroes & Villains: Gill-man – Nominated Villain

Home media: In 1980, Universal released *The Creature From The Black Lagoon* on video cassette in an anaglyph 3D version, using the Deep Vision anaglyph 3D release as its source. Later releases on VHS, Beta and DVD were in the 2D version.

On October 2, 2012, Universal Studios Home Entertainment released the film on Blu-ray as a 2D / Blu-ray 3D dual format disc as part of the "Universal Classic Monsters: The Essential Collection" box set. On June 4, 2013, the *The Creature From The Black Lagoon* Blu-ray disc was released as a stand alone title.

In other media: *Novelization: The Creature From The Black Lagoon* was novelized in 1954 by John Russell Fearn under the pseudonym of "Vargo Statten". Later in 1977, as a mass market paperback under the pseudonym of "Carl Dreadstone". This was part of a short-lived series of books based on the classic Universal horror films. The 1977 book was introduced by Ramsey Campbell, but was written by Walter Harris.

The 1977 novel offers a completely different Gill-man, who in this version of the story is gigantic, almost as big as the Rita herself, weighing in at 30 tons. It is both coldblooded and warmblooded, is a hermaphrodite, and also possesses a long whip-like tail. The gigantic creature is dubbed "AA", for "Advanced Amphibian", by the expedition team members. After slaying most of the team members, destroying a Silkorsky helicopter, and kidnapping Kay more than once, the creature is finally killed by the crew of a United States Navy torpedo boat.

The 1977 novel also differs greatly with respect to the human characters. Only David Reed and Kay Lawrence remain the same. Mark Williams is a German named "Bruno Gebhardt", and dies not as a result from drowning but by the monster falling on him.

Lucas is named "Jose Goncalves Fonseca de Souza" and is a mostly sympathetic character, until his suggestion of throwing the wounded and unconscious Reed to the monster makes an enraged Gebhardt throw "him" to the beast instead. Dr. Thompson and Dr. Maia both die grisly deaths, whereas in the movie they survive. Maia is eaten by the monster, and Thompson is impaled on a long tree branch flung at him by the creature like a spear.

Reboots and remakes: Sequels: The Creature From The Black Lagoon spawned two sequels: *Revenge of The Creature* (1955), which was also filmed and released in 3D in hopes of reviving the format; and *The Creature Walks Among Us* (1956), filmed in 2D. A comedic appearance with Abbott and Costello on an episode of *The Colgate Comedy Hour* aired prior to the film's release. The appearance is commonly known as *Abbott and Costello Meet the Creature From The Black Lagoon*.

Cancelled remakes: In 1982, John Landis wanted Jack Arnold to direct a remake of the film, and Nigel Kneale was commissioned to write the screenplay. Kneale completed the script, which involved a pair of creatures, one destructive and the other calm and sensitive, being persecuted by the United States Navy.

A decision to make the film in 3D led to the remake being canceled by producers at Universal, both for budgetary concerns and to avoid a clash with *Jaws 3-D*. In 1992, John Carpenter tried to develop the remake at Universal. He had hired Bill Phillips to write the script while Rick Baker was hired to create the 3D model of the Creature, but the project never got green-lit.

Herschel Weingrod and Timothy Harris wrote a new script, and Universal offered Peter Jackson the director's position in 1995, but he chose to work on *King Kong* instead. In February of 1996, Ivan Reitman was planning to direct the remake, but the outing never materialized. With the financial success of *The Mummy* remake in May of 1999, development of the *The Creature From The Black Lagoon* remake was revived.

In December 2001, Gary Ross signed on to write and produce the remake with his father Arthur A. Ross, one of the original film's writers. He told <u>The Hollywood Reporter</u>, "The story my father wrote embodies the clash between primitive men and civilized men, and that obviously makes it a fertile area for re-examination."

In August 2002, Guillermo del Toro, a fan of the original film, was attached as director. He had hoped to do a story focused more on the Creature's perspective and letting him have romantic success, which he would later turn into the 2017 film *The Shape of Water*, but Universal heads rejected this concept.

Because of these creative clashes and his commitments to numerous other projects, Universal was forced to go without del Toro and hired Tedi Sarafian to write a script in March of 2003.

In October of 2005, Breck Eisner signed on as director. "As a kid, I remember loving Jack Arnold's original version of this film", he explained. "What I really want to do is update an iconic image from the '50s and bring in more of the sci-fi sensibility of Alien or John Carpenter's *The Thing* (1982)." Ross said in March of 2007 that the Gill-man's origin would be reinvented, with him being the result of a pharmaceutical corporation polluting the Amazon. "It's about the rainforest being exploited for profit", he said.

However, the production was delayed by the 2007–2008 Writers Guild of America strike. As a result, Eisner made *The Crazies* (2010) the number one on his priority list instead. His new goal was to finish filming *The Crazies* and then begin filming *The Creature From The Black Lagoon* in Manaus, Brazil and on the Amazon River in Peru. Eisner was inspired to shoot on location by the film *Fitzcarraldo* (Werner Herzog), and the boat set had already been built. Eisner continued to rewrite the script, which was to be a summer blockbuster full of "action and excitement, but [still] scary". Eisner spent 6 months designing the new incarnation of the Gill-man with Mark McCreery (*Jurassic Park* and *Davy Jones'* designer). The director said the design was "very faithful to the original, but updated" and that the Gill-man would still be sympathetic.

In 2009, it was reported that Carl Erik Rinsch would direct a 2010 remake that would be produced by Marc Abraham, Eric Newman and Gary Ross. However, the project featuring this ensemble had been abandoned by late 2011.

In March of 2012, Universal announced that a remake was in production, and would simply be titled *The Black Lagoon* rather than *The Creature From The Black Lagoon* in order to distinguish the two versions.

In October of 2012, the studio hired Dave Kajganich to write the film. The film was expected to hit theaters by May of 2014, but was ultimately cancelled. And so another "blockbuster" film outwore its welcome.

Reboot: Universal Pictures is developing a shared universe of rebooted modern day versions of their classic Universal Monsters, with various films in different stages of development. The series begins with *The Mummy* (2017) and will continue with *Bride of Frankenstein* (2019). *The Creature From The Black Lagoon* has a story written by Jeff Pinkner and a script written by Will Beall. In June of 2017, Kurtzman revealed that the Gill-man will be from the Amazon. But on November 8, 2017, Alex Kurtzman and Chris Morgan moved on to other projects, leaving the future of the Dark Universe in doubt.

On January 15, 2018, it was reported by Omega Underground that the production team for the *Bride of Frankenstein* has reassembled and are now eyeing Gal Gadot for the lead role. Wouldn't that be nifty.

Legacy: The 2017 film *The Shape of Water* was partly inspired by Guillermo del Toro's childhood memories of *The Creature From The Black Lagoon*. He wished to see the Gill-man and the film's co-star Julie Adams succeed in their "romance".

Using that premise, he embarked in producing an engaging and sympathetic treatment of the creature from the point of view of a female worker tasked with keeping the lab stocked with towels, soaps, and food for the creature, which has already been captured and is kept in a tank. Somehow she manages to help the creature escape into the water system beneath the city. The only way she can escape her interrogators is to drown herself. The creature comes to her rescue. At the end, the woman turns out to be a hybrid herself, and turns into a mermaid to join her fishy lover. Romantic, yes; realistic, no. But that is for a future book.

DEVIL GIRL FROM MARS (1954)

Directed by David MacDonald
Produced by Edward J. Danziger and Harry Lee Danziger
Written by James Eastwood and John C. Maher
Music by Edwin Astley
Cinematography by Jack Cox
Edited by Peter Taylor
Production company: Danziger Productions (UK)
Distributed by British Lion Films; release date: May 2, 1954 (UK); April 27, 1955 (US)
Running time: 76 min.

Cast:
Patricia Laffan as Nyah, the Devil Girl from Mars
Hugh McDermott as Michael Carter
Hazel Court as Ellen Prestwick
Peter Reynolds as Robert Justin/Albert Simpson
Adrienne Corri as Doris
Joseph Tomelty as Professor Arnold Hennessey
John Laurie as Mr. Jamieson
Sophie Stewart as Mrs. Jamieson

Plot: A flying saucer is seen flying over several cities in Europe, then passes over the English Channel into Britain. A squadron of fighters is dispatched to intercept the craft. But the saucer is accidentally struck by one of the fighters and is forced to land in a Scottish moor near the local village of Inverness-shire.

At a local public house called The Bonnie Prince Charlie, life is carrying on as usual. A newspaper reporter, Michael Carter (Hugh McDermott), has struck up a casual affair with the barmaid Ellen Prestwick (Hazel Court), who has fled to this new life from a married man with whom she had an affair. A regular customer named Albert Simpson (Peter Reynolds) has returned to the village to resume his courtship with the barmaid Doris (Adrienne Corri), who is the love of his life. In reality he is an escaped convict from Stirlingshire Prison named Robert Justin, who was serving time for murdering his wife. A local scientist, Prof. Arnold Hennessey (Joseph Tomelty), is visiting to take a break from his experiments, and holds a small court with the Jamiesons, who are the owners of the pub. Carter pursues an angle as he persters Hennessey with questions about his work.

The whole atmosphere is pleasantly cozy and domestic at first, when a strange woman appears in the doorway.

She is dressed head to toe in shiny black leathers, with a cape which goes down to the floor. Her features are sharp and mature. She introduces herself as Nyah (Patricia Laffan). She announces to the patrons in the pub that she is from Mars, and that she has arrived on Earth to secure men to take with her back to Mars.

She trains a raygun on the patrons while she calmly explains that on Mars the emancipation of women eventually led to warfare. The women won, gaining political power, but the men soon became

216

impotent and the birthrate began to decline. In order to circumvent this potential disaster, Mars developed technologies to enable Martians to have more children, but the technologies proved unreliable where fertility was concerned. As a result the decline of population continued unabated.

It becomes clear that the local Scotsmen are not the least bit interested in going with her to Mars, and the local women are not about to give them up without a fight. Reluctantly, she leaves, saying that she will be back.

Hennessey is excited about her. He says that he would like to know more. But Carter is not so impressed. He makes a call to the local constabulary but finds that the phone is dead. The patrons become frightened. Some leave to go home, and the Jamiesons arm themselves. Simpson and Carter form their own vigilante committee with Ellen and Doris, while Hennessey makes notes about the Martian visitor.

Meanwhile, Nyah returns to her damaged craft and summons her robot Chani to make repairs to it. While the craft has self-regenerating technology, it will take time for the repairs to take effect. She decides that if the men will not volunteer to go with her, she will kidnap them to complete her mission.

She returns to the pub to threaten the patrons once more. Hennessey asks her to show him the spacecraft, to prove that her words are true. She agrees readily, thinking that having a scientist in her larder would give her people a better gene pool. While Hennessey is inpecting the interior of her craft, Nyah turns her robot loose in the village and returns to the pub.

There, Nyah is confronted by guns. Mr. Jamieson shoots at her, but her personal cloaking shield deflects the bullet. She responds by shooting and incinerating their hunchbacked handyman, whom she considers "defective". Then she kidnaps the Jamiesons' nephew Tommy and leaves with him, while the robot destroys the manor house and most of the surrounding village.

Realizing that the only road to victory over Nyah means employing guile and treachery, Hennessy suggests that one of the men at the inn should volunteer to go to Mars in exchange for the safe return of Tommy. This selfless volunteer, after a bit of coaching from Hennessy, will then fatally sabotage the Devil Girl's spacecraft after takeoff. Hennessy himself volunteers, but Carter convinces him that he is much too old to appeal to Nyah and has no chance of being accepted. Carter means to go instead, but at the last minute, Justin leaves and manages to convince Nyah to accept him. While Carter chases after him, Justin goes inside with Nyah and the craft takes off.

Soon afterward, the craft explodes. Justin had managed to sabotage the controls, atoning for his wife's accidental death by sacrificing himself to save Earth from the Devil Girl from Mars. END

Analysis and additional notes: This was not the most serious gem. There was a little exposition which set up the situation, but beyond that there were problems with the plotline. For one, the appearance of a single female Martian armed with little but a raygun and a robot seemed a bit silly. I certainly would not have taken her threats seriously. However, it appeared that the robot was not remote controlled and capable of making some decisions on its own, which is an improvement on previous models.

I thought that the time-honored social model of an alien planet ruled by women was interesting for a change. Instead of outlawing or killing their men, the Martians simply subdued them or took their place in power. We are not allowed to know why the decline in birthrate, however, and if this was a conscious decision on the part of the male population or genuine impotency. There is simply not enough time in the film to determine which. But the main line, that of regenerating the population using alien DNA, is sound science. That is, if one is to believe the whole scenario to begin with.

For its daring plotline and dramatic pacing I give this film 2.5 stars out of 4. IMdb gives it 5.0/10, while Rotten Tomatoes gives it a page, but no rating, and only 23% of their audience liked it.

Production: In an interview with Frank J. Dello Stritto, screenwriter John Chartres Mather claimed that *Devil Girl From Mars* came about while he was working with The Danzigers, who were producing *Calling Scotland Yard* that appeared as both an American television series and as featurettes in Great Britain and the British Commonwealth. When production finished ahead of schedule, Maher said he was ordered to use up the remaining film studio time already booked and paid for by working on a feature film for the Danzigers. The interview also claimed that Patricia Laffan's devil girl costume was economically made by designer John Sutcliffe.

The film was made on a very low budget, with no retakes except in cases where the actual film stock became damaged. It was shot over a period of 3 weeks, often filming well into the night. Actress Hazel Court later said, "I remember great fun on the set. It was like a repertory company acting that film."

The robot, named Chani, was constructed by Jack Whitehead and was fully automated, although it suffered breakdowns during the filming.

Since the alien Klaatu, posing as "Mr. Carpenter" in *The Day The Earth Stood Still* (1951), was intended by screenwriter Edmund H. North to evoke Jesus Christ, so too are there indications that the Martian woman Nyah was intended to evoke an anti-Virgin Mary image. But Nyah comes off as a true soldier instead of a meek woman.

Mars's sound editor was Gerry Anderson, who went on to create the popular UK science fiction television series for children, *Supercar, Fireball XL-5, Thunderbirds, Stingray,* and others. He was listed as "Gerald Anderson" in the film's screen credits.

To save time and money, composer Edwin Astley reused his *Saber of London* score for the film.

Reception: <u>Rolling Stone</u> columnist Doug Pratt called *Devil Girl From Mars* a "delightfully bad movie". The "acting is really bad and the whole thing is so much fun you want to run to your local community theatre group and have them put it on next, instead of Brigadoon."

American film reviewer Leonard Maltin said the film is a "hilariously solemn, high camp British imitation of U. S. cheapies."

The reviewer for the <u>British Monthly Film Bulletin</u> (1954) wrote that the "settings, dialogue, characterisation and special effects are of a low order, but even their modest unreality has its charm. There is really no fault in this film that one would like to see eliminated. Everything, in its way, is quite perfect."

In the book *Going To Mars* the authors described the film as "an undeniably awful but oddly interesting" film. They noted that the plot was "more a reflection of the 1950s view of politics and the era's inequality of the sexes than a thoughtful projection of present or future possibilities."

Eric S. Rabkin likens the character Nyah to a dominatrix and even a neo-Nazi. He said of the film that, "a host of charged images and subconscious fears" are handled with a broad camp irony. Otherwise, "without some underlying psychological engagement, how could anyone sit through a movie so badly made?"

The film inspired Hugo and Nebula award-winning author Octavia Butler to begin writing science fiction. After watching the motion picture at age 12, she declared that she could write something better. Likewise, the Los Angeles avant-garde artist Gronk lists this film as the crucial factor that guided him in his career choice.

GOJIRΛ (GODZILLA) (1954)

Directed by Ishirō Honda
Produced by Tomoyuki Tanaka
Screenplay by Takeo Murata and Ishirō Honda
Story by Shigeru Kayama
Music by Akira Ifukube
Cinematography by Masao Tamai
Edited by Taichi Taira
Production company: Toho
Distributed by Toho
Release date: October 27, 1954 (Nagoya); November 3, 1954 (Japan)
Running time: 96 minutes; budget: ¥100 million
Box office; ¥183 million (Japan) I $562,711 (USA)

Cast:
Akira Takarada as Hideto Ogata
Momoko Kōchi as Emiko Yamane
Akihiko Hirata as Dr. Daisuke Serizawa
Takashi Shimura as Dr. Kyohei Yamane
Fuyuki Murakami as Dr. Tanabe
Sachio Sakai as Hagiwara
Ren Yamamoto as Masaji Yamada
Toyoaki Suzuki as Shinkichi Yamada
Toranosuke Ogawa as President of the Nankai Shipping Company
Hiroshi Hayashi as Chairman of Diet Committee
Seijiro Onda as Oyama, Diet Committee member
Kin Sugai as Ozawa, Diet Committee member
Kokuten Kōdō as The Old Fisherman
Tadashi Okabe as Assistant of Dr. Tanabe
Jiro Mitsuaki as Employee of Nankai Salvage Company

Ren Imaizumi as Radio Officer Nankai Salvage Company
Sokichi Maki as Chief at Maritime Safety Agency
Kenji Sahara as partygoer
Haruo Nakajima as Godzilla and a reporter
Katsumi Tezuka as Godzilla & newspaper deskman

Plot: When the Japanese freighter Eiko-maru is destroyed near Odo Island, another ship, the Bingo-maru, is sent to investigate, only to meet the same fate with few survivors. A fishing boat from Odo is also destroyed, with one survivor. Fishing catches mysteriously drop to zero, blamed by an elder on the ancient sea creature known as "Godzilla".

Reporters arrive on Odo Island to investigate. A villager tells one of the reporters that something in the sea is ruining the fishing. That evening, a storm strikes the island, destroying the reporters' helicopter, and Godzilla, though very briefly seen, destroys 17 homes, kills 9 people and 20 of the villagers' livestock.

Odo residents travel to Tokyo to demand disaster relief. The evidence describes damage consistent with something large crushing the village. The government sends paleontologist Kyohei Yamane to lead an investigation on the island, where giant radioactive footprints and a trilobite are discovered. The village alarm bell is rung, and Yamane and the villagers rush to see the monster, retreating after seeing that it is a giant dinosaur.

Yamane presents his findings in Tokyo, estimating that Godzilla is 50 meters (164') tall, and is evolved from an ancient sea creature which has crossed over into a terrestrial animal. He concludes that Godzilla has been disturbed from its deep underwater natural habitat by underwater hydrogen bomb testing. [There is simply not enough science present in the film to verify this.]

Debate ensues about notifying the public about the danger of the monster. Meanwhile, 17 ships are lost at sea.

Ten frigates are dispatched to attempt to kill the monster using depth charges. The mission disappoints Yamane, who wants Godzilla to be studied. Having survived the attack, officials appeal to Yamane for ideas to kill the monster, but Yamane tells them that Godzilla is unkillable, having survived H-bomb testing, and must be studied, not killed, to learn its unique properties.

Yamane's daughter, Emiko, decides to break off her arranged engagement to Yamane's colleague, Dr. Daisuke Serizawa, because of her love for Hideto Ogata, a salvage ship captain. When a reporter arrives and asks to interview Serizawa, Emiko escorts the reporter to Serizawa's home.

After Serizawa refuses to divulge his current work to the reporter, the reporter goes away. Once he is gone, Serizawa gives Emiko a demonstration of his recent project on the condition she must keep it a secret. The demonstration horrifies her and she leaves without breaking off the engagement. Shortly after she returns home, Godzilla surfaces from Tokyo Bay and attacks Shinagawa; then, after attacking a passing train, Godzilla returns to the ocean.

After consulting with international experts, the Japanese Self-Defense Forces construct a 30 meter tall (100'), 50,000 volt electrified fence along the coast and deploy their forces to stop and kill Godzilla.

Yamane returns home, dismayed that there is no plan to study Godzilla for its resistance to radiation, where Emiko and Ogata await hoping to get his consent for them to wed. When Ogata disagrees with Yamane, arguing the threat Godzilla poses outweighs any potential benefits from studying the monster, Yamane tells him to leave.

Later, Godzilla resurfaces and breaks through the fence to Tokyo with its atomic breath, unleashing more destruction across the city. Further attempts to kill the monster with tanks and fighter jets fail. After the battle, Godzilla once again returns to the ocean. The day after, hospitals and shelters are crowded with the maimed and the dead, with some survivors suffering radiation sickness.

Distraught by the devastation, Emiko tells Ogata about Serizawa's research, a weapon called the "Oxygen Destroyer" which disintegrates oxygen atoms. The organisms die of a rotting asphyxiation. Emiko and Ogata go to Serizawa to convince him to use the Oxygen Destroyer but he refuses at first. But after watching a TV program which displays the nation's current tragedy, Serizawa finally accepts their pleas. As Serizawa burns his notes, Emiko breaks down crying with relief.

A navy ship takes Ogata and Serizawa to plant the device in Tokyo Bay. After finding Godzilla asleep in its underwater nest, Serizawa unloads the device and then cuts off his air support, taking the secrets of the Oxygen Destroyer to his grave.

Godzilla is destroyed but many mourn Serizawa's death.

Yamane believes that if nuclear weapons testing continues, another Godzilla may rise in the future. END

Analysis and additional notes: I remember that as a child I saw a theatrical re-release of this film during a Saturday matinee. It was one of many monster films I saw during my formative years. I really did not know much about Japanese culture at the time, but I was slowly learning about their art and food. This one stood out as a really impressive story about the results of nuclear testing and its aftermath, though I knew it was fictional and bore no actual resemblence to nuclear science. Still, the idea that a monster could be born of nuclear fission and survive was intriguing.

As the years went by there were many sequels and remakes. I did not like the 2004 version of *Godzilla* because the lizard they used for the monster looked nothing like the original.

Later, I liked the first *Pacific Rim* (2013) in which Godzilla battles with a pair of Kaiju (monsters) to help out the giant tech armored pilots. To make him into a hero, they had him gently nudging several ships aside, then diving under a bridge to reach the city. But of course the battle is more destruction of city buildings as the Kaiju are no respecters of property. When the last Kaiju dies, Godzilla is exhausted and collapses on the beach, there to snooze until he is rested. Then he quietly slips back into the sea.

In the intervening years, Godzilla was resurrected from his watery death to battle other kaidju monsters. But gradually over time, his terrible threat to Tokyo was "dumbed" down until he became a friend to children, even having a son and an adopted cousin. During this time I stopped watching them more than once. Somehow it was not the same as the first. As a result my skepticism grew with the number of Godzilla movies.

Sure, they were fun, but were they science fiction? That question has not been answered to my satisfaction. The standard radiation excuse does not wash with the other monsters. Some come from outer space, but does that make it science fiction?

For its seriously terrifying plot and scientific resolution I give *Gojira* (Godzilla) 3 stars out of 4. IMdb gives it 7.6/10, but Rotten Tomatoes gives it nothing. There is not even a page. I suppose someone will mention it to them at some point. It is one of the most famous monster movies in the film pantheon.

Themes: In the film, Godzilla symbolizes nuclear holocaust from Japan's perspective and has since been culturally identified as a strong metaphor for nuclear weapons. Producer Tomoyuki Tanaka stated that, "The theme of the film, from the beginning, was the terror of the bomb. Mankind had created the bomb, and now nature was going to take revenge on mankind." Director Ishirō Honda filmed Godzilla's Tokyo rampage to mirror the Atomic bombings of Hiroshima and Nagasaki, stating, "If Godzilla had been a dinosaur or some other animal, he would have been killed by just one cannonball. But if he were equal to an atomic bomb, we wouldn't know what to do. So, I took the characteristics of an atomic bomb and applied them to Godzilla."

Academics Anne Allison, Thomas Schnellbächer, and Steve Ryfle have stated that Godzilla contains political and cultural undertones that can be attributed to what the Japanese had experienced in World War II, and that Japanese audiences were able to connect emotionally to the monster. They theorized that these viewers saw Godzilla as a victim and felt that the creature's backstory reminded them of their experiences in World War II. These academics have also claimed that as the atomic bomb testing that woke Godzilla was carried out by the United States, the film in a way can be seen to blame the United States for the problems and struggles that Japan experienced after World War II had ended. They also felt that the movie could have served as a cultural coping method to help the people of Japan move on from the events of the war.

Brian Merchant from Motherboard called the film "a bleak, powerful metaphor for nuclear power that still endures today" and on its themes, he stated: "it's an unflinchingly bleak, deceptively powerful film about coping with and taking responsibility for incomprehensible, manmade tragedy. Specifically, nuclear tragedies. It's arguably the best window into post-war attitudes towards nuclear power we've got—as seen from the perspective of its greatest victims."

Terrence Rafferty from The New York Times stated that Godzilla was "an obvious gigantic, unsubtle, grimly purposeful metaphor for the atomic bomb" and felt the film was "extraordinarily solemn, full of earnest discussions."

Mark Jacobson from <u>Vulture</u> stated that Godzilla "...transcends humanist prattle. Very few constructs have so perfectly embodied the overriding fears of a particular era. He is the symbol of a world gone wrong, a work of man that once created cannot be taken back or deleted. He rears up out of the sea as a creature of no particular belief system, apart from even the most elastic version of evolution and taxonomy, a reptilian id that lives inside the deepest recesses of the collective unconscious that cannot be reasoned with, a merciless undertaker who broaches no deals." Regarding the film, Jacobson stated, "Honda's first Godzilla... is in line with these inwardly turned post-war films and perhaps the most brutally unforgiving of them. Shame-ridden self-flagellation was in order, and who better to supply the rubber-suited psychic punishment than the Rorschach-shaped big fella himself?"

Tim Martin from <u>The Daily Telegraph</u> stated that the original 1954 film was "...a far cry from its B-movie successors. It was a sober allegory of a film with ambitions as large as its thrice-normal budget, designed to shock and horrify an adult audience. Its roster of frightening images — cities in flames, overstuffed hospitals, irradiated children — would have been all too familiar to cinemagoers for whom memories of Hiroshima and Nagasaki were still less than a decade old, while its script posed deliberately inflammatory questions about the balance of postwar power and the development of nuclear energy."

Martin also noted how the film's themes were omitted in the American version, stating, "Its thematic preoccupation with nuclear energy proved even less acceptable to the American distributors who, after buying the film, began an extensive reshoot and recut for Western markets."

Production: In 1954, Toho originally planned to produce *Eiko-no Kagi-ni* (In The Shadow of Glory), a Japanese-Indonesian co-production about the aftermath of the Japanese occupation of Indonesia. However, anti-Japanese sentiment in Indonesia forced political pressure on the government to deny visas for the Japanese filmmakers. Producer Tomoyuki Tanaka flew to Jakarta to renegotiate with the Indonesian government but was unsuccessful, and on the flight back to Japan, conceived the idea for a giant monster film inspired by the 1953 film *The Beast From 20,000 Fathoms* and the Daigo Fukuryū Maru incident that happened March of that year.

During his flight, Tanaka wrote an outline with the working title *The Giant Monster from 20,000 Leagues Under The Sea* and pitched it to executive producer Iwao Mori. Mori approved the project in April 1954 after special effects director Eiji Tsuburaya agreed to do the film's effects and confirmed that the film was financially feasible. Mori also felt the project was a perfect vehicle for Tsuburaya and to test the storyboarding system that he instituted at the time.

Mori also approved Tanaka's choice to have Ishirō Honda direct the film and shortened the title of the production to *Project G* (G for Giant), as well as giving the production classified status and ordered Tanaka to minimize his attention on other films and mainly focus on *Project G.*

Writing: Tsuburaya submitted an outline of his own, written three years before; it featured a giant octopus attacking ships in the Indian ocean. In May 1954, Tanaka hired science fiction writer Shigeru Kayama to write the story. Only 50 pages long and written in 11 days, Kayama's treatment depicted Dr. Yamane wearing dark shades, a cape and living in a European style house from which he only emerged at night. Godzilla was portrayed as more animalistic by coming ashore to feed on animals, with an ostensibly gorilla-like interest in females. Kayama's story treatment also featured less destruction and borrowed a scene from *The Beast From 20,000 Fathoms* by having Godzilla attack a lighthouse.

Takeo Murata and director Ishiro Honda co-wrote the screenplay in three weeks, confining themselves in a Japanese Inn in Tokyo's Shibuya ward. On writing the script, Murata stated, "Director Honda and I... racked our brains to make Mr. Kayama's original treatment into a full, working vision." Murata stated that Tsuburaya and Tanaka also pitched their ideas as well. Tanaka requested that they do not spend too much money while Tsuburaya encouraged them to "do whatever it takes to make it work".

Murata and Honda redeveloped key characters and elements by adding the Emiko-Ogata-Serizawa love triangle, while in Kayama's treatment, Serizawa was depicted as merely a colleague of Dr. Yamane's.

In Kayama's treatment, Godzilla's full appearance was to be revealed during the Odo Island hurricane but Honda and Murata instead opted to hold back on revealing Godzilla by simply showing parts of the creature as the film built up to his full reveal.

Honda and Murata also introduced the characters Hagiwara and Dr. Tanabe in their draft but the role of Shinkichi, who had a substantial role in Kayama's treatment, was cut down.

Creature design: The filmmakers took inspiration from various dinosaurs to shape Godzilla's final iconic design.

Godzilla was designed by Teizo Toshimitsu and Akira Watanabe under Eiji Tsuburaya's supervision. Early on, Tanaka contemplated on having the monster be similar to gorilla or whale in design due to the name "Gojira" (a combination of the Japanese words for gorilla, gorira, and whale, kujira) but eventually settled on a dinosaur design.

Kazuyoshi Abe was hired earlier to design Godzilla but his ideas were later rejected due to Godzilla looking too humanoid and mammalian, with a head shaped like a mushroom cloud. However Abe was retained to help draw the film's storyboards.

Toshimitsu and Watanabe decided to base Godzilla's design on dinosaurs and, by using dinosaur books and magazines as a reference, combined elements of a Tyrannosaurus, Iguanodon and the dorsal fins of a Stegosaurus.

Tsuburaya wanted to rely on stop-motion animation, but reluctantly settled on "suitmation". Toshimitsu sculpted three clay models on which the suit would be based. The first two were rejected but the third was approved by Tsuburaya, Tanaka, and Honda.

The Godzilla suit was constructed by Kanji Yagi, Koei Yagi, and Eizo Kaimai, who used thin bamboo sticks and wire to build a frame for the interior of the suit and added metal mesh and cushioning over it to bolster its structure and finally applied coats of latex. Coats of molten rubber were also applied, followed by carved indentations and strips of latex glued onto the surface of the suit to create Godzilla's scaly hide. This first version of the suit weighed 100 kg (220 lbs). For close-ups, Toshimitsu created a smaller scale, mechanical, hand-operated puppet that sprayed streams of mist from its mouth to show Godzilla's atomic breath.

Haruo Nakajima and Katsumi Tezuka were chosen to perform in the Godzilla suit, due to their strength and endurance. At the first costume fitting, Nakajima fell down while inside the suit, due to the heavy and inflexible materials used to create the suit. This first version

227

of the suit was cut in half and used for scenes requiring only partial shots of Godzilla or close-ups, with the lower-half fitted with rope suspenders for Nakajima to wear.

A second identical suit was created for full body shots, which was made lighter than the first suit; but Nakajima was still only able to be inside for 3 minutes before passing out. As a result, Nakajima lost 20 pounds during the production of the film. Nakajima would go on to portray Godzilla and other monsters until his retirement in 1972.

Tezuka filmed scenes in the Godzilla suit but was unable to fully commit to the physical demands required of the role due to his age. Few of his scenes made it to the final cut. Tezuka filled in for Nakajima when he was unavailable or needed relief from the physically demanding role.

Special effects: Tsuburaya had wanted to use stop motion for the film's special effects but realized it would have taken seven years to complete, based on the staff and infrastructure at Toho. Settling on suitmation and miniature effects, Tsuburaya and his crew scouted the locations Godzilla was to destroy and were nearly arrested after a security guard overheard their plans for destruction but were released after showing police their Toho business cards.

Kintaro Makino, the chief of miniature construction, was given blueprints by Akira Watanabe for the miniatures and assigned 30 to 40 workers from the carpentry department to build them, which took a month to build the scaled down version of Ginza. A majority of the miniatures were built at 1:25 scale but the Diet building was scaled down to a 1:33 scale to look smaller than Godzilla.

The buildings' framework were made of thin wooden boards reinforced with a mixture of plaster and white chalk. Explosives were installed inside miniatures that were to be destroyed by Godzilla's atomic breath, while some were sprayed with gasoline to make them burn more easily. Others included small cracks so they could crumble easily. Optical animation techniques were used for Godzilla's glowing dorsal fins by having hundreds of cells drawn frame by frame.

Haruo Nakajima perspired inside the suit so much that the Yagi brothers had to dry out the cotton lining every morning and sometimes reline the interior of the suit and repair damages. The special effects crew spent 71 days on filming.

Filming: Most of the film was shot in the Toho lot. Honda's team also filmed on location in the Shima Peninsula in Mie Prefecture to film the Odo Island scenes, which used 50 Toho extras and Honda's team establishing their base in the town of Toba. Toho had negotiated with the Japan Self-Defense Forces to film scenes requiring the military and filmed target practices and drills for the film. Honda's team followed a convoy of JSDF vehicles for convoy dispatch scene. 32,000 girls were used from an all female high school for the prayer for peace scene. Honda's team spent 51 days shooting the film.

Release: Box office: Godzilla was first released in Nagoya, Japan on October 27, 1954. A week later, it was released nationwide on November 3, 1954. It sold approximately 9,610,000 tickets and was the 8th best attended film in Japan that year. It remains the second most attended "Godzilla" film in Japan, behind *King Kong vs. Godzilla*. The film grossed ¥183 million during its initial theatrical run in Japan.

In 1957, the film was released in France, where it drew 835,511 box office admissions. The film's limited North American releases in the early 21st century grossed $562,711, with the 2004 release grossing $412,520, and the 2014 release grossing $150,191.

North America: In 1955 and in the 1960's, *Godzilla* played in theaters catering to Japanese-Americans in predominantly Japanese neighborhoods in the United States. An English subtitled version was shown at film festivals in New York, Chicago, and other cities in 1982.

To coincide with *Godzilla's* 50th anniversary, art-house distributor Rialto Pictures gave the film a traveling tour limited release, coast to coast across the United States on May 7, 2004. It ran uncut with English subtitles until December 19, 2004. Starting out in only two theaters, the film grossed $38,030 in its opening weekend. It never played on more than six screens at any given point during its limited release. By the end of its 2004 run, it had grossed $412,520. The film played in roughly 60 theaters and cities across the United States during its 7½ month release.

On April 18, 2014, Rialto re-released the film in the United States using another limited traveling tour. This coincided with not only *Godzilla's* 60th anniversary, but also celebrated Legendary's *Godzilla* film released that same year. To avoid confusion with the Hollywood feature, the Rialto release was subtitled "The Japanese Original". The film opened with a $10,903 gross while playing on only one screen in

New York City. It went on to play in roughly 66 theaters in 64 cities from April 18 to October 31, 2014. After its run, the film grossed $150,191.

Critical reception: Initial reception: The film received mixed to negative reviews in Japan. Japanese critics accused the film of exploiting the widespread devastation that the country had suffered in World War II, as well as the Daigo Fukuryū Maru (Lucky Dragon) incident that occurred a few months before filming began. Ishiro Honda lamented years later in the Tokyo Journal, "They called it grotesque junk, and said it looked like something you'd spit up. I felt sorry for my crew because they had worked so hard!". Honda also stated "At the time they wrote things like 'This movie is absurd, because such giant monsters do not exist.'"

Others said that depicting a fire breathing organism was "strange." Honda also believed Japanese critics began to change their minds after the good reviews the film received in the United States. He stated "The first film critics to appreciate Godzilla were those in the U.S. When Godzilla was released there as Godzilla, King of the Monsters! in 1956, the critics said such things as, 'For the start, this film frankly depicts the horrors of the Atomic Bomb.', and by these evaluations, the assessment began to impact critics in Japan and has changed their opinions over the years."

As time went on, the film gained more respect in its home country. In 1984, Kinema Junpo magazine listed *Godzilla* as one of the top 20 Japanese films of all time, while a survey of 370 Japanese movie critics published in *Nihon Eiga Besuto 150* (Best 150 Japanese Films), had *Godzilla* ranked as the 27th best Japanese film ever made.

The film was nominated for two Japanese Movie Association awards: one for Best Special Effects and the other for Best Film. It won Best Special Effects but lost Best Picture to Akira Kurosawa's *Seven Samurai.*

2004 release: On *Metacritic,* which assigns a weighted average based on selected critic reviews, the film has a score of 78/100, based on 20 critics, indicating "generally favorable reviews".

In Entertainment Weekly, Owen Glieberman, who gave the film an A rating, wrote: "Godzilla, an ancient beast roused from the ocean depths and irradiated by Japanese H-bomb tests, reduces Tokyo to a pile of ash, yet, like Kong, he grows more sympathetic as his rampage goes on. The characters talk about him not as an enemy but as a force of destiny, a 'god'. The inescapable subtext is that Japan, in some bizarre way, deserves this hell. Godzilla is pop culture's grandest symbol of nuclear apocalypse, but he is also the primordial spirit of Japanese aggression turned, with something like fate, against itself."

In the <u>Dallas Observer</u>, Luke Y. Thompson wrote: "A lot of people are likely to be surprised by what they see. The 1954 Japanese cut is shot like a classic film noir, and the buildup to Tokyo's inevitable thrashing is quite slow by today's standards. The echoes of World War II are very strong, and the devastation wrought by Godzilla (played by Haruo Nakajima) is not sugar coated; it eerily mirrors that of Hiroshima and Nagasaki, and the deaths and injuries are dwelt upon. The monster himself is not fully revealed for quite a while, and even when he finally shows up, he's a malevolent black predator with glistening skin, who stays mostly in the shadows, many times more fearsome than the green-skinned cookie monster who showed up in the various sequels to layeth the smacketh down on the candyasses of numerous alien invaders in ugly leotards."

One of the few recent mixed reviews was written by Roger Ebert in the <u>Chicago Sun-Times</u>. Ebert admitted the film was "an important one" and "properly decoded, was the Fahrenheit 9/11 of its time", but he also said: "In these days of flawless special effects, Godzilla and the city he destroys are equally crude. Godzilla at times looks uncannily like a man in a rubber suit, stomping on cardboard sets, as indeed he was, and did. Other scenes show him as a stuffed, awkward animatronic model. This was not state-of-the-art even at the time; King Kong (1933) was much more convincing. When Dr. Serizawa demonstrates the Oxygen Destroyer to his fiancee, Emiko [sic], the super weapon is somewhat anticlimactic. He drops a pill into a tank of tropical fish, the tank lights up, he shouts, "stand back!", the fiancée screams, and the fish go belly-up. Yeah, that'll stop Godzilla in his tracks."

Since its release, *Godzilla* has been regarded not only as one of the best giant monster films ever made but an important cinematic achievement. The film was ranked #31 in <u>Empire</u> magazine's "The 100 Best Films Of World Cinema" in 2010. In 2015, Variety named it one of the "10 Best Monster Movies of All-Time".

Home media: The 1956 *Godzilla, King of The Monsters!* version of the film was released on DVD by Simitar in 1998 and Classic Media in 2002. A DVD of the original Japanese version of the film was released in Japan in 2002. The quality of the print used for the Japanese version was partially restored and remastered, including three audio tracks (the original mono track, an isolated audio track, and an isolated track and special effects track), and an interview with Akira Ifukube.

In 2006, Classic Media and Sony BMG Music Entertainment Home Entertainment released a two-disc DVD set titled *Gojira: The Original Japanese Masterpiece*. This release features both the original 1954 Japanese *Gojira* film and the 1956 American *Godzilla, King of The Monsters!* version, making the original Japanese version of the film available on DVD in North America for the first time. This release also restores the original ending credits of the American film which, until recently, were thought to have been lost.

In the fall of 2005, BFI released the original Japanese version in the UK theatrically, and later in the same year on DVD. The DVD includes the original mono track and several extra features, such as documentaries and commentary tracks by Steve Ryfle, Ed Godziszewski, and Keith Aiken. The DVD also includes a documentary about the Daigo Fukuryu Maru, a Japanese fishing boat that was caught in an American nuclear blast and partially inspired the creation of the movie. A DVD was released in Australia by Madman Co. Ltd in 2004 for the film's 50th Anniversary.

In 2009, Classic Media released *Godzilla* on Blu-ray. This release includes the same special features from the 2006 Classic Media DVD release, but does not feature the 1956 American version.

On January 24, 2012, The Criterion Collection released a "new high-definition digital restoration" of *Godzilla* on Blu-ray and DVD. This release includes a remaster of the 1956 American version, *Godzilla, King of The Monsters*, as well as other special features such as interviews with Akira Ikufube, Japanese film critic Tadao Sato, actor Akira Takarada, Godzilla performer Haruo Nakajima, effects technicians Yoshio Irie and Eizo Kaimai, and audio commentaries on both films by David Kalat, author of *A Critical History and Filmography of Toho's Godzilla Series*.

GOG (1954)

Directed by Herbert L. Strock
Produced by Ivan Tors
Written by Tom Taggart (screenplay), Ivan Tors (story), Richard G. Taylor (dialogue)
Music by Harry Sukman
Cinematography by Lothrop B. Worth
Edited by Herbert L. Strock
Production company: Ivan Tors Productions
Distributed by United Artists; release date June 5, 1954 | August 13, 1954 (New York)
Running time: 83 minutes; budget: $250,000

Cast:
Richard Egan as David Sheppard
Constance Dowling as Joanna Merritt
Herbert Marshall as Dr. Van Ness
John Wengraf as Dr. Zeitman
Steve Roberts as Maj. Howard
Marian Richman as Technician Helen
Phillip Van Zandt as Dr. Pierre Elzevir
Valerie Vernon as Madame Elzevir
Byron Kane as Dr. Carter
David Alpert as Dr. Peter Burden
Michael Fox as Dr. Hubertus
William Schallert as Dr. Engle
Aline Towne as Dr. Kirby
Jean Dean as Marna Roberts
Al Bayer as Helicopter Pilot
Tom Daly as Secretary
Andy Andrews as Security Guard Andy
Julian Ludwig as Security Guard Julie

Plot: Unaccountable and deadly malfunctions begin occurring at a top secret government facility located under the New Mexico desert, where a space station is being constructed to launch into orbit. Dr. David Sheppard (Richard Egan), from the Office of Scientific Investigation (OSI) in Washington, D.C., is called in. Working with

Joanna Merritt (Costance Dowling), another OSI agent already at the facility, Sheppard determines that the deaths among the laboratory's 150 top scientists are due to deliberate sabotage of the facility's Nuclear Operative Variable Automatic Computer (NOVAC), which controls and coordinates all the equipment in the underground facility.

It is far more difficult, however, to determine how the sabotage is being done. The unseen enemy strikes again and again, snuffing out the lives of 5 scientists and 2 human test subjects in quick succession, as well as Major Howard (Steve Roberts), the complex's Chief of Security. In addition, both Madame Elzevir (Valerie Vernon), a solar engineering scientist, and Dr. Peter Burden (David Alpert), the chief atomic engineer, are attacked. They manage to survive, but are seriously injured.

Eventually, Sheppard determines that a powerful radio transmitter and receiver were secretly built into NOVAC during its construction in Switzerland, without the knowledge or consent of its designer, Dr. Zeitman (John Wengraf).

A robot plane, whose fiberglass body does not register on radar, has been flying overhead, beaming precisely focused, ultrahigh frequency radio signals into the complex to control NOVAC's every function. The computer controls Gog and Magog, two huge mobile robots with multiple arms, powerful gripping tools, and other implements. The robots are designed to go where no human can, so they roll autonomously throughout the facility and even enter radioactive compartments.

Magog goes to the complex's nuclear reactor control room and pulls a safety rod out of the atomic pile, starting a chain reaction that will build to a nuclear explosion, which in turn will destroy the entire facility. Sheppard suits up and arrives in time to push the safety rod back into the pile. Magog seems to "detect" this action and stalks Sheppard before he can leave the control room. Sheppard responds by attacking the robot with a flame thrower, disabling it. But Gog soon follows its twin to the reactor room to finish the job. Sheppard's flame thrower runs out of fuel as the robot advances on him.

Dr. Van Ness (Herbert Marshall) arrives with another flame thrower, but the control valve sticks, and now Gog turns on him. Sheppard desperately uses the nozzle of his flame thrower as a bludgeon, trying to smash the robot's electronic tubes. The crippled robot begins spinning back and forth, its arms thrashing about wildly. Then. Gog suddenly comes to a halt, its metal arms falling limply to its sides. Both robots are inert.

It turns out that American F-86 and F-94 jet fighters have found and destroyed the enemy plane, ending NOVAC's reign of destruction. Van Ness then realizes that Sheppard and Merritt have been exposed to an overdose of radiation from the reactor. Sheppard takes Merritt into his arms and heads for the complex hospital. There he learns that their radiation exposure was not serious and that they will both soon recover.

A few days later, Dr. Van Ness explains the situation to the Secretary of Defense, informing him that, in spite of all the setbacks, the project is still on schedule, and that a working model of the space station is about to be launched into orbit. The new "baby space station" will be equipped with telescopes and television cameras that will spot any further attempts to sabotage the complex.

The Secretary notes with satisfaction: "Nothing will take us by surprise again!"

The following morning, the launch goes off successfully. END

Analysis and additional notes: This adventure could be labeled a documentary and still garner some interest as a science fiction film. In fact, the story could be called "a day in the life" of the space program. Here, the robots Gog and Magog are merely tools, controlled by the computer NOVAC instead of through remote control by a human. They do functions which are dangerous to the human scientists at the complex.

But the computer itself was vulnerable to hacking, a practice which has grown to dangerous levels here in the 21st century. We don't know why the security team at the complex did not detect the control plane itself early on. It would have had to patrol the grounds at a relatively low altitude to be able to transmit, opening itself to detection. The radio waves could then have been detected easily, and they could have just pulled the plug to the computer and reboot once the sabotage was discovered. Easy peasy.

No, we are witnesses to various murders throughout the film, gladiator combat between the humans and the robots, and danger of nuclear annihilation. And yet the Secretary of Defense barely bats an eyelash to the destruction, taking it all in with the calmness of a Buddha, instead of screaming his head off about the costs. There is a strange atmosphere of detachment about the deaths and injuries of people working on the complex. The robots, being representative of modern technology, seem more emotional about each other than the humans around them.

So it is actually espionage and not the space program which takes the center of the stage. The computer and the robots are rendered as mere symbols of the technology and its improvements.

For its rather pedantic and almost unemotional presentation, I give it only 2 stars out of 4. IMdb gives it 4.4/10, and Rotten Tomatoes shows no rating, but only 22% of their audience liked it.

Production: GOG was filmed on just two sets at Hal Roach Studios, with the exteriors shot at the former military outpost George Air Force Base, near Victorville, California. It took just 15 days to shoot all of the footage. GOG's final cost was estimated to be $250,000.

Shortly after filming was completed, Constance Dowling married Ivan Tors and retired from acting. Another actor in the film, William Schallert, made his debut in the science fiction genre with this low budget feature. He later appeared in other film genres, ranging from comedies to dramas and back again to science fiction. He also appeared in TV episodes, including the popular Patty Duke series.

Although shot in the 3D process, GOG was released at the tail end of the first 3-D fad (1953–1954). As a result, it was often projected "flat" in its widescreen aspect ratio of 1.66:1, made standard by Hollywood the year before, despite prints being available in the stereoscopic format.

Reception: The film was previewed in 3D for the press at a United Artists' screening room. Initial critical response to the film ranged from "good" to "very good".

Critical response was generally positive, with many critics noting the story's basis in science fact, rather than science fiction; this was a staple of Tors's science fiction films. His 1955 television series *Science Fiction Theatre* had the same period verisimilitude, and often lifted props and some situations from GOG and the other two OSI films he produced.

<u>Motion Picture Herald</u>'s William R. Weaver said of GOG, "The production moves steadily forward, keeping interest growing at a

steady pace, and exciting the imagination without overstraining credulity."

Home video: GOG has been released on Blu-ray in 3D from Kino and contains an audio commentary by Tom Weaver, Bob Furmanek and David Schecter.

KILLERS FROM SPACE (aka The Man Who Saved Earth)(1954)

Produced and directed by W. Lee Wilder
Written by William Raynor and Myles Wilder
Music by Manuel Compinsky
Cinematography by William H. Clothier
Edited by William Faris
Production company: Planet Filmplays, Inc. and RKO Radio Pictures
Distributed by RKO Radio Pictures
Release date: January 23, 1954; running time: 71 minutes

Cast:
Peter Graves as Dr. Douglas Martin
Frank Gerstle as Dr. Curt Kruger
James Seay as Col. Banks
Steve Pendleton as FBI Agent Briggs
Barbara Bestar as Ellen Martin
Shepard Menken as Major Clift, M.D.
John Merrick as Denab and The Tala
Jack Daly as Powerhouse Supervisor
Ron Kennedy as Sentry Sergeant
Ben Welden as Tarbaby 2 Pilot
Burt Wenland as Unspecified Sergeant
Lester Dorr as Gas Station Attendant
Robert Roark as Unspecified Guard
Ruth Bennett as Miss Vincent
Mark Scott as Narrator
Roy Engel as 1st Police Dispatcher (uncredited)
Coleman Francis as Power Plant Phone Operator (uncredited)

Plot: Dr. Douglas Martin (Peter Graves) is a nuclear scientist working on atomic bomb tests. While collecting aerial data on an atomic blast at Soledad Flats, he and his pilot lose control of their aircraft and it crashes.

The next day, Martin's wife Ellen (Barbara Bestar) is discussing what happened to her husband to Col. Banks (James Seay), who explains that when the air rescue squad got to the crash site, Martin had disappeared. Ellen is insistent that the search must not be abandoned. She is one of those Air Force wives who maintains an even strain, even though she is desperate for news. Banks tells her that everything that can be done will be.

Meanwhile, Martin stumbles his way to the entrance to the air base and is intercepted by the MP officer at the gate.

Once he is taken to the base hospital, Martin appears to have survived unhurt, walking back to the air base with no memory of what happened. On his chest is a strange scar that was not there before the crash. It appears to be almost completely healed, unusual for operations of that time. After a series of tests, Martin is pronounced healthy and fit by the base doctor, Dr. Clift (Shepard Mencken), but he wants to keep Martin there for observation.

Ellen is allowed to visit her husband but he acts so strangely that she is shooed away by Clift and Banks, who want to control what is going on. She vows to return to find out what is wrong. They assure here that Martin is still in shock and must have some rest. Meanwhile, the Air Force brings in an FBI agent named Briggs (Steve Pendleton) to investigate. Their belief is that Martin is an impostor sent to spy on their operations. But the scientist is cleared of all affiliations and told to take some time off.

Martin protests being excluded from his project while on leave. He must know when the next scheduled bomb test is to take place. But Banks tells him to forget about it. Ellen persuades her husband to go home with her.

That evening, Martin experiences a strange nightmare, waking Ellen. He is restless and unable to calm down. Finally he says he will drink some milk to settle his nerves. Ellen follows him, and while she goes into the kitchen, Martin calls the base to find out if there is any new data to record. The receptionist on call says he cannot divulge any details; that information is classified. Frustrated, Martin hangs up, then slips out the door and drives back to the base. There, he discovers that another bomb test was conducted without his knowledge.

Desperate to get the data, he pretends to be retrieving several things from his office, where a strange woman has taken his place behind his desk. He finds out that she is someone else's secretary who needed a quiet place to work. Finally she leaves, saying that she did not know he would be there that day.

He spends a couple of hours waiting in his office, while watching the office across the way. There, Dr. Curt Kruger has a safe room, where the most secret documents are kept. Martin thinks that the data may be there. A few minutes later, Dr. Kruger seals up the safe and departs.

Martin sneaks out of his own office and enters the other one, opens the safe and rifles through the documents. He finds what he wants and copies it down in a notepad, then leaves without closing the safe. Then he drives back to Soledad Flats and places the information under a stone, when Briggs snatches it from him and asks what he is doing with it. Martin punches him out, then runs to his car and takes off. He speeds along the highway until he encounters a baleful pair of eyes coming toward him. He swerves off the pavement and crashes into a tree.

Now back at the hospital, he is given sodium ametol to discover the truth. Deep under the drug's influence, Martin tells a story about being held captive by space aliens, led by Denab (John Merrick), in their underground base, which is in a cavern deep underground.

The aliens, with large, bulging eyes, are from the planet Astron Delta, ruled by a being called The Tala (also John Merrick). They had revived Martin's lifeless body since he had actually died in his aircraft. Apparently they had created an artificial heart and replaced the dead one.

Denab explains that their sun became too weak and threatened Astron Delta with extinction. The plant life on their planet had died out and climate change threatened the surviving population, which now stood at about 1 billion. The alien explained that The Tala's supreme plan is to invade the Earth, which is as close to their native planet as they have been able to determine. But there is a catch: in order to populate Earth they are going to render humanity extinct.

Martin panics and says he will do nothing to help them, then runs away. But despite his efforts to find a way out of the cavern, he encounters a series of gigantic Earth denizens: spiders, gila monsters, scorpions, lizards, grasshoppers, and so on. Martin is horrified. Everywhere he goes he met by cannibalism and battle among the monsters. When he tries yet another tunnel he is met by various Deltans who ignore him as if he does not exist. Before long he finds himself back at square one, where Denab calmly tells him that all his efforts will be fruitless.

Finding some sense of rationality amidst the fear, Martin determines to discover some way to neutralize the alien's plan. He asks how this conquest will be done.

Denab shows him some of the instrumentality at their command. All is powered by the electrical grid and nuclear energy, stolen from the bomb tests and also a local power plant nearby. Martin intuits this from observation, but was unable to impart what he knew. Apparently the aliens wiped his memory and hypnotized him to force him to collect the data.

The FBI agent Briggs (Steve Pendleton) and the base commander (James Seay) are skeptical of this story and keep him confined at the hospital "for his own safety". Nevertheless, the attending physician says that Martin genuinely believes that what he told them is true. It would be impossible for Martin to say otherwise, because the drug robbed him of the imagination to lie.

Ellen Martin insists on seeing her husband so they allow her in on the project with the proviso that she must not tell anyone else. When she comes into Martin's hospital room, he has recovered from the truth serum but is agitated and eager to resume his work.

With calculations made using a slide rule, Martin determines that if he shuts off the power to Soledad Flats for just 10 seconds, it will create an overload in the aliens' equipment. Armed with this information, he escapes from the hospital and goes to the nearby electrical power plant, where he searches for the main power control, intending to shut off the power.

His three friends and his wife chase after him, and they invade the plant looking for him. He dodges them easily, then approaches the control room and enters it. There, he threatens the technicians with harm if they do not show him the main power control switches. The supervisor manages to escape and calls the police.

Martin forces the other technician to turn off the power at gunpoint. His friends enter the room and plead with him to stop what he is doing and surrender. But Martin is implacable. While he threatens the technician Briggs circles around the control equipment and tries to take the gun away from him. Martin refuses to let go, exhorting the technician to do as he is told.

The technician finally obeys. Martin counts down softly from 10 to 0, when the power plant rocks with an earthquake. Thunder alerts everyone to look out a side window, where an atomic explosion has just been detonated. The massive explosion has destroyed the alien base and its menagerie of giant monsters. END

Analysis and additional notes: When I studied the notes from this one I was forced to watch it again, because the plot given was far too short and sketchy to make it memorable. Not to mention accurate. We are witness to the results of nuclear testing but there is no blame for it.

We are told that aliens from another planet want to conquer ours to migrate here. It would have been nice if they had merely asked, but apparently they were too arrogant to realize that their other planets all died the same way. Denab made it clear that once their resources were exhausted, his race preferred to migrate elsewhere rather than find planetoids in their own system to inhabit. And they would prefer to be the only population to inhabit any planet they wanted to colonize.

The pacing of the film was actually quite exciting. Our hero Martin makes the rational decisions many are afraid to make: it's us or them. To save himself, his wife; indeed his whole planet, he must act in accordance with his moral compass. No doubt, bomb testing was not really his goal. He wanted to study the effects bomb testing produced, possibly to determine if such testing is harmful to the environment. But we do not get to follow along with that part of the storyline.

I must say that the quality of the film was primitive. Shots of the animals were a bit distant. Martin's cavern exploration consisted of several key shots which were repeated several times, ostensibly to show that the cavern really is huge. Some medium shots of the characters were placed against blank backgrounds, and one had a character towering over the camera. But overall, the film was consistent in plotting and pacing.

For this aspect of film making, I can give Killers From Space 2.5 stars out of 4. IMdb gives it 3.2/10, while Rotten Tomatoes gives it no rating but 27% of their audience liked it.

Production: Under the working title of *The Man Who Saved The Earth*, production took place from early to mid July 1953 at KTTV Studios. Scenes featuring the cavern hideout of the aliens were shot in Bronson Canyon in Hollywood. Bronson Caves were two entrances to what is a rock outcrop, and have been used in many productions.

Reception: *Killers From Space* was released as a B movie, hampered by low production values and a minuscule budget.

Film reviewer Thomas Scalzo also noted: "Killers From Space is an enjoyable, if slow-going, sci-fi / horror diversion, and if these killers from space had somehow found a way to stop their yammering long enough to get on with some actual killing, the combination of Peter Graves, mutant insects and amphibians, a palpable atmosphere of '50s atomic fear, and the directorial efforts of Billy Wilder's brother, would have been enough to bump the film into the upper echelon of early sci-fi essentials."

In 2006, skeptic Dr. Aaron Sakulich noted similarities between the film and many alien abduction stories that would first appear over a decade later, such as the medical testing done by the aliens, the protagonist's strange scar, his memory erasure, the aliens' giant eyes, and their way of mind control.

There are no further notes on the film.

MONSTER FROM THE OCEAN FLOOR (1954)
Directed by Wyott Ordung
Produced by Roger Corman
Written by Bill Danch
Music by Andre Brummer
Cinematography by Floyd Crosby
Edited by Edward Sampson
Production company: Palo Alto
Distributed by Lippert Pictures; release date: May 21, 1954
Running time: 64 minutes
Budget: $30,000; box office: $850,000

Cast:
Anne Kimbell as Julie Blair
Stuart Wade as Steve Dunning
Dick Pinner as Dr. Baldwin

Wyott Ordung as Pablo
Inez Palange as Tula
Jonathan Haze as Joe
David Garcia as Jose
Roger Corman as Tommy

Plot: Julie Blair (Kimbell) is an American vacationing at a seaside village in Mexico. She hears stories from several people about a creature dwelling in the cove, and that other people have disappeared. She meets Dr. Baldwin (Dick Pinner), a marine biologist who is woking to preserve the environment of the cove. They fall for one another as they explore the cove's features together, but the mysterious death of a diver inspires Julie to investigate further. Baldwin is skeptical, yet he cannot deny that the disappearances warrant some delving for the truth.

Julie is herself a skilled diver. She goes alone to the cove at night and sits near the dark waters, where she sees a giant creature rising from the ocean. It is like nothing she has ever seen before, a giant shadow with one baleful eye gazing down at her. It then sinks under the water and disappears.

When she returns to the local cantina she encounters the storyteller Pablo and says that she has seen what he was talking about. But he sluffs the whole thing off by saying that he was telling tourists nonsense to make the whole place attractive. He himself does not believe his own story.

The next day, Julie returns to the cove and dives into its sunlit water. There she encounters a hungry shark and drives it off with a bowie knife. But when it goes away she sees an entirely different creature. It appears to be a giant octopus. As its giant tentacles reach for her, Julie swims rapidly back toward the beach. She exits the water before it can catch her.

Baldwin sees the monster in time to save her by driving it away with an oar from a beached boat. Together, they run to shelter in the nearby cantina.

Later, Baldwin, Julie and another diver named Steve Dunning (Stuart Wade) go out in a boat to look for clues. While walking on the sea floor, Dunning finds an empty diving suit with a helmet which is missing its glass. He takes it back to the boat saying that there was no sign of its user. He also notes that there is some kind of slime down there, and produces a sample bottle. Baldwin examines the slime and discovers it is from a one-celled organism. He puzzles over this. His scientist friend is also skeptical, but accepts that it is very unusual.

When Julie learns this she is convinced that what she saw the night before must have been some kind of mutant, created by nuclear testing. How many more creatures of this kind must inhabit the depths?

She and Baldwin argue over what to do, when the one-eyed creature rises from the surf. It is a gigantic amoeba, ready to invade the surface world once again. It chases them up the beach until it stops. Apparently it can go no further. Baldwin manages to set it on fire, where it burns down and leaves a pile of sludge on the sand. END

Analysis and additional notes: I must admit that this one was a yawner. The actual excitement does not occur until about half way through, when Julie does her first dive. After that, we see that the science is not as thorough as it should have been, and there is no military intervention to save the villagers from their giant predators. It comes across as a vacation romance interrupted by nuclear mutants, with no explanations or timelines to explain the story further.

I thought it interesting that the protagonist was female, and the men in her life were only secondary, but I think she could have been a bit more adventurous than she was. True, she had the chutzpah to dive into shark infested waters on her own, but was this wise? I guess we will never know. The standard diving rule is: **take a buddy with you**. You never know when you might run into a giant octopus or two.

For its slow plodding plotline up to the final reveal, I can't give it a rating. It simply did not engage me. IMdb gives it 3.3/10, and Rotten Tomatoes gives it no rating at all, and only 14% of their audience liked it. If it was possible, I would call it a C movie, even if the plot was somewhat sensible, but it was too short and too primitive in terms of production values to give it a B.

Production: Alan Frank listed *Monster From The Ocean Floor's* budget as $30,000. However, Roger Corman stated that the film was made for $12,000 over six days. So, he claimed more than twice as much. According to Corman, $4,000 of the film's budget came from Ordung, $3,500 from from the sale of the *Highway Dragnet* story to

Allied Artists, $5,000 in deferrment from Consolidated Labs, and money raised privately by selling $500 and $1,000 shares.

Ordung later claimed that he hocked his life insurance policy and sold his apartment to raise $15,000 to pay for the film. Corman's brother, Gene Corman, estimated the budget at $35,000.

Roger Corman had seen an article on a new electric powered one-man submarine, and was able to use it in the picture for free in exchange for the publicity and an on-screen credit ("Submarine built by Aerojet General").

The film's original title was *It Stalked The Ocean Floor*, but was changed by the distributor for being too artsy.

Release: Gene Corman negotiated the sale of the film to a distributor. Although Herbert Yates of Republic Pictures had an interest in the film, *Monster From The Ocean Floor* was sold to Lippert Pictures for $110,000. Gene Corman later said that Lippert had renegotiated his deal on the film once he found out that Roger Corman had not spent the whole $100,000 on making it, but considerably less.

Roger Corman received a $60,000 advance for *Monster*, which enabled him to make his next film, *The Fast And The Furious* (1955).

Reception: Critical: TV Guide found the movie lacking and criticized the directing. However, its critic said the movie was interesting historically as the "beginning of something big and cheap".

Variety was kinder, calling the movie "a well made quickie". *Creature Feature* by John Stanley gave the movie 2 out of 5 stars citing minimal mood, the film's dubbing, and a cast of unknowns.

RIDERS TO THE STARS (1954)
Directed by Richard Carlson and Herbert L. Strock(uncredited)
Produced by Maxwell Smith (associate producer: Scientific Research), Herbert L. Strock (associate producer), and Ivan Tors (producer)
Written by Curt Siodmak and Ivan Tors (story)
Music by Harry Sukman
Cinematography by Stanley Cortez and Joseph F. Biroc
Edited by Herbert L. Strock
Production company: Ivan Tors Productions, Inc.
Distributed by United Artists; release date: January 14, 1954
Running time: 81 minutes

Cast:

William Lundigan as Dr. Richard Donald Stanton
Herbert Marshall as Dr. Donald L. Stanton / Narrator
Richard Carlson as Dr. Jerome "Jerry" Lockwood
Martha Hyer as Dr. Jane Flynn
Dawn Addams as Susan Manners
Robert Karnes as Walter J. Gordon
Lawrence Dobkin as Dr. Delmar
George Eldredge as Dr. Paul Drayden
Dan Riss as Dr. Frank Warner
Michael Fox as Dr. Klinger the Shrink
King Donovan as James F. O'Herli, Security
Kem Dibbs as David Wells
James Best as Sidney K. Fuller

Plot: A group of highly qualified single men, including Dr. Richard Stanton (William Lundigan) and Dr. Jerome "Jerry" Lockwood (Richard Carlson), are recruited for a top secret project. They undergo a series of rigorous physical and psychological tests, during which time Stanton becomes attracted to the beautiful Dr. Jane Flynn (Martha Hyer), one of the scientists testing the candidates.

After most of the candidates have been eliminated from consideration, the four remaining subjects are told about the purpose of the project.

Stanton's father, Dr. Donald Stanton (Herbert Marshall), is the man in charge. He and his colleagues are working on manned space travel. They have found, however, that even the best quality metal alloys eventually turn brittle in the harsh environment of outer space. Since metal based meteors are not vulnerable to these metal fatigue stresses, the scientists want to recover samples before they enter the Earth's atmosphere to discover how the meteors' surface shells protect them.

To accomplish this, there is the need to send men into space, something that has never been done before. Stanton, Lockwood, and Walter Gordon (Robert Karnes) accept the dangerous assignment after some consideration; while the fourth candidate quits declaring that he is not going to sacrifice his life to a doomed venture in the first place.

After launching an unmanned craft into the magnetosphere, we see it returned to the Earth containing 2 lab rats. An internal camera has photographed them looking quite calm in the weightless environment. They have also survived unharmed, which is the chief concern of the lead scientists.

Three one man rockets are launched about 2 hundred miles into space in order to intercept an incoming meteor swarm.

Gordon makes the first run to capture a meteor. It turns out to be too large for his spaceship's nose scoop, and the ship is destroyed in the collision that follows.

Lockwood suffers a mental breakdown when his view screen shows Gordon's suit floating amid the debris toward him. Panicked and delusional, he fires his rocket engines and blasts away from Earth, heading into deep space to his doom.

Stanton then misses the main swarm, but a stray meteor crosses his orbital path. He decides to pursue it, despite a warning from ground control. He may use too much fuel in the attempt and burn up upon re-entry. But Stanton snags the meteor in time and manages to survive a crash landing safely intact. He is rewarded for his heroism with a kiss from Dr. Flynn.

When the meteor is examined, it is found to have an outer coating of crystalline pure carbon whose molecular structure is such that it is almost impervious to cosmic rays and heat stresses. With this discovery, the U. S. can now build safer rockets and space stations for the inevitable conquest of space. END

Analysis and additional notes: This may have seemed like a dud but it was actually quite engaging. We see a scientific presentation of the problem, the solution, and the result. There is a brief nudge toward romance but that is the extent of it. While the actual rockets are primitive in their interiors, there is some effort to make them look more scientific. And yet, critics saw it as a dull "documentary" with little to make it believable. I can dismiss this as a result of their bent to see science fiction as rock'em, sock'em adventures to entertain the audience, but this one stayed on topic and diverted little from its main premise. It was a serious attempt to create serious science fiction, in spite of its ridiculously low budget. It was also the film which started the trend toward making science exciting and adventurous, inspiring other film makers to pay more attention to the science.

For this and the several real-life shots interspersed throughout *Riders To The Stars*, I give it 2.5 stars out of 4. IMdb gives it 3.5/10, while Rotten Tomatoes gives it no rating so far, but there is a page for it.

Production: *Riders To The Stars* was the first film from director and star Richard Carlson, who starred in several previous science fiction films. Carlson played the lead in *The Magnetic Monster* (1953) which led to him finding a niche in the emergent genres of science fiction and horror. He followed it with leads in *The Maze* (1953), *It Came From Outer Space* (1953), and *Creature From The Black Lagoon* (1954).

In order to create a more authentic feel for the story, contemporary newsreel footage of WAC Corporal spacecraft was used. The WAC Corporal was a sounding stratospheric rocket that flew as the 2nd stage on a rocket booster developed from the German V-2 rocket, designed by Wernher von Braun. One actual sequence shows two white rats in a rocket beyond the force of gravity... one of the most startling series of photographs ever made.

Five years later, actor William Lundigan would go on to star in the syndicated future space television series *Men Into Space* (1959), which could be considered a sequel to or at least a continuation of the ideas explored in *Riders To The Stars*.

The movie was filmed and released theatrically in color provided by Color Corporation of America, but prints struck for television syndication were in black and white. Turner Classic Movies aired the color version in an attempt to revive its original presentation. Nice of them to do that.

Reception: Critically reviewed in The New York Times, *Riders To The Stars* was considered lackluster and gimmicky. "Spliced in to give all the idiotic, pseudo-scientific mumbo-jumbo a precarious footing in fact are newsreel shots ..."

Later reviews, however, noted that the film makers had created a "near-documentary" by using rocket footage and scientific equipment as a precursor to the coming space age, all within an "unremarkable film". At the time, they did not realize that what science fiction predicts may often come true.

STRANGER FROM VENUS (UK; 1954) (aka "Immediate Disaster" and "The Venusian" in the US)
Produced and directed by Burt Balaban
Produced by Gene Martel and Roy Rich
Written by Desmond Leslie (story) and Hans Jacoby (screenplay)
Music by Eric Spear
Cinematography by Kenneth Talbot
Edited by Peter R. Hunt
Production company: Princess Pictures Inc.
Release date: December 31, 1954; running time: 75 minutes

Cast:
Patricia Neal as Susan North
Helmut Dantine as The Stranger
Derek Bond as Arthur Walker
Cyril Luckham as Dr. Meinard
Willoughby Gray as Tom Harding
Marigold Russell as Gretchen Harding
Arthur Young as Scientist
Kenneth Edwards as Charles Dixon
David Garth as First Police Officer
Stanley Van Beers as General
Nigel Green as Second Police Officer
Graham Stuart as Police Chief Richards

Plot: A flying saucer is seen in the sky above the countryside by various eyewitnesses, including an American woman driving in her car. She is Susan North (Patricia Neal). She crashes into a tree after being blinded by the craft's landing lights and deafened by its loud propulsion system.

A stranger (Helmut Dantine) walks up to the car and sees that she is injured. He takes her out of the wreckage and walks away with her unconscious body.

Later, the stranger enters a country inn very near where the sighting and accident took place. He is able to read people's thoughts, and when asked says he has no name. He asserts that he is responsible for saving the life of Susan North, the car accident victim, and that she is safe. After the mysterious stranger explains that he comes from the planet Venus, a guest at the inn, Arthur Walker (Derek Bond), a high-ranking government official (and Susan's fiancé), calls the war ministry.

Susan walks into the inn a little dazed, but with her crash wounds nearly healed. With the stranger's permission, Dr Meinard (Cyril Luckham) examines him and says, "there is no pulse. There are two possible explanations for this. I am drunk, or you are dead."

The area surrounding the inn is quickly cordoned off by the military. No one may leave or enter the area without permission.

Journalist Charles Dixon (Kenneth Edwards) tries to learn more about the man from Venus. Dixon learns that the stranger is able to speak several human languages, and that his people have learned quite a bit about humanity by listening to radio broadcasts and viewing television transmissions. He also explains how Venusians use 'magnetic brilliance' for their spaceship propulsion, supplied by the magnetic energy fields of the other planets as they revolve in their various orbits.

When governmental officials arrive at the inn, the man from Venus outlines his purpose for coming to Earth: to prepare the way for the arrival of his superiors, who have a dire warning for humanity's leaders. Humans are developing dangerous technologies without measuring their long term destructive consequences.

Should 50 hydrogen bombs be exploded in the same general location during a future atomic war, the explosions and radiation could alter the Earth's orbit, thereby affecting its gravitational field. This disruption would then affect the orbits and gravitational fields of all the other planets in the solar system.

The stranger makes a promise that if Earth eliminates these dangers, Venus will share some of its higher scientific knowledge. During the meeting, however, the man from Venus concludes that humanity is not yet ready to receive such advanced knowledge.

After a communication disc is stolen, which allows him to contact the approaching Venusian ship, the stranger quickly realizes that an interplanetary meeting of minds can never take place. He also learns that such a meeting will be turned into a trap by the British government, in order to seize the Venusian ship to study it for its advanced space technology.

He achieves a sort of rapprochement with Susan, seeing her as more reasonable than her male colleagues. She gives him some insight to what he will be facing if he tries to unify all governments of the world to impart his warning. She accepts him readily as a denizen from another world, not afraid to share her fear and her reserve as a citizen of her own. Susan treats him with compassion, a far different view than that of the men. From her insights and observations, he learns that his assignment is nothing more than an uphill battle.

After the short conference with Susan, the stranger threatens that, should the British government carry out this warlike action, the stranger assures Walker that an immediate retaliation from an orbiting Venusian mother ship would terminate all life in Britain.

Walker tries to warn the war ministry of the stranger's declaration, without success, since the telephone system is now out of order. But he returns the stolen communication disc, and the stranger is able to warn away the approaching scout ship. A deadly interplanetary conflict is avoided. But discussion with Earth's leaders has been derailed by the British government's shortsighted ploy to gain Venusian technology. The future is now uncertain, and his peaceful mission a failure. The stranger from Venus abruptly vanishes. END

Analysis and additional notes: Despite this film being a British production, the screenplay reads very much like the plot to *The Day The Earth Stood Still* (1951), only it lacks an all destructive robot to aid the stranger in his quest. So far the stranger looks and behaves very much like a human being, apart from the fact that he originates from our sister planet; but unlike Klaatu he does not have much time to complete his assignment. Some deadline is looming on the horizon.

Let's face it, *Stranger From Venus* is a poor man's version of *The Day The Earth Stood Still*, and let me say here that I would have preferred if the Venusians installed an atmospheric bullhorn to make their warning clear, rather than send one of their agents to threaten a few people in an isolated inn in the middle of nowhere. It lacked... impact. I was disappointed when I saw the ending. There was no climax and no denouement. It was like someone ended a sentence without the preposition. And? And?? What happened next?

For the actors' sake, I give *Stranger From Venus* 2 stars out of 4. I cannot say much else about the rest of it. IMdb gives it 5.4/10, no doubt for the acting, and Rotten Tomatoes has a page for it, but no rating and no audience score.

US theatrical and television releases: the film was released theatrically in the UK and in other countries under the titles *Stranger From Venus* and *Immediate Disaster*. In the U.S., it was only released to television by Flamingo Telefilm out of New York City, under the title *Immediate Disaster*. This was because of the possibility of legal action from 20th Century Fox, due to its similarity in plot to the earlier Patricia Neal film *The Day The Earth Stood Still*, which in 1954 was still in theatrical release. But of course this would have been an unwise move, since *Stranger* did not copy the previous film exactly.

The rights were sold to Wade Williams Distribution, and the film was made available theatrically under the title *Stranger From Venus*. It has been licensed for home use for several decades, both on VHS and DVD.

There are no other notes on this production.

TARGET EARTH (1954)
Directed by Sherman A. Rose
Produced by Herman Cohen
Screenplay by James H. Nicholson, Wyott Ordung, and William Raynor
Story by Paul W. Fairman
Music by Paul Dunlap
Cinematography by Guy Roe
Edited by Sherman A. Rose
Production company: Abtcon Pictures, Inc.
Distributed by Allied Artists Pictures Corporation
Release date: November 7, 1954; running time: 75 minutes
Budget: $85,000

Cast:
Richard Denning as Frank Brooks
Kathleen Crowley as Nora King
Virginia Grey as Vicki Harris
Richard Reeves as Jim Wilson
Robert Roark as Davis
Whit Bissell as Tom, Chief research scientist

Arthur Space as Lt. General Wood
Steve Pendleton as Colonel
Mort Marshall as Charles Otis
House Peters Jr. as Technician
Steve Calvert as the Robot

Plot: After a failed attempt at suicide by taking an overdose of sleeping pills, Nora King (Kathleen Crowley) regains consciousness and discovers that she is alone in an empty building. After making a cursory exploration, she learns that her building has no electricity or water. There is no sign to explain what is going on.

Nora returns to her apartment and looks out the window. There is no traffic, no city activity, no one on the street in what was supposed to be Chicago. She dresses to go out and learn what has happened. As she walks along the street, stores and restaurants are empty of customers and their doors are left wide open. There is no traffic anywhere and there are very few cars left parked on the streets.

Upon stumbling over the body of a dead woman, she encounters Frank Brooks (Richard Denning), who has just recently revived after being beaten in a robbery. He, too is puzzled by the lack of population in what would ordinarily be a busy, bustling city. She helps him up and brushes him off. After brief introductions, Frank and Nora decide to team up and look for other survivors, if there are any.

Hearing music coming from a nearby restaurant, they come upon a couple, Jim Wilson (Richard Reeves) and Vicki Harris (Virginia Grey), who are still drunk. They tell the two newcomers that they were too inebriated to join an evacuation of Chicago's population, which was conducted suddenly and overnight. They together figured that whatever was going to happen, they were perfectly suited to be together no matter what.

Proceeding as a group, all four continue to search the deserted streets, when they come upon a car that will not start. Another survivor, Charles Otis (Mort Marshall), sees them and tells them that the same applies to all the other cars he has tried. Nothing will work.

A growing apprehension takes hold of the group as they begin to appreciate that they are alone with an unknown menace that has caused everyone to evacuate the city. Then, Charles finds a newspaper in a hotel lobby that proclaims that a "mystery army" is attacking the city. In it, he learns that the army evacuated every soul they could find in the precious little time they had.

In a panic, he runs out into the street to look for the others and warn them, only to be killed by a death ray from a nearby alien robot.

While trying to defend the city, a military force led by Lt. Gen. Wood (Arthur Space), sets up a command post at the outskirts. After Air Force bombers are easily destroyed by the invaders, the use of atomic weapons is contemplated. A group of scientists, including the chief research scientist called Tom (Whit Bissell), are finally able to work on a captured robot to find out if the alien machines have any vulnerabilities. But the group in the city are not aware of this.

By now, the four survivors are busy trying to evade the attacking robots. Soon they are joined by Davis (Robert Roark), a psychotic killer who has his own plans for survival. While Frank is out scouting the area for an escape route, Davis fixates on Nora, while Jim and Vicki defend her as best they can. The problem is, Davis is armed with a revolver. During their argument Davis shoots Jim to death. Nora and Vicki manage to disable Davis temporarily and escape.

Davis chases after them and finally shoots Vicki to death, then tries to force Nora to stay with him. He thinks he will defeat the robots and set himself up as the Emperor of Earth. Nora rejects him easily. She figures that she is going to die anyway.

Frank comes upon Davis on the roof, who has Nora in a chokehold. Frank manages to distract Davis to allow Nora to escape. Together, they manage to escape Davis, when two robots arrive on the roof of the building. They disintegrate Davis when he shoots at them.

Alone, Frank and Nora escape from the robots on the roof by climbing down a fire escape to get to the ground. There they meet with an army unit which has arrived, bearing weapons which are able to destroy the invading army of robots. END

Analysis and additional notes: This movie reminded me of a short story I wrote when I was 16 about a mysterious fog which envelops a small town, and it was associated with nuclear war. I had the first draft written but never got farther than that. I learned later that it was a wise decision not to go on with it, because I found out that there were several different television shows which approached the subject on several occasions. This film is very much like that but on a larger and grander scale. Perhaps I may have seen in when I was a little girl and then forgot about it.

Nevertheless, *Target Earth* was a straightforward movie, with little science in it but the invading robots. We don't get to see who is in command of them. We don't get to see anything of outer space while our heroes' shoes are planted firmly on the ground. The scientists at the laboratories are only concerned with reverse engineering the robots and we don't get to see much of that. So the whole film turns into an adventure/romance story with scientific underpinnings.

Still it was an excellent character study. Each one had a full life to tell, even though we see only an hour's worth of them. There was the issue of morality, compassion, and cooperation.

Only Davis appeared to be the single dark point in the story, and he did nothing to redeem himself, turning himself into the villain. Against the backdrop of a robot invasion, we actually cheer when he gets destroyed.

For its intriguing story line and pacing, I give *Target Earth* 2.5 stars out of 4. IMdb gives it 5.7/10, while Rotten Tomatoes has no rating for it yet and only 26% of its audience liked it.

Production: The screenplay for *Target Earth* is based on the 1953 science fiction short story "Deadly City" by Paul W. Fairman, which first appeared in the March 1953 issue of <u>If</u> magazine under Fairman's pseudonym, Ivar Jorgensen.

Principal photography began in mid July of 1954 at Kling Studios, for a shooting schedule of a tight 7 days, which also included outdoor shooting. While the story is set in Chicago, *Target Earth* was actually filmed in Los Angeles. Empty street scenes were filmed during the very early morning hours before normal traffic began.

Casting: Actor Robert Roark was given a role because his father was a chief investor in *Target Earth.*

Even though a "robot army" is mentioned several times during the film, only one robot was constructed for the production, which was then used in all scenes to depict the invasion. When actor Steve Calvert, who played the robot, was not working on B films, he regularly worked as a bartender at Ciro's on the Sunset Strip. He also played the apes in *Bride of the Gorilla* (1951) and *Bela Lugosi Meets a Brooklyn Gorilla* (1952).

Reception: Target Earth was considered to be a typical product of 1950s science fiction but could never rise above its low budget underpinnings. One of the few notable aspects of the production was that the film was one of the first to explore the subgenre of alien invasions, following the success of George Pal's *The War Of The Worlds* (1953).

Target Earth was also produced by Herman Cohen, making his producing debut, who would become one of the most prominent B movie producers of the 1960s. Director Sherman A. Rose, who was a prolific editor in both television and film, would go on to make only two other films.

TV Guide later rated it 1 out of 4 stars, writing, "The robots are just plain disappointing." David Maine of PopMatters rated it 6/10 stars and called it "a tight, engaging little thriller that focuses more on character than special effects."

THEM! (1954)

Directed by Gordon Douglas
Produced by David Weisbart
Screenplay by Ted Sherdeman and Russell Hughes
Story by George Worthing Yates
Music by Bronislau Kaper
Cinematography by Sidney Hickox
Edited by Thomas Reilly
Production company: Warner Bros. Pictures, Inc.
Distributed by Warner Bros. Pictures, Inc.
Release dates: June 16, 1954 (New York); June 19, 1954 (US)
Running time: 94 minutes; box office: $2.2 million (rentals)

Cast:
James Whitmore as Sgt. Ben Peterson
Edmund Gwenn as Dr. Harold Medford
Joan Weldon as Dr. Pat Medford
James Arness as FBI Agent Robert Graham
Onslow Stevens as General O'Brien
Sean McClory as Major Kibbee
Chris Drake as Trooper Ed Blackburn
Sandy Descher as Ellinson girl

Mary Ann Hokanson as Mrs. Lodge
Don Shelton as Captain Fred Edwards
Fess Parker as Alan Crotty
Olin Howlin as Jensen, the alcoholic
Dorothy Green as police matron

Cast notes: Leonard Nimoy has a small, uncredited part as a U.S. Army Staff Sergeant in the communications room.

- Other actors who appear in small parts include John Beradino, Willis Bouchey, Booth Colman, Richard Deacon, Lawrence Dobkin, Ann Doran, William Schallert, Douglas Spencer, Dub Taylor, Dorothy Green, Harry Wilson and Dick York.

- When casting his planned Davy Crockett episode of the Disneyland television series, Walt Disney viewed the film to see James Arness, who had been recommended for the role. However, Disney was more impressed by a scene with Fess Parker as an inmate in a mental ward of the Texas hospital. Watching Parker's performance, Disney realized he had found his Davy Crockett.

- John Wayne saw the film and, impressed with Arness's performance, recommended him for the role of Marshal Matt Dillon in the new *Gunsmoke* TV series, a role that Arness went on to play from 1955 to 1975.

Plot: New Mexico State Police Sgt. Ben Peterson (James Whitmore) and Trooper Ed Blackburn (Chris Drake) discover a little girl wandering aimlessly in the desert near Alamogordo, in shock and in a catatonic state. They take her to a nearby vacation trailer, located by a spotter aircraft, where they find evidence that the little girl had been there when it was attacked and nearly destroyed. In the galley section of the trailer is a strange footprint and a quantity of sugar which has spilled onto the ground.

It is later discovered that the trailer was owned by an FBI Special Agent named Ellinson, on vacation with his wife, son, and daughter. The other members of the girl's family remain missing. Now in an ambulance, the child briefly reacts to a pulsating chirring sound from the desert by sitting up in the stretcher. No one else notices her reaction, and she lies back down when the noise stops.

At a general store owned by "Gramps" Johnson, Peterson and Blackburn find him dead, and a wall of his store is partially torn out.

There, they find more sugar, with a few of the strange prints surrounding it. After a quick look around, Peterson leaves Blackburn behind to secure the crime scene. Blackburn later goes outside to investigate a strange, pulsating chirring sound. Gun shots are fired, the sound grows faster and louder, and then Blackburn goes missing.

Peterson's chief later points out that both Johnson and Blackburn had fired their weapons at their attacker. More puzzling is the coroner's report on Johnson's brutal death, which includes a huge amount of formic acid found in his body.

The FBI sends Special Agent Robert Graham (James Arness) to New Mexico to investigate. After a strange footprint is found near the Ellisons' trailer, the Department of Agriculture sends myrmecologists Dr. Harold Medford (Edmund Gwenn) and his daughter, Dr. Pat Medford (Joan Weldon), to assist in the investigation. The elder Medford exposes the Ellinson girl to formic acid fumes, which rips her from her catatonia into a state of panic. She screams, "Them! Them!" The nurses move in and try to quiet her down, and she does. But she is an orphan now.

Medford's suspicions are validated by her reaction, but he will not reveal his theory prematurely. He must gather more evidence.

Later, at the Ellinson campsite, Pat encounters a giant, eight foot long foraging ant. It begins to chase her down an embankment. Following instructions from the elder Medford, Peterson and Graham shoot off the ant's antennae, blinding it, Then, using a Thompson submachine gun, they kill it.

Medford then reveals his theory: a colony of giant ants, mutated by radiation from the first atomic bomb test near Alamogordo, is responsible for the human deaths. As he speaks, we see a giant ant emerging from the nest and it dumps two skeletons onto the sand. One of them sports a gun belt with ammunition, missing the gun.

General O'Brien orders an Army helicopter search, and the ants' nest is found. Cyanide gas bombs are tossed inside. Then Graham, Peterson, and Pat descend into the nest to check for survivors. Deep inside, Pat finds evidence that two queen ants have hatched and escaped to establish new colonies. Medford is excited about this. It means to him that the ants have merely grown in size but are still just ants. Peterson is alarmed at his attitude. As far as he is concerned they are still killers.

Peterson, Graham, and the Medfords join a government task force which covertly begins to investigate reports of unusual activity.

In one situation a civilian pilot (Fess Parker) has been committed to a mental hospital after claiming that he was forced down by UFOs shaped like giant ants. "They had wings and everything!" he exclaims.

Next, the Coast Guard receives a report of a giant queen hatching her brood in the hold of a freighter at sea in the Pacific. The giant ants have attacked the ship's crew, and there are few survivors. The freighter is later sunk by U.S. Navy gunfire. [Ants can drown if they are far from dry land.]

A third report about a large sugar theft at a railroad yard leads Peterson, Graham, and Major Kibby to Los Angeles. An alcoholic in a hospital "drunk tank" claims he had seen giant ants outside his window. Of course nobody believed him. Kibby says he can go home, but he would rather not.

The mutilated body of a father is recovered, but his two young sons are missing. His wife is distraught with worry, thinking that he was robbed at gunpoint. But she insists that the men must find and apprehend them.

Peterson, Graham, and Kibby find evidence that the father and his sons were flying a model airplane in the Los Angeles River drainage channel near the hospital. Peterson points to the giant culverts facing onto the shallow river and thinks they would make good burrows for giant ants.

Martial law is declared in Los Angeles, and troops are assigned to find the ant nest in the vast storm drain system under the city. The mother of the two boys has the presence and will to insist on going with the soldiers to search for her boys.

While searching for the ants' nest in a culvert, Peterson finds the two missing boys alive, trapped by the ants in a concrete ditch. As long as they are there the ants cannot reach them. Peterson calls for reinforcements and lifts both boys to safety, just before being attacked himself. The boys are restored to their mother, who whisks them away before more damage can be done.

Graham arrives with reinforcements and kills the ants, but Peterson dies from his injuries as other ants swarm to protect the nearby nest. While Graham and the soldiers fight off the ants, a tunnel collapse traps Graham. Several ants charge, but he is able to hold them off with his submachine gun just long enough for troops to break through and kill them all.

On a lower level, the queen and her eggs are discovered and quickly destroyed with flamethrowers.

Dr. Medford offers a philosophic observation: "When Man entered the Atomic Age, he opened the door to a new world. What we may eventually find in that new world, nobody can predict." END

Analysis and additional notes: This film was shortened somewhat from its original length for television. One scene which was notably omitted was the shot of an ant dumping the two skeletons. The editors were probably told that the scene was too disturbing for younger viewers. However, it was critical to the plot in that it demonstrated typical ant behavior, and we learn what happened to the missing men.

Overall, the film was a full-length exploration of an adventure featuring an aberration of science. The plotline is very credible and almost realistic, even though the ants themselves were a bit crude in their construction. It was believable in that it was treated with the seriousness that other science fiction films of the 50s lacked. It had a beginning, a middle, and an end. At the center was a "what if" scenario which made it true science fiction. It was to presage a whole raft of giant monster movies of the fantastic.

I only have one bugaboo, and that is that ants and other insects do not have vocal cords. When they make noise they do so with their wings and their legs, not with their throats. Yet, when the noise is heard in the film it is presumed that the noise is produced vocally. This may be true for frogs and toads, but not for ants. There is no feature in the film which explains the vocal sound except for its effect on humans.

As for the culverts in Los Angeles, they have been covered over and their lids decorated with various designs. If there were ever any ants in them, they are no longer dangerous to humans. I have seen them in person, and when I see them, I am reminded of this film.

For its reasonably logical plotline and credible acting, I give *Them!* 3 stars out of 4. IMdb gives it 7.3/10, while Rotten Tomatoes gives it a rating of 100% fresh! 76% of their audience liked it. The website's consensus reads, "One of the best creature features of the early atomic age, Them! features effectively menacing special effects and avoids the self-parody that would taint later monster movies."

Production: When *Them!* began production in the fall of 1953, it was originally conceived to be in 3D and Warner Color. During pre-production, tests were to be shot. A few color tests were shot of the large scale ant models, but when it was time to shoot the 3D test, Warner Bros.' "All Media" 3D camera rig malfunctioned and no footage could be filmed.

The next day a memo was sent out that the color and 3D aspects of the production were to be scrapped. Widescreen black and white would now be the film's presentation format. Warner Bros. hoped to emulate the "effective shock treatment" effect of its previous science fiction thriller *The Beast From 20,000 Fathoms*. However, that film was never shot in widescreen. For the preparation of certain scenes, many of the camera setups for 3D still remain in the film, like the opening titles and the flamethrower shots aimed directly at the camera.

Although Warner Bros. was dissatisfied with the color results, the film's titles were printed in a vivid red and blue against a black and white background in order to give the film's opening a dramatic "punch". This effect was achieved by an Eastman Color section spliced into each release print. The 1985 VHS tape release, the subsequent LaserDisc and later DVD release have retained this black and white with two-color title effect.

The entrance to the ants' final nest was shot along the concrete spillways of the Los Angeles River, between the First and Seventh Street Bridges, east of downtown. The depiction of the Chihuahuan Desert of southern New Mexico is actually the Mojave Desert near Palmdale, California. Mercy Hospital was a real institution and is now Brownsville Medical Center.

James Whitmore wore "lifts" in his shoes to compensate for the height difference between himself and James Arness. It has also been noted that Whitmore employed bits of "business" (hand gestures and motions) during scenes in which he appeared in order to draw more attention to his character when not speaking.

The Wilhelm scream, created three years earlier for the film Distant Drums, is used during the action sequences: when a sailor aboard the freighter is grabbed by an ant, when James Whitmore's character is caught in an ant's mandibles, and when an overhead wooden beam falls on a soldier in the Los Angeles storm drain sequence.

The giant ants, painted a purplish green color, were constructed and operated by unseen technicians as supervised by Ralph Ayers. During the climactic battle sequence in the Los Angeles storm drains, there is a brief shot of one ant moving in the foreground with its side removed, revealing its mechanical interior. This blunder has been obscured in the DVD releases of the film.

The film poster shows a gigantic ant with menacing human-like eyes rather than the normal compound eyes of an ant. They could have photoraphed a real ant's head instead, and saved themselves some money on art.

The sounds the giant ants emit in the film were the calls of Bird-voiced tree frogs mixed in with the calls of a wood thrush, hooded warbler and red-bellied woodpecker. It was recorded at Indian Island, Georgia, on April 11, 1947 by the Cornell Lab of Ornithology. Again, I protest strongly whether it was necessary.

Reception: Them! was released in June of 1954, and by the end of that year had accrued $2 million (US) in distributors' domestic (U.S. and Canada) rentals, making it the year's 51st biggest earner. According to an article in The Slate, this was Warner Bros. highest grossing film that year. However, 1954 In Film lists two other films from Warner Bros. that earned more gross receipts.

From contemporary reviews, the Monthly Film Bulletin stated that despite the science fiction film genre being new, it had developed several subdivisions, including "the other-worldly, the primaeval-monstrous, the neo-monstrous, the planet-ary-visitant, etc." and that "Them! is a "well-built example of the neo-monstrous", "less absurdly sensational than most" Discussing the ant monsters in the film, the review referred to them as "reasonably horrible--they do not entirely avoid the impression of mock-up that is almost inevitable when over-lifesize creatures have to be constructed and moved", while noting that they were "considerably more conceivable than those prehistoric remnants that have recently been emerging from bog and iceberg."

The review commented on the cast as "like most science-fiction, [the film] is on the whole serviceably rather than excitingly cast" and the crew was noted, stating the direction was "smoothly machined" and the film has "decent writing" though "more short cuts might have been [taken]", finding that the start of the film was too slow.

A. H. Weiler's review in <u>The New York Times</u> noted "... from the moment James Whitmore, playing a New Mexico state trooper, discovers a six-year-old moppet wandering around the desert in a state of shock, to the time when the cause of that mental trauma is traced and destroyed, Them! is taut science fiction".

The reviewer in <u>Variety</u> opined it was a "top-notch science fiction shocker. It has a well-plotted story, expertly directed and acted in a matter-of-fact style to rate a chiller payoff and thoroughly satisfy the fans of hackle-raising melodrama."

John McCarten of <u>The New Yorker</u> wrote, "If you're willing to let your imagination off its leash, you may have a fairly good time at 'Them!'"

Since its original release, *Them!* has become generally regarded as one of the best science fiction films of the 1950s.

Bill Warren described it as " ... tight, fast-paced and credible ... [T]he picture is suspenseful."

Phil Hardy's *The Aurum Film Encyclopedia: Science Fiction* noted, "Directed by [Gordon] Douglas in semi-documentary fashion, Them! is one of the best American science fiction films of the fifties."

Danny Peary believed the film "Ranks with The Thing and Invasion of the Body Snatchers as the best of the countless '50s science fiction films."

In the <u>Time Out Film Guide</u>, David Pirie wrote, "By far the best of the 50s cycle of 'creature features' ... retains a good part of its power today."

Them! was nominated for an Oscar for its special effects and won a Golden Reel Award for best sound editing.

Remake: Screenwriter Neil Ruttenberg and producer Richard Donner pitched a remake in which the ants would be intelligent and terrifying. Warner Bros. decided instead upon on Bob Gale's pitch, which included mechanical effects.

In popular culture: Van Morrison's band Them was named after this film.

Joey and Chandler watch the film on TV in the 1995 Friends episode "The One Where Rachel and Ross... You Know."

New Jersey punk band the Misfits has a song titled "Them!", with lyrics directly inspired by the film, on their release Famous Monsters (1999).

The video game series "It Came From The Desert" was inspired by *Them!*

Eight Legged Freaks features a scene in which sequences from the film are included.

The Counterstrike expansion for Westwood Studios' *Command & Conquer: Red Alert* had a secret 4 part mini-campaign called *It Came From Red Alert!*, in which the primary antagonists are giant ants.

Lilo & Stitch 2: Stitch Has A Glitch features the film on a TV that Lilo, Stitch, Nani and David watch along with Jumba and Pleakley.

Fallout 3, which takes place in a post apocalyptic irradiated wasteland, has a side quest involving giant mutated fire ants called "Those!" in homage to the film.

In Tim Burton's film *Ed Wood* (1994), Bela Lugosi (Martin Landau) explains to Ed (Johnny Depp), "Nobody wants vampires anymore. Now all they want is giant bugs". The scene takes place in 1952, but the actual movie came out two years later. Who knew?

In the 1950s E.C. Comics parody comic, *Panic*, a companion to the highly successful *Mad*, there is a parody of this film titled *Them! There! Those!* featuring art by Wally Wood.

The 1960s Remco toy line titled "Hamilton Invaders" featured giant bugs versus military defenders. One of the larger mechanical bugs, "The Spooky Spider", was designed after the giant ants in *Them!*, even though the creature sports only six legs. Another creature in this line also featured a giant bug, called "Horrible Hamilton", designed after the giant wasps from the 1950s feature *Monster From Green Hell*.

The scene where Pat is attacked by the foraging ant appears as a movie replay in the 2018 Marvel film *Ant-Man And The Wasp*.

TOBOR THE GREAT (1954)

Directed by Lee Sholem
Produced by Richard Goldstone
Written by Carl Dudley and Philip MacDonald
Music by Howard Jackson
Cinematography by John L. Russell
Edited by Basil Wrangell
Production company: Dudley Pictures Corporation
Distributed by Republic Pictures; release date: September 1, 1954
Running time: 77 minutes

Cast:
Charles Drake as Dr. Ralph Harrison
Karin Booth as Janice Roberts
Billy Chapin as Brian "Gadge" Roberts
Taylor Holmes as Professor Arnold Nordstrom
Alan Reynolds as Gilligan, Reporter
Steven Geray as Foreign spy chief
Henry Kulky as Paul, spy henchman
Franz Roehn as Karl
Hal Baylor as Max, spy henchman
Peter Brocco as Dr. Gustav
Norman Field as Commissioner
Robert Shayne as General
Lyle Talbot as Admiral
Emmett Vogan as Congressman
William Schallert as Johnston
Helen Winstonas Secretary
Lew Smith as Tobor
Jack Daly as Scientist
Maury Hill as Scientist

Plot: At his underground laboratory in Los Angeles, Professor Nordstrom (Taylor Holmes) is worried that manned space exploration is too dangerous, and enlists the help of Dr. Ralph Harrison (Charles Drake), who recently left the new government appointed Civil Interplanetary Flight Commission to work on his own experiments in semi-retirement..

The two scientists embark on a research project to create a robot that can replace a human for space flight. While the project goes rather smoothly, Nordstrom's daughter, Janice Roberts (Karin Booth), and her 11 year old son Brian (Billy Chapin), nicknamed "Gadge", become very interested in the project and pester Nordstrom for more information. Gadge is especially interested and continues to monitor his grandfather's progress, even in secret when the scientists leave the lab for meals.

When a press conference is called to announce the creation of "Tobor", reporters, such as the inquisitive journalist named Gilligan (Alan Reynolds), are invited to Professor's Harrison's home to see the remarkable invention. There they are taken on a short tour of the control systems which will control the robot. Harrison explains that, In order to undertake space travel, the remote controlled robot has been given some human capabilities, including the ability to "feel" emotions and react via a telepathic device built into its robotic brain.

Under the watchful eyes of Harrison's trusted assistant Karl (Franz Roehn), the giant robot Tobor is unveiled and then demonstrated. Unknown to the scientists, a foreign spy chief (Steven Geray) has quietly joined the group of reporters. He draws up a plan to steal the robot. When the other reporters depart to write their articles, he is still there, studying the robot through the curtain which shelters it.

During efforts to perfect the robot's control systems, Gadge sneaks into the laboratory and discovers how to turn on Tobor. He learns that the robot can make emotional connections with people. Gadge not only controls the robot, but when he is accidentally tossed about, Tobor appears to comfort him, as if it is sorry for hurting the boy. Nordstrom and Harrison come upon him conversing with the robot. Gadge reveals his discovery to them, and demonstrates by commanding the robot to make several gestures.

The robot, not knowing its own strength, proceeds to destroy several pieces of equipment and furniture, until Gadge commands it to stand down. It backs up onto its platform and waits until Gadge turns it off. Gadge does not appear to be frightened of the monster robot. So far it has demonstrated compassion where Gadge is concerned.

After cleaning up, the scientists realize that an additional chair had to be brought to the news conference, leading them to believe that someone had infiltrated the closely guarded laboratory. Aware that their robot could fall into the wrong hands, they construct a small transmitter in a fountain pen that will be able to communicate with Tobor. They give the pen to Gadge, now that they have learned that Tobor imprinted on the boy as its control commander.

When an organized attack by foreign agents is thwarted by the defensive devices at the Nordstrom's home, the spies hit on another scheme. They send Gadge and his grandfather an invitation to a space flight presentation at the Griffith Park Planetarium. They intend to hold them as hostages when they show up for the presentation.

Gadge and Nordstrom arrive but find themselves alone in the vacant planetarium, which has been locked up for the weekend. Confused, they turn away to go home, when the spies are successful and kidnap their targets.

Dr. Gustav (Peter Brocco) tries to force Nordstrom to give them the crucial information needed to control the robot. But Nordstrom refuses, and Gadge secretely activates the pen transmitter, which he gives to Nordstrom.

When Nordstrom and Gadge do not return to the laboratory for a demonstration of Tobor to military officials, Dr. Harrsion contacts the local sheriff with his concerns that something dire has happened to them.

Suddenly, Tobor is activated remotely, reacts to commands sent by Nordstrom, and storms out of the house, driving off in a military Jeep parked in front.

One of the spies realizes the pen is important and snatches it away, breaking it.

Realizing that Tobor is going to rescue the professor and Gadge, Harrison and the military officials follow it in their cars. Near the enemy agents' lair, when the transmissions stop Tobor comes to an abrupt halt where it is, but Harrison successfully activates the robot using telepathic commands and overrides its lack of control.

The spies threaten to hurt Gadge, who instinctively reacts and uses his mind to call out to Tobor to help him, as Nordstrom relents and starts to write out the information the spies want.

In company with Harrison and the military men, Tobor breaks down the lair's door in the planetarium and attacks the enemy agents, rescuing the professor. One of the spies tries to escape with the coerced information, forcing Gadge to go with him. Tobor yanks him out of his car, injuring him badly. Gadge is then gently carried out of the car by the robot.

Later, when the robot has been successfully reprogrammed, a spacecraft is launched with Tobor at the controls. END

Analysis and additional notes: This one was rather interesing. Not only do we see a robot with "enhanced" control features, but it has emotions which allow it to assess a situation and act where necessary. That it imprints on Gadge is coincidental, since Gadge spends the most time with it. A supposed "bond" has been established between the two disparate entities. There is some discussion as to whether Tobor has a soul, but it seems to be empathically connected to the boy, which is completely different from all previous robots. It has no ambitions of its own and is protective of the scientists as part of its programming. Even survival does not deter it from doing its duty.

The boy himself is something of a wunderkindt, more intelligent for his age and scientifically inquisitive than most. We presume that he is a product of his breeding, since he is exposed to science early by dint of the scientists he hangs around with, one of whom is his grandfather. He is also rather precocious, and accidentally discovers all the things Tobor can do.

The robot itself is not designed terribly well. A clunky metallic shell connected by rivets, with a head that sits on its shoulders like just another attachment. It has two eyes and a mouth which is a flat panel. In the publicity poster it is shown carrying an unconscious woman on its extended arms, but there it no such scene in the film itself. In fact, Gadge's mother shows up in very small scenes to establish that he has one. Apart from that it is mostly male territory.

For its rather avant garde plotline and fast pacing, I give *Tobor The Great* 3 stars out of 4. IMdb gives it 5.3/10. Rotten Tomatoes has no rating for it yet, but 56% of its audience liked it.

Production: Principal photography for *Tobor The Great* took place from early to mid January 1954, on location at the Iverson Movie Ranch in Chatsworth, California.

Tobor's design was the brainchild of Robert Kinoshita, the television and film effects man and prop designer. Kinoshita went on to design Robby the Robot for the classic 1956 film *Forbidden Planet*, as well as the B-9 Environmental Control Robot for the mid 1960s hit science fiction television series *Lost In Space*.

The original Tobor prop and remote control device is still in existence, having been stored away safely in a private collection for more than 50 years. There is an online company, Fred Barton Productions, that sells screen accurate, full size replicas of Tobor as seen in the film.

Reception: In a review in <u>The New York Times</u> *Tobor The Great* is characterized as "This children's sci-fi adventure [that] chronicles the friendship between an 11-year-old and his grandfather's robot Tobor, who was designed to explore deep space."

In <u>DVD Savant</u> film reviewer Glenn Erickson called it, "Like other low budget Republic shows of its day, the film is sturdy, slow and straightforward, taking little advantage of the ideas in its script. Yet it was a kiddie favorite simply because it was about a boy who shared an adventure with a massive metal man."

In an appraisal of *Tobor The Great* film historian and reviewer Leonard Maltin noted "the film missed out on becoming an important sci-fi classic ... terrible acting and dialogue. A botched attempt at a heartwarming sci-fi comedy-thriller."

Legacy: The film inspired a *Tobor The Great* comic book story series, written by Denis Gifford and with artwork by James Bleach. It appeared in Star Comics #1-2 (1954), from Marvel Publications. Star Comics was an imprint of Marvel featuring children's stories.

Here Comes Tobor was a proposed American science fiction TV series. Produced for the 1956–1957 season, the project was never picked up and only a pilot episode was filmed but never aired.

A new film company, Diamond World Pictures, announced in 2011 that a sequel to *Tobor The Great* was to be the first film from the company. Plans were to star Patrick Dempsey and Christopher Plummer, and use the classic combination of live-action and stop-motion animation. To date, no film has been released.

Home video: *Tobor The Great* was released on DVD on May 13, 2008 by Lionsgate Home Entertainment. The standard DVD, containing the film only, had an incorrect open matte transfer; it was originally shot for theatrical exhibition using the 1.66:1 widescreen aspect ratio.

In December of 2016, the film was announced for both DVD and Blu-ray reissue by Kino Lorber.

20,000 LEAGUES UNDER THE SEA (1954)

Directed by Richard Fleischer
Produced by Walt Disney (uncredited)
Screenplay by Earl Felton
Based on *Twenty Thousand Leagues Under The Sea* by Jules Verne
Music by Paul Smith and Joseph S. Dubin (orchestration)
Cinematography by Franz Planer
Edited by Elmo Williams
Production company: Walt Disney Productions
Distributed by Buena Vista Distribution, release: December 23, 1954
Running time: 127 minutes
Budget: $5 million; box office: $28.2 million

Cast:
Kirk Douglas as Ned Land
James Mason as Captain Nemo
Paul Lukas as Professor Pierre Aronnax
Peter Lorre as Conseil
Robert J. Wilke as Nautilus's First Mate
Ted de Corsia as Captain Farragut
Carleton Young as John Howard
J. M. Kerrigan as Billy
Percy Helton as Coach driver
Ted Cooper as Abraham Lincoln's First Mate
Fred Graham as Casey
Laurie Mitchell as Hooker

Note: Beside several television series, Walt Disney embarked on making films for families. The very first film ever produced by Disney was a compilation of animated scenes to promote the debut of *Snow White And The Seven Dwarfs* in 1937. During the 1940s, Disney produced several combined animated and live-action films as well as musical anthologies. Then during the 1940s and 50s, Disney began producing more live-action films, among which was *20,000 Leagues Under The Sea*.

Plot: In 1868, rumors of a sea monster attacking ships in the Pacific Ocean have disrupted shipping lanes. The United States invites Professor Pierre M. Aronnax (Lukas) and his assistant Conseil (Lorre) to participate in a Navy expedition to prove the monster's existence. On board with them is the cocky master harpooner Ned Land (Douglas). He has no opinion one way or another of the monster's existence, but he is there for the "fortune and glory" alone.

After months of searching, the "monster" is spotted shortly before it rams the warship. Ned and Aronnax are thrown overboard, and Conseil goes in after Aronnax. The helpless, crippled frigate drifts away, and no one aboard responds to their cries for help. They are left treading water and helpless to stop any sea beast who deigns to eat them. They are also arguing bitterly about who is at fault for it.

Soon afterward, the three men find a strange looking metal vessel has hoved underneath them, and realize the "monster" is a man made "submerging boat". Arronax discovers the top hatch on the deck. During their wandering through the seemingly deserted vessel, Aronnax finds a large viewport in the forward cabin and sees an underwater funeral well underway.

Ned, Aronnax, and Conseil try to leave in a lifeboat, but the submarine crew stops the castaways. The captain introduces himself as Nemo (Mason), master of the submarine vessel which he calls Nautilus. He returns Ned and Conseil to the top deck, presuming to submerge beneath them; while offering Prof. Aronnax, whom he recognizes for his work, the chance to stay. After Aronnax proves he is willing to die with his companions, Nemo allows Ned and Conseil to remain with him. They are now all guests of Nemo.

Nemo takes them to the penal colony island of Rura Penthe. Nemo was once a prisoner there, as were many of his crew. There, the island prisoners are loading a munitions ship. The Nautilus rams it, destroying its cargo and killing the crew. Arronax is dismayed. Has Nemo any pity for the innocents killed in the action?

An anguished Nemo tells Aronnax that his actions have saved thousands from death in war. He also discloses that this "hated nation" tortured his wife and son to death while trying to force him to reveal the secrets of his work, both on the submarine and on the munitions he uses. He is a superior mechanical and electrical engineer, whose plans are decades ahead of his time. The enemy nations of the world have condemned him to the life of a submariner, without a nation to call his own.

Ned discovers the coordinates of Nemo's secret island base, Vulcania, and releases messages in bottles during his free time, hoping somebody will find them. The messages contain the truth about Nemo but also reveal his plans to any who find them.

Off the coast of New Guinea, the Nautilus becomes stranded on a reef. Ned is surprised when Nemo allows him to go ashore with Conseil, ostensibly to collect specimens of flora and fauna, while strictly admonishing them to stay on the beach. Despite his caution, Ned goes off alone, deserting Conseil to explore other avenues of escape. The island is lush, verdant jungle. Green darkness.

While drinking from a pool, he sees human skulls mounted on stakes. It means there are other humans there, and they may be cannibals. Just then, a face appears in the foliage, and then another. Ned runs for his life to rejoin Conseil on the beach.

They row away frantically, pursued by the cannibals in their canoes. Aboard ship, the cannibals are repelled by electrical charges through its hull. Nemo is furious with Ned for disobeying his express orders, then confines him to the brig.

A warship approaches, firing upon Nautilus, which descends into the depths. There it attracts a giant squid, which wraps the sub in its tentacles. After a similar electric charge fails to repel the monster, Nemo and his men surface during a storm to dislodge it. Nemo is caught in one of its tentacles, soon to be crushed to death. Ned, having just escaped from captivity, severs the tentacle and saves Nemo from drowning.

Later, Nemo has had a change of heart and claims he wants to make peace with the world.

As the Nautilus nears Vulcania, Nemo finds the island surrounded by warships, whose marines are converging on his base. As Nemo goes ashore, Ned tries to identify himself as the author of the bottled messages. Aronnax is furious with Ned, recognizing that Nemo will destroy all evidence of his discoveries and rob the world of his vast knowledge, thanks to Ned's interference.

Nemo enters the base and activates a time bomb. But on the way back he is mortally wounded by a bullet to his back. After navigating Nautilus away from Vulcania, Nemo announces he will be "taking the Nautilus down for the last time". He exhorts his mates to leave and save themselves, but all of the crew declare they will accompany their captain to his watery death.

Aronnax, Conseil, and Ned are forcibly confined to their cabins. The Nautilus's crew also retreat to their cabins at Nemo's order. Ned manages to escape (again) and tries to surface the Nautilus on his own. But the sub collides with a reef in the process and begins to flood.

Nemo staggers alone to his salon viewport, watching his beloved living sea beyond the glass as he dies.

When Ned frees Aronnax and Conseil, Aronnax tries to retrieve Nemo's detailed journal from Nemo's cabin, but the urgency of their escape obliges Ned to knock him unconscious and carry him out. The companions watch from a lifeboat as Vulcania explodes, while Ned apologizes to Aronnax for hitting him. As the Nautilus disappears beneath the waves, Nemo's last words to Aronnax echo: "There is hope for the future. And when the world is ready for a new and better life, all this will someday come to pass, in God's good time". END

Analysis and additional notes: In general I loved the movie, but I hated Ned Land. His "loose cannon" approach to life may have made him the hero, but it also made him dangerous to all who stood near him. He acted without thinking of the consequences. He was opinionated and harsh toward his companions, little realizing that he has damaged all hope for the future. His refusal to stay cautious of his surroundings landed him in hot water several times, and it was only Nemo who seemed reluctant to punish him. In that Land was extremely lucky, because anything he did was in the moment.

I remember that when I first saw the film I was about 10 years old. I loved the model of the submarine Nautilus then. It became my anchor in life, and for a time I wished I could be a submariner. From then on I made sure to see submarine films, including the television series *Voyage To The Bottom Of The Sea*. After that, Seaview replaced Nautilus. It seemed I was enamored of the Coming Thing. After that I began watching any science fiction film I could find.

The production values of the film were superior for the time. I am sure that had the techonology of the 21st century existed then, it would have been a real blockbuster. There is no credit listed for special effects. The animation of the giant animatronic(!) squid was as credible as stop-motion animation could be for the time. I can't believe that no one person would claim any credit for it, apart from Walt Disney.

For the fast-paced plotting and credible acting, I give this film 3 stars out of 4. IMdb gives it 7.2/10, and Rotten Tomatoes rates it 89% fresh, while 74% of their audience liked it.

Production: In 1950, Sig Rogell announced he had bought the rights to the novel as well as to an adaptation prepared by Robert L. Lippert's production company. He was going to make the film independently. The rights were later sold to Disney.

20,000 Leagues Under The Sea was filmed at various locations in The Bahamas and Jamaica, with the cave scenes filmed beneath what is now the Xtabi Resort on the cliffs of Negril. Filming began in spring of 1954. Some of the location filming sequences were so complex that they required a technical crew of more than 400 people.

The film presented many other challenges, as well. The famous giant squid attack sequence had to be entirely reshot, as it was originally filmed as taking place at dusk and in a calm sea. It was filmed again, this time taking place at night and during a huge gale, both to increase the drama and to better hide the cables and other mechanical workings of the animatronic squid.

With a total production cost of $9 million, the film was the most expensive in Hollywood to that date and presented a serious financial risk to the studio should it flop. However, the subsequent box office receipts proved otherwise.

Reception: Upon release: The New York Times film critic Bosley Crowther gave it a generally positive review by stating that, "As fabulous and fantastic as anything he has ever done in cartoons is Walt Disney's 'live action' movie made from Jules Verne's '20,000 Leagues Under the Sea.' Turned out in CinemaScope and color, it is as broad, fictitiously, as it is long (128 minutes), and should prove a sensation — at least with the kids."

In his 1967 biography *The Disney Version*, the critic Richard Schickel stated that James Mason was "superbly cast as the mad inventor Captain Nemo." Never mind that the original Nemo was an Indian prince whose loss of his wife and daughter caused him to make war on his fellow man. Mason was Mason, and that was that.

The film was also praised for the performances of the leading actors. This was the first time that major international stars such as

Kirk Douglas, James Mason, and Peter Lorre had appeared in a Disney film, although Robert Newton, a well-known actor in British films, had played Long John Silver in Disney's *Treasure Island* (1950), and Richard Todd, another well-known British actor, had appeared in Disney's Technicolor live-action version of *The Story of Robin Hood and His Merrie Men* (1952). Mason especially was singled out for his performance as Captain Nemo. Many people who had first seen him on-screen in the film identify him most strongly with this role.

20,000 Leagues Under The Sea received positive reviews from critics, and was the 2nd highest grossing film of the year (behind *White Christmas*), earning $8 million in box office attendance in North America. It has become a notable classic film for the Disney Corporation.

Critical opinion: Film critic Steve Biodrowski said that the film is "far superior to the majority of genre efforts from the period (or any period, for that matter), with production design and technical effects that have dated hardly at all." Biodrowski also added that the film "may occasionally succumb to some of the problems inherent in the source material (the episodic nature does slow the pace), but the strengths far outweigh the weaknesses, making this one of the greatest science-fiction films ever made."

Audiences remember it primarily for its giant squid battle sequence as well as the Nautilus itself; and James Mason's portrayal of Nemo.

Awards and nominations: The film won two Academy Awards and was nominated for one more.

Academy Awards (1954):

Won: Best Art Direction – Color (John Meehan, Emile Kuri)

Won: Best Special Effects (John Hench, Joshua Meador)

Nominated: Best Film Editing (Elmo Williams)

The film's primary art designer, Harper Goff, who designed the Nautilus, was not a member of the Art Directors Union in 1954 and therefore, under a bylaw within the Academy of Motion Pictures, he was unable to receive his Academy Award for Art Direction. [Boooo!]

Record albums: Rather than an authentic soundtrack recording of the film's score or dialogue, two vinyl studio cast record albums were released to coincide with the film's first two releases. Both albums contained condensed and heavily altered versions of the film's script without the usage of any of the film's cast for character voices.

In addition, both albums were narrated by Ned Land as opposed to Aronnax, who narrated the film and the original novel. Neither album mentioned Nemo as actually being "cracked" (i.e. insane), as the film does, and considerably sanitized the character by omitting any mention of him killing anyone and even having him sing sea chanties with his crew. The albums also had Nemo surviving at the end and releasing Ned, Arronax, and Conseil out of gratitude for their saving his life. In this version, Ned, Aronnax and Conseil were not shipwrecked because the Nautilus rammed the ship they were on, but because a hurricane came up and the Nautilus "rescued" them.

The first album was issued in 1954 in conjunction with the film's original release, and starred William Redfield as the voice of Ned Land. This album, a book and record set, was issued as part of RCA Victor's "Little Nipper" series on two 45-RPM records.

The second album, released by Disneyland Records in 1963 (in conjunction with the film's first re-release), was issued on one 33⅓ RPM 12" LP with no accompanying booklet and no liner notes – the usual practice with most Disney label albums. It contained much more of the film's plot, but with many of the same alterations as the first album, so this recording was technically a remake of the earlier one. The cast for the 1963 album was uncredited. Neither album listed the film's credits or made any mention of the film's cast.

A single for the film's most memorable song "A Whale of a Tale", written by Norman Gimbel and Al Hoffman, and sung by Kirk Douglas, was also released in 1954 under the Decca Children's Series label. The song "And The Moon Grew Brighter and Brighter", which Douglas had sung in the movie *Man Without A Star* (written by Lou Singer and Jimmy Kennedy), was on the B-side. Both songs can be found on the 2008 digital release of the film's soundtrack.

In the film, Johann Sebastian Bach's "Toccata and Fugue in D minor" is played by Nemo on the Nautilus's pipe organ, but James Mason's playing is actually dubbed by an anonymous organist.

Additional: Disneyland used the original sets as an attraction from 1955 to 1966. Walt Disney World Resort's Magic Kingdom also had a dark ride named 20,000 Leagues Under The Sea: Submarine Voyage from 1971 to 1994, which consisted of a submarine ride complete with the giant squid attack, and an arrangement of the main theme from the 1954 film playing on Captain Nemo's organ in the background.

For this ride, voice artist Peter Renaday stood in for James Mason in the role of Captain Nemo. In 1994, an attraction at Disneyland Paris, named Les Mystères du Nautilus, opened, and a dark ride at Tokyo DisneySea was created in 2001.

Remake: On January 6, 2009, Variety reported that a remake titled *20,000 Leagues Under The Sea: Captain Nemo* was being planned with Joseph McGinty Nichol attached to direct. The film serves as an origin story for the central character, Captain Nemo, as he builds his warship Nautilus. "McG" remarked that it will be "much more in keeping with the spirit of the novel" than Richard Fleischer's film, in which it will reveal "what Aronnax is up to and the becoming of Captain Nemo, and how the man became at war with war itself." It was written by Bill Marsilli, with Justin Marks and Randall Wallace brought in to do rewrites. The film was to be produced by Sean Bailey with McG's Wonderland Sound and Vision.

McG once suggested that he wanted Will Smith for the Captain Nemo role, but Smith turned down the part. As a second possible choice, McG had mentioned Sam Worthington, whom he worked with on *Terminator: Salvation*, though they never discussed it seriously. The project was later shelved in November 2009 with McG backing out of directing the project.

During the 2010 San Diego Comic Con, director David Fincher announced plans to direct *20,000 Leagues Under The Sea* for Walt Disney Pictures, based on a script by Scott Z. Burns. While Fincher was wrapping up *The Girl With The Dragon Tattoo* (2011), it was speculated that *20,000 Leagues Under The Sea* would enter principal photography by late 2012. In the meantime, Fincher began courting Brad Pitt to play the role of Ned Land while the film was placed on hold for casting. However, in February 2013, it was announced that Pitt had officially turned down the role.

In April 2013, the Australian government said it would provide a one-off incentive of $20 million in order to secure the production rights. The film was put on hold yet again in May due to complications of casting. On July 17, 2013, Fincher dropped out of the film to direct the adaptation of *Gone Girl*. Fincher revealed in an interview that he left the film because he wanted Channing Tatum for Ned Land, but

Disney wanted Chris Hemsworth for the role. (In my humble opinion, I believe Hemsworth would have been perfect. He of the six pack abs and quirky personality.) Finally, the money originally allocated for the production of this film was redirected towards *Pirates of the Caribbean: Dead Men Tell No Tales*.

In February of 2016, Disney announced that it was planning a film titled *Captain Nemo*, with James Mangold directing. No further news have been released. To date, Disney continues to shield its project with no data to be available.

And so, a good project gets stuck like Nautilus on a reef.

✦

And so ends *Science Fiction Films of The 20th Century: 1950 - 1954*. I hope you enjoyed it and will purchase the next volume, *1955 - 1959*. Thanks very much for your interest. ✦